Surreal South

Surreal South

edited by

Laura Benedict
&
Pinckney Benedict

Press 53
Winston-Salem, North Carolina

Press 53
PO Box 30314
Winston-Salem, NC 27130

First Edition

This book is a complete work of fiction. All names, characters, places and incidents are products of the authors' imagination. Any resemblances to actual events, places or persons, living or dead, are coincidental.

Cover design by Kevin Watson

Cover art, *Tulip,*
copyright © 2007 by Adela Leibowitz,
used by permission of the artist

Printed on acid-free paper

ISBN 978-0-9793049-7-2

Acknowledgments

"The Era of Great Numbers" by Lee K. Abbott. First published in *Epoch Magazine*

"Pig Helmet & The Wall of Life" by Pinckney Benedict. First published in *StoryQuarterly 42*

"Help Me Find My Spaceman Lover" by Robert Olen Butler. First published in *Tabloid Dreams:Stories* (Owl Books, 1997)

"Poem in the Ninth Month" by Beth Ann Fennelly. First published in *The Believer*

"Smonk Gets Out Alive" from the novel *Smonk*, by Tom Franklin (HarperCollins, 2006)

"The Paperhanger" by William Gay. First published in *Harper's*

"Dinner Date" and "Silver Man" by Joy Beshears Hagy. First published in *Caesura*

"Crazy Ladies" by Greg Johnson. First published in *Distant Friends: Stories* (University of Georgia Press, 1997)

"The Bingo Master" by Joyce Carol Oates. First published in the anthology *Dark Forces* (Viking, 1980)

"Dog Song" by Ann Pancake. First published in *Shenandoah*

"Sautéing the Platygast" by Dean Paschal. First published in *Boulevard* (Spring 2002)

"Swans" by Benjamin Percy. First published in *The Idaho Review*

"The Corpse Bird" by Ron Rash. First published in *The South Carolina Review*

"The Bear Bryant Funeral Train" by Brad Vice. First published in *The Carolina Quarterly* (Volume 55, Number 1, Winter 2003)

"The Echo of Neighborly Bones" by Daniel Woodrell. First published in *Murdaland* (Issue #1, 2007)

Contents

For Barry Hannah,
godfather of the surreal south

Introduction

"Our Southern reality hatched as surrealism."
—Rodney Jones

Welcome to the dream world. This is not the faintly comfortable scientific dream world, in which our nighttime visions are only chance firings of unthinkably minuscule neurons, a pointless hollow panoply of random images. Nor is this the therapeutic dream world of the good doctor Freud, where all is symbol and figurative significance, a direct, elegant and ultimately reductive correspondence between the hidden fears and desires of the dreamer and their expression within the dream. No, this is neither the uninterpretable dream of the post-Enlightenment materialist, made harmless by its meaninglessness; nor is it the interpreted dream, which must make reference to and thus privilege the waking world over itself. What you are about to encounter is the unfiltered stuff of the dream, and that is wild, terrifying, provocative, and unsettling material.

Far be it from us, the editors, to advise you as to how you should undertake to read these pieces. We're just happy that you're encountering them at all. But if we were to make a suggestion, it would be this: Put away literary notions. Put away schoolchild considerations of theme and symbol and interpretation. Forget notions of allegory. If there is allegory here, it is the allegory of the self, as we find it in the best work of Poe, for instance: the hidden self of the writer and the unrealized self of the reader. It's the sort of allegory that not only does not require analysis, but that actively struggles against it. Go back to the roots of storytelling and simply experience the stories the way you experience your dreams: directly, with unqualified immediacy, and with an admixture of fear and terrible joy.

A dream consists of absolute specifics, a profusion of unambiguous details and precise sensory impressions. Its internal logic is perfect and undeniable, its physics ineluctable if bizarre. While we're in the dream, we are whole and do not question our existence there. Only when the dream is done do we see it revealed as a fiction. There is sublimity in the dream: its order is both inevitable and entirely surprising. It places in shocking juxtaposition the familiar and the never-before-seen. As a consequence it makes the familiar new (sometimes in jarring and terrifying ways—the lover becomes a monster, the parent a predator, the child a stranger; inanimate objects speak and the long-dead rise to life once again) and reveals the pure inner nature of both.

The best literature works in precisely this way. It speaks in an appealing and distinctive voice, certainly, but it breaches aesthetic barriers, reaches past the intellect, reaches past consensus notions of rightness and the common moral order, and lays its hand directly on the exposed raw nerve of the soul. It strikes straight at the base of the human experience with images that have stalked and chivvied our poor fragile kind since our earliest beginnings as sentient beings. It refuses utterly to pander to our selfish, solipsistic, simplistic demands and desires, fulfilling instead some deeper, more savage, and more desperate need. It does not allow for false comfort. It does not tell us what we think we need to know; it does not provide us with the false comforts that we desire most to hear.

Instead, it tells us what we have already come to know deep within ourselves, what we have always known, but what we are too afraid to say out loud in the full light of day. It tells us what we are: and what we are is a race of chimeras, beings made up of the incompatible parts of innumerable mutually antagonistic creatures. Our pieces do not fit together. We are, when we're willing to tell the truth about ourselves, surreal at our hearts.

This is, to us, what literature is, what literature does, when it is doing what it does best. We don't pretend that this anthology is an exhaustive exploration of the South or of surrealism. We freely admit (actually, we privately glory in the fact) that our selection process was highly idiosyncratic. The criteria for consideration were simple: writers had to be alive at the time of their selection; they had to be from, associated with, or writing about the geographical South; they had to be more or less our contemporaries; and they had to be folks whose work we like and admire. And they had to be willing to send us intimate and potentially embarrassing, potentially alienating work of surpassing strangeness and vividness.

Many of these writers are our personal friends and helped us in this labor of love because of that friendship. We thank all of them for their invaluable contributions. Despite the eccentric method of our selection, we feel confident in asserting that we've brought together in this volume an assortment of some of the best writing that we've seen, by southerners or about the South.

The South itself is a kind of dream, isn't it? For Southerners, it is the dream of the nation within the nation, spiritually fiercely independent from and materially entirely reliant on and indebted to the parent country, the conqueror realm. If the North is tough, harsh reality and bright blazing daylight, then the South is the uneasily slumbering mind of the U.S, a cupboard filled with the country's dark dreams. The world within the world, shadowed by all the unmitigated horrors and illuminated by all the dubious glories of its distant (and growing distanter with every passing day, praise God) and ill-remembered past.

Its inhabitants—herein depicted as beautiful, cruel, wistful, mad, egotistical, sentimental to a fault—often struggle with infinite sadness and rage and shame (frequently guilt as well) over the one, and infinite, usually unspoken longing and nostalgia for the other. The South is not alone in its nightmare legacies of slavery, poverty, violence, and ignorance, but (*pace* those who believe that the South has never changed its character nor ever will), it is—perhaps like post-Nazi Germany in this way—uniquely aware of them and almost preternaturally sensitive to their influences.

For Northerners, the South is that poorly defined and unfamiliar region of the United States over which the mists of imagination and legend still hover, nearly 150 years after the end of the barbarous civil war that broke the nation into two distinct and distinctly unequal halves, while forevermore welding it into a single unwieldy and impossible-to-govern unit. It is a contradiction and a conundrum, the South: the haunted house; the fallen aristocrat cheek by jowl with the impoverished, stalwart yeoman; the cavalier, the beggar, the slave; the beloved, Christ-obsessed, and still-handsome aunt, as well as the grinning over-friendly cousin with bluish skin and webbed fingers whose presence you cannot stand, whose family relationship to you is undeniable (you can see it in the eyes and in the shape of the nose, the distinctive widow's peak and the cleft in the chin), and about whom you tell all your friends and colleagues in a hushed voice and with a half-ashamed grin. It is a slightly smutty joke and a burning scourge; a ruined but still awesome, still dreadful, giant; a reminder of the best and worst that dwells within us all, just below our oh-so-thin skin.

Everywhere and to everyone, to judge by the ubiquity of Southern literature, in this country and around the world, the American South is a puzzle, a slightly gruesome enticement, a boundless ambiguity, an enduring paradox, and an endless source of myth.

That's what you'll find in this volume. Myths of astonishing and universal power. Legends. Ghosts. Monsters. Murderers. Sexual deviants. Villains. Heroes. Wars and rumors of wars. Football. Grand Guignol. Melodrama. Gothic tales. Even robots. The best dreams and the worst dreams of many of the finest writers we know, collected here for your perusal. This is the world we grew up in; this is the world we live and work in. This is the world to which we return endlessly in our dreams, in our fantasies, in our stories and our poems.

This is the Surreal South.

Laura Benedict
Pinckney Benedict
Carbondale, IL
May 2007

Daniel Woodrell

The Echo of Neighborly Bones

Once Boshell finally killed his neighbor he couldn't seem to quit killing him. He killed him again whenever he felt unloved or blue or simply had empty hours facing him. The first time he killed the man, Jepperson, an opinionated foreigner from Minnesota, he kept to simple Ozark tradition and used a squirrel rifle, bullet to the heart, classic and effective, though there were spasms of the limbs and even a lunge of big old Jepperson's body that seemed like he was about to take a step, flee, but he died in stride and collapsed against a fence post. Boshell took the body to the woods on his deer scooter and piled heavy rocks on the man, trying to keep nature back from the flesh, the parts of nature that have teeth or beaks. For most of a week Boshell was content with killing his neighbor just once, then came a wet spattering Sunday, the dish went out and he couldn't see the ball game on TV, so he snuck away to the pile and cleared the rocks from the head and chest. Jepperson had died with a sort of sneer on his face, thick lips crooked to the side, his dead eyes yet looking down his nose in calm contempt. That look and Jepperson's frequent sharp comments had months ago prompted Boshell to put a sticker on his truck bumper that read, I Don't Give a Damn HOW You Did It Up North! Even dead the man goaded a fella. The falling wet slicked his hair back from his greening face and his lips seemed to move under the drops, flutter, like he had still another insult he was about to let fly. Boshell hunted a stout stick and thumped the corpse. Thumped the stick enough times to snuff a live man, thumped enough to feel better about the rain and the washed-out ball game, then went home to his wife, Evelyn.

She said, "Wherever'd you get off to?"

"Oh, you know. I just can't get to feelin' done with the son-of-a-bitch."

"In all this rain?"

"I'm gonna have to move him. He's goin' high now the cold snap broke. Someplace further from the fire road."

"Well, his wife's got herself some company today over there, and they been sniffin' about, lookin' places." She pointed across the creek where there was a big metal barn, four penned horses, and a mess of guineas running loose, pecking and gabbling. Four people in raincoats and sagging hats stood near the horses with their boots on the bottom fence rail and their elbows on the top. "Best wait 'til they leave."

"I'll try."

Only two days later Boshell checked the can for morning coffee and found it empty, so he went out to kill the man again, kill himself awake without any joe to drink. Bird droppings had spotted the rocks over the man, and one of the hands had moved somehow so that a pinky stuck from between the rocks. The little bit of the pinky that showed had been chewed at, nibbled, torn. Boshell pulled the rocks away until Jepperson was open to the October sky. He went back to his truck for a hatchet, a beat-up hatchet with a dinged, uneven blade and a cracked handle. He stood over the corpse and said, "Say it. Go on and say it, why don't you?" Then he sank the hatchet into the chest area and stood back to admire the way the handle stood up straight from the wound. The handle was directly below Jepperson's nose and his eyes appeared to find it to be kind of funny business, having a hatchet in his chest.

"Glad you like it."

Boshell left the blade in the man's chest, then dragged the corpse to his truck. He tossed a tarp over the raised handle and all, but knew he wouldn't likely run into anybody, not where he was going. He steered the truck downhill going west, onto a creek bed with shallow puddles but no flow, and eased south over the pale and reddish rocks, the truck bucking during the rougher patches. He turned uphill below the old home place, the land now overgrown by brambles and deserted by residents, and parked on the slope. One wall of a house with an askew window could be seen still standing back in the thicket. Boshell's people had lived on this dirt until the government annexed it for the National Forest in the 1950's, and lazy old time had slowly reclaimed the place for trees and weeds and possums. He came here often, to sit and wonder, and feel robbed of all these acres.

He shoved the corpse from the truck bed, and the hatchet fell loose when the body thumped to ground. Boshell set the blade back into the wound, then tamped it in snug with a boot stomp. The hatchet fell free twice more before he got Jepperson up to where his grandma's garden had been laid and she'd grown the tangiest okra he'd ever had and oddly shaped but sweet tomatoes you just couldn't find anymore. The corpse nodded when dragged and the head bent a bit to the side, like he was taking an interest in this trip, noting the details, setting the picture in his mind.

Boshell said, "This all was ours, ours up until foreigners like you'n yours got here from up north with fancy notions'n bank money and *improved* everything for us." He looked on Jepperson, with his face yet smug in death, and remembered when the dead man said in that voice that came from way high in the nose, "If I come across one more eaten guinea, I'll shoot your dog." And Boshell had said, "That ain't the neighborly way, mister. If'n Bitsy was to rip a guinea or two, just tell us." And the dead man, so much younger and bigger and flush with money and newcomer attitudes, said, "I don't give two shits about being neighborly with you people. Have you not noticed that?"

Now Boshell nudged the corpse with a boot, put the toe to the chin and shoved the head until the face was up again. He started to crouch but the scent was too high, and he stood back a step to say, "They go for about a dollar fifty a bird, neighbor—still seem worth it?"

The old, original well was sided by short, stacked walls of stones. The well had gone dry long ago, in Grandpa's time, before the coughing killed him, and a slab rock the color of dirt had been slid over the gap so no playing child or adult drinking moon in the dark would wander over and fall into the hole, bust a leg or a neck. The hole was but eight feet deep, and there were a few shards of glass and earthenware shattered about the bottom where the spout had sealed shut after the water table dropped.

"Your new home, neighbor. Maybe I'll be back to tell you about this place. Family history."

Evelyn made his favorite dish that night. She'd thawed a couple of quail, split them and fried them in the black skillet, served them with sides of chow-chow and bean salad. Boshell had whiskey, she had her daily glass of beer, and they watched the evening news on an east coast channel the satellite dish pulled into their front room. The traffic reports made them laugh, shake their heads, and the weather was interesting to watch, what with the cold northern temperatures and snowflakes swirling down between sun-thwarting buildings into gray canyons, but of no use. When a segment about lost dogs in Brooklyn came on he tried to turn the TV off, but Evelyn was bawling before he could find the button.

She ran outside and Boshell followed. She rushed past the ranks of firewood, the chopping block, a wheelless Nova that would never be fixed, and sagged against an oak tree lightning had split. Bitsy had crawled home hurt and collapsed beneath the split tree, gutshot, vomiting, looking up at Ev with baffled, resigned eyes, and it took two hours for her to bleed out and die with a last windy sound and a little flutter. Strands of silver hair waved across Evelyn's face and her hands clenched onto her dress and squeezed the wad. The horses across the creek neighed in their pen, and the big house beyond was dark.

"Oh, Ev," he said, "we'll soon get you another."

"There wasn't never but the one Bitsy. Just the one."

Later, when the moon had settled, Boshell slid from bed and dressed. He fetched a big flashlight and went out back to the tool shed. He shoved cobwebs in the corner aside and searched among hoes, rakes, a busted scythe, until he came across his old three-tined frog gig. He tapped the ground with the gig as he walked, and started down the dry creek bed, splashing light over all those rocks, whistling like a child.

Susan Woodring

Sales Call

Sorry to keep you waiting," the woman says, arriving breathless at the door. She has been sleeping in a nest she made from her grandmother's tattered mink stole, her husband's old work dungarees, and a few bits of lace and ribbon, an old pin cushion, this and that from around the house. The doorbell rang five minutes ago, or it has been more than an hour. The stranger beaming at her from across the threshold might have been waiting for her to answer since the beginning of the new millennium. The woman, cooped up for decades, has lost her sense of time. The whites of her eyes are green-tinged, like a wedge of cheese just starting to mold.

The man smiles, pulling his thin red lips back to reveal stubby white teeth like hacked off tree stumps. "Delighted to meet a pretty girl at any wait." The woman winces at that, and the man bows slightly, removing his hat with a flourish. The hat is threaded silver and iridescent, winking brilliantly in his hands. His purple eyes sparkle.

The woman is wearing a plain terrycloth robe, her face and neck bare. Behind her, the cat clock strikes nine, its rhinestone eyes twitching in sync with its ticking tail. The room is shabbily furnished, the couch threadbare and sinking. A pair of child-sized saddle shoes lay abandoned a small distance from the door. There is a dusty giant piano in the corner and the room seems to tilt a bit in its direction. A rickety end table sinks under the weight of old newspapers, days high. The air inside the house is dense and yellow, terribly aged.

"Bentley Connor," the man says, extending his hand. "Ma'am?"

"Mrs. Dale Myers." She looks into his eyes, his crystalline irises, and reads of his past loves, his life of sales calls. She knows instinctively that the man has a wife somewhere, long abandoned and gone to drink, and an aging mother, sitting up in a bath chair reading a cinema rag, alone.

"Mrs. Myers. A moment of your time?"

The salesman is clearly from far away; his manner and style of dress are too outlandish for the straight-and-narrow ways of all the local housing developments and the tiny, Baptist-run factory towns beyond. His black hair is done up in greasy pomade that shines a swirl of shifting, glinting colors under the glare of midmorning sunlight burning through the open door. He wears a clean, black suit with flashy cufflinks. Behind him, the woman glimpses the vehicle in which he arrived, now parked at the curb. It is a low, slender metal contraption, perhaps aluminum, with an exhaust pipe jutting out the back several inches wide in diameter. At the man's side is a gleaming silver machine with a long, tapered neck and thin, sleek shoulders, similar in composition to his vehicle on the street. The man grasps its handle, rubbing his thumb slowly across, lovingly. He winks at the woman and raises his eyebrows suggestively. The woman finds all this a bit too familiar. The man, she can tell, is slippery, not to be trusted for an instant. She tries to think, where is her husband?

The salesman wheels his machine past her, into the filthy living room. A lazy plump fly ascends from the house's discord and drifts languidly out the front door, and the woman closes it. Inside the house, the man pulls a long cord from the interior chrome folds of his silver machine. He touches the neck of the machine with his index finger, and bends down to kiss it, his eyes closed in rapture. Looking up, he gives the woman an intoxicated, oily grin.

"Your rugs will be the envy of the neighborhood."

"Oh, no," the woman starts, cinching her bathrobe closed at her neck. "You can't do that in here, Mr. . . . uh…Mr. . . ." She cannot recall the man's name. A clumsy, dull memory comes to her, though, of long ago, or it could have been just the day before, but the floors were clean and she was walking purposefully across them, her smart navy pumps clicking through the living room, into the kitchen. She prepared the children's things for school, and set out her husband's lunchbox, a meatloaf sandwich, a thermos of coffee, and an apple inside.

"You are going to thank me for this," the man says, winking at her. "You'll want to kiss me, I promise." He locates an outlet behind the piano and the woman is reminded: Tuesday afternoons, piano lessons. Thursday nights, Bridge at the Parkers'. Saturday, the lodge, and she and the children—there are two!—stay home.

The man sets his briefcase on the chair, snaps it open, and stands over it, rubbing his hands together. The girl and the boy, she remembers now, have been switched off and stored in the closet. Her husband, her Dale, has passed over into another time, but it is not too late. She can yet call him back. The cat on the wall lets out a tiny mew and Mrs. Dale Myers catches her breath. She doesn't know how to begin. The end table sags further, finally dropping its newspapers to the floor. They swoosh down and scatter. She has left a bundt in the oven for forty-seven years. The ladies of the neighborhood had warned her not to use the off switch. It's too much, they had said, too *easy*, but then, those ladies were so old-fashioned. The last day of her old life, when she turned the children off in her exasperation with the endless demands of mothering, was a Tuesday. It was time to leave and she could not get them, the older girl and the little boy, to stop their bickering, to put their shoes on. The children are years overdue for their piano lessons.

"I'm saving your life here," the man says, extracting a jeweler's pouch. "I'm keeping you from a million errant dust particles."

"I really don't think," the woman begins to protest, but the salesman doesn't pay mind to her words.

He begins to loosen the drawstring opening of the velvet pouch. His fingers work the folds, then push through, easing the bag open. The woman clutches at her bathrobe. He peers inside the rich layers of black velvet, then glances up with his otherworldly eyes. "You have been waiting for this, Mrs. Dale Myers," he whispers. He turns the bag over and ordinary dirt falls to the faded rug of muted colors.

"No," she pleads, "don't."

"Shh," he says and switches the machine on. It swells and roars, and the salesman takes aim. The spilt dirt disappears into the machine; then, with a great suction and gulp, it consumes the rug, upending the furniture as it pulls, then takes the chair, the couch, the end table, the newspapers. The woman tries to hold back her daughter's saddle shoes, but they too are sucked away. The man, sweating with the effort, points the machine in this direction, then turns it, aims it in another. The refrigerator unplugs itself from the wall in the kitchen and scoots through, suctioned up into the machine. Also, the piano, clunking and clattering and playing a few plucked notes as it goes, the mattress from the bedroom, the framed family photos on the wall. The kitchen cupboards unhinge themselves and come. The oven door is lost. Her nest makings come also, one by one—the stole, the dungarees, the pin cushion—all hurdling through the air and then pulled into the machine's slick opening, the salesman at the machine's controls. Finally, the walls succumb, with their closets still attached, and the woman screams for the children. Too late, she remembers the silky warmth of their little heads under her hands, her guiding them to bed at night, or laying on a touch for a comfort. The woman is dizzy and weak, watching it all disappear. The salesman glances at her in the midst of his labors, and for an instant, his eyes are blank—it seems he has lost himself in his work and has forgotten she is there. The machine whirs to its finale, taking in the roofing tiles and a few dropped nails. It leaves her alone on a square of concrete, the machine gone, the salesman vanished, only an ancient orange cat with jeweled eyes, circling and weaving through the woman's bare legs.

Robert Olen Butler

Help Me Find My Spaceman Lover

I never thought I could fall for a spaceman. I mean, you see them in the newspaper and they kind of give you the willies, all skinny and hairless and wiggly-looking, and if you touched one, even to shake hands, you just know it would be like when you were about fifteen and you were with an earth boy and you were sweet on him but there was this thing he wanted, and you finally said okay, but only rub-a-dub, which is what we called it around these parts when I was younger, and it was the first time ever that you touched...well, you know what I'm talking about. Anyway, that's what it's always seemed like to me with spacemen, and most everybody around here feels about the same way, I'm sure. Folks in Bovary, Alabama, and environs—by which I mean the KOA camp off the interstate and the new trailer park out past the quarry—everybody in Bovary is used to people being a certain way, to look at and to talk to and so forth. Take my daddy. When I showed him a few years ago in the newspaper how a spaceman had endorsed Bill Clinton for president and they had a picture of a spaceman standing there next to Bill Clinton—without any visible clothes on, by the way—the spaceman, that is, not Bill Clinton, though I wouldn't put it past him, to tell the truth, and I'm not surprised at anything they might do over in Little Rock. But I showed my daddy the newspaper and he took a look at the spaceman and he snorted and said that he wasn't surprised people like that was supporting the Democrats, people like that don't even look American, and I said no, Daddy, he's a spaceman, and he said people like that don't even look human, and I said no, Daddy, he's not human, and my daddy said, that's what I'm saying, make him get a job.

But I did fall for a spaceman, as it turned out, fell pretty hard. I met him in the parking lot at the twenty-four-hour Wal-Mart. We used to have a regular old Wal-Mart that would close at nine o'clock and when they turned it into a Super Center a lot of people in Bovary thought that no good would come of it, encouraging people to stay up all night. Americans go to bed early and get up early, my daddy said. But I have trouble sleeping sometimes. I live in the old trailer park out the state highway and it's not too far from the Wal-Mart and I live there with my yellow cat Eddie. I am forty years old and I was married once, to a telephone installer who fell in love with cable TV. There's no cable TV in Bovary yet, though with a twenty-four-hour Wal-Mart, it's probably not too far behind. It won't come soon enough to save my marriage, however. Not that I wanted it to. He told me he just *had* to install cable TV, telephones wasn't fulfilling him, and he was going away for good to Mobile and he didn't want me to go with him, this was the end for us, and I was understanding the parts about it being the end but he was going on about fiber optics and things that I didn't really follow. So I said fine and he went away, and even if he'd wanted me to go with him, I wouldn't have done it. I've only been to Mobile a couple of times and I didn't take to it. Bovary is just right for me. At least that's what I thought when it had to do with my ex-husband, and that kind of thinking just stayed with me, like a grape-juice stain on your housedress, and I am full of regrets, I can tell you, for not rethinking that whole thing before this. But I got a job at a hairdresser's in town and Daddy bought me the trailer free and clear and me and Eddie moved in and I just kept all those old ideas.

So I met Desi in the parking lot. I called him that because he talked with a funny accent but I liked him. I had my insomnia and it was about three in the morning and I went to the twenty-four-hour Wal-Mart and I was glad it was there and it was open—I'd tell that right to the face of anybody in this town—I was glad for a place to go when I couldn't sleep. So I was coming out of the store with a bag that had a little fuzzy mouse toy for Eddie, made of rabbit fur, I'm afraid, and that strikes me as pretty odd to kill all those cute little rabbits, which some people have as pets and love a lot, so that somebody else's pet of a different type can have something to play with, and it's that kind of odd thing that makes you shake your head about the way life is lived on planet earth—Desi has helped me see things in the larger perspective—though, to be honest, it didn't stop me from buying the furry cat toy, because Eddie does love those things. Maybe today I wouldn't do the same, but I wasn't so enlightened that night when I came out of the Wal-Mart and I had that toy and some bread and baloney and a refrigerator magnet, which I collect, of a zebra head.

He was standing out in the middle of the parking lot and he wasn't moving. He was just standing still as a cow and there wasn't any car within a hundred feet of him, and, of course, his spaceship wasn't anywhere in sight, though I wasn't looking for that right away because at first glance I didn't know he was a spaceman. He was wearing a long black trench coat with the belt cinched tight and he had a black felt hat with a wide brim. Those were the things I saw first and he seemed odd, certainly, dressed like that in Bovary, but I took him for a human being, at least.

I was opening my car door and he was still standing out there and I called out to him, "Are you lost?"

His head turns my way and I still can't see him much at all except as a hat and a coat.

"Did you forget where you parked your car?" I say, and then right away I realize there isn't but about four cars total in the parking lot at that hour. So I put the bag with my things in the seat and I come around the back of the car and go a few steps toward him. I feel bad. So I call to him, kind of loud because I'm still pretty far away from him and also because I already have a feeling he might be a foreigner. I say, "I wasn't meaning to be snippy, because that's something that happens to me a lot and I can look just like you look sometimes, I'm sure, standing in the lot wondering where I am, exactly."

While I'm saying all this I'm moving kind of slow in his direction. He isn't saying anything back and he isn't moving. But already I'm noticing that his belt is cinched *very* tight, like he's got maybe an eighteen inch waist. And as I get near, he sort of pulls his hat down to hide his face, but already I'm starting to think he's a spaceman.

I stop. I haven't seen a spaceman before except in the newspaper and I take another quick look around, just in case I missed something, like there might be four cars *and* a flying saucer. But there's nothing unusual. Then I think, oh my, there's one place I haven't looked, and so I lift my eyes, very slow because this is something I don't want to see all the sudden, and finally I'm staring into the sky. It's a dark night and there are a bunch of stars up there and I get goose bumps because I'm pretty sure that this man standing just a few feet away is from somewhere out there. But at least there's no spaceship as big as the Wal-Mart hanging over my head with lights blinking and transporter beams ready to shine down on me. It's only stars.

So I bring my eyes down—just about as slow—to look at this man. He's still there. And in the shadow of his hat brim, with the orangey light of the parking lot all around, I can see these eyes looking at me now and they are each of them about as big as Eddie's whole head and shaped kind of like Eddie's eyes.

"Are you a spaceman?" I just say this right out.

"Yes, mam," he says and his courtesy puts me at ease right away. Americans are courteous, my daddy says, not like your Eastern liberal New York taxi drivers.

"They haven't gone and abandoned you, have they, your friends or whoever?" I say.

"No, mam," he says and his voice is kind of high-pitched and he has this accent, but it's more in the tone of the voice than how he says his words, like he's talking with a mouth full of grits or something.

"You looked kind of lost, is all."

"I am waiting," he says.

"That's nice. They'll be along soon, probably," I say, and I feel my feet starting to slide back in the direction of the car. There's only so far that courtesy can go in calming you down. The return of the spaceship is something I figure I can do without.

Then he says, "I am waiting for you, Edna Bradshaw."

"Oh. Good. Sure, honey. That's me. I'm Edna. Yes. Waiting

for me." I'm starting to babble and I'm hearing myself like I was hovering in the air over me and I'm wanting my feet to go even faster but they seem to have stopped altogether. I wonder if it's because of some tractor beam or something. Then I wonder if they have tractor beam pulling contests in outer space that they show on TV back in these other solar systems. I figure I'm starting to get hysterical, thinking things like that in a situation like this, but there's not much I can do about it.

He seems to know I'm struggling. He takes a tiny little step forward and his hand goes up to his hat, like he's going to take it off and hold it in front of him as he talks to me, another courtesy that even my daddy would appreciate. But his hand stops. I think he's not ready to show me his whole spaceman head. He knows it would just make things worse. His hand is bad enough, hanging there over his hat. It's got little round pads at the end of the fingers, like a gecko, and I don't stop to count them, but at first glance there just seems to be too many of them.

His hand comes back down. "I do not hurt you, Edna Bradshaw. I am a friendly guy."

"Good," I say. "Good. I figured that was so when I first saw you. Of course, you can just figure somebody around here is going to be friendly. That's a good thing about Bovary, Alabama—that's where you are, you know, though you probably do know that, though maybe not. Do you know that?"

He doesn't say anything for a moment. I'm rattling on again, and it's true I'm a little bit scared and that's why, but it's also true that I'm suddenly very sad about sounding like this to him, I'm getting some perspective on myself through his big old eyes, and I'm sad I'm making a bad impression because I want him to like me. He's sweet, really. Very courteous. Kind of boyish. And he's been waiting for me.

"Excuse me," he says. "I have been translating. You speak many words, Edna Bradshaw. Yes, I know the name of this place."

"I'm sorry. I just do that sometimes, talk a lot. Like when I get scared, which I am a little bit right now. And call me Edna."

"Please," he says, "I am calling you Edna already. And in conclusion, you have no reason to be afraid."

"I mean call me *just* Edna. You don't have to say Bradshaw every time, though my granddaddy would do that with people. He was a fountain pen salesman and he would say to people, I'm William D. Bradshaw. Call me William D. Bradshaw. And he meant it. He wanted you to say the whole name every time. But you can just call me Edna."

So the spaceman takes a step forward and my heart starts to pound something fierce, and it's not from fright, I realize, though it's some of that. "Edna," he says. "You are still afraid."

"Telling you about my granddaddy, you mean? How that's not really the point here? Well, yes, I guess so. Sometimes, if he knew you for a while, he'd let you call him W.D. Bradshaw."

Now his hand comes up and it clutches the hat and the hat comes off and there he stands in the orange lights of the parking lot at three in the morning in my little old home town and he doesn't have a hair on his head, though I've always liked bald men and I've read they're bald because they have so much male hormone in them, which makes them the best lovers, which would make this spaceman quite a guy, I think, and his head is pointy, kind of, and his cheeks are sunken and his cheekbones are real clear and I'm thinking already I'd like to bake some cookies for him or something; just last week I got a prize-winning recipe off a can of cooking spray that looks like it'd put flesh on a fence post. And, of course, there are these big eyes of his and he blinks once, real slow, and I think it's because he's got a strong feeling in him, and he says, "Edna, my name is hard for you to say."

And I think of Desi right away, and I try it on him, and his mouth, which hasn't got anything that look like lips exactly, moves up at the edges and he makes this pretty smile.

"I have heard that name," he says. "Call me Desi. And I am waiting for you, Edna, because I study this planet and I hear you speak many words to your friends and to your subspecies companion and I detect some bright-colored aura around you and I want to meet you."

"That's good," I say, and I can feel a blush starting in my chest, where it always starts, and it's spreading up my throat and into my cheeks.

"I would like to call on you tomorrow evening, if I have your permission," he says.

"Boy," I say, "do a lot of people have the wrong idea about spacemen. I thought you just grabbed somebody and beamed them up and that was it." It was a stupid thing to say, I realize right away. I think Desi looks a little sad to hear this. The corners of his mouth sink. "I'm sorry," I say.

"No," he says. "This is how we are perceived, it is true. You speak only the truth. This is one reason I want to meet you, Edna. You seem always to say what is inside your head without any attempt to alter it."

Now it's my turn to look a little sad, I think. But that's okay, because it gives me a chance to find out that Desi is more than courteous. His hands come out toward me at once, the little suckers on them primed to latch on to me, and I'm not even scared because I know it means he cares about me. And he's too refined to touch me this quick. His hands just hang there between us and he says, "I speak this not as a researcher but as a male creature of a parallel species."

"You mean as a man?"

His eyes blink again, real slow. "Yes. As a man. As a man I try to say that I like the way you speak."

So I give him permission to call on me and he thanks me and he turns and glides away. I know his legs are moving but he glides, real smooth, across the parking lot and I can see now that poor Desi didn't even find a pair of pants and some shoes to go with his trench coat. His legs and ankles are skinny like a frog's and his feet look a lot like his hands. But all that is unclear on the first night. He has disappeared out into the darkness and I drive on home to my subspecies companion and I tell him all about what happened while he purrs in my lap and I have two thoughts.

First, if you've never seen a cat in your entire life or anything like one and then meet a cat in a Wal-Mart parking lot in the middle of the night all covered with fur and making this rumbling noise and maybe even smelling of mouse meat, you'd have to make some serious adjustments to what you think is pretty and sweet and something you can call your own. Second—and this hits me with a little shock—Desi says he's been hearing how I talk to my friends and even to Eddie, and that sure wasn't by hanging around in his trench coat and blending in with the furniture. Of course, if you've got a space ship that can carry you to earth from a distant galaxy, it's not so surprising you've got some kind of radio or something that lets you listen to what everybody's saying without being there.

And when I think of this, I start to sing for Desi. I just sit for a long while where I am, with Eddie in my lap, this odd little creature that doesn't look like me at all but who I find cute as can be and who I love a lot, and I sing, because when I was a teenager I had a pretty good voice and I even thought I might be a singer of some kind, though there wasn't much call for that in Bovary except in the church choir, which is where I sang mostly, but I loved to sing other kinds of songs too. And so I say real loud, "This is for you, Desi." And then I sing every song I can think of. I sing "The Long and Winding Road" and "Lucy in the Sky with Diamonds" and "Everything is Beautiful" and a bunch of others, some twice, like "The First Time Ever I Saw Your Face." Then I do a Reba McIntire medley and I start with "Is There Life Out There" and then I do "Love Will Find its Way to You" and "Up to Heaven" and "Long Distance Lover." I sing my heart out to Desi and I have to say this surprises me a little but maybe it shouldn't because already I'm hearing myself through his ears—though at that moment I can't even say for sure if he has ears—and I realize that a lot of what I say, I say because it keeps me from feeling so lonely.

The next night there's a knock on my door and I'm wearing my best dress, with a scoop neck and it shows my cleavage pretty good and on the way to the door I suddenly doubt myself. I don't know if spacemen are like earthmen in that way or not. Maybe they don't appreciate a good set of knockers, especially if their women are as skinny as Desi. But I am who I am. So I put all that out of my mind and I open the door and there he is. He's got his black felt hat on, pulled down low in case any of my neighbors are watching, I figure, and he's wearing a gray pinstripe suit that's way too big for him and a white shirt and a tie with a design that's dozens of little Tabasco bottles floating around.

"Oh," I say. "You like hot food?"

This makes him stop and try to translate.

"Your tie," I say. "Don't you know about your tie?"

He looks down and lifts the end of the tie and looks at it for a little while and he is so cute doing that and so innocent-like that my heart is doing flips and I kind of wiggle in my dress a bit to make him look at who it is he's going out with. If the women on his planet are skinny, then he could be real real ready for a woman like me. That's how I figure it as I'm waiting there for him to check out his tie and be done with it, though I know it's my own fault for getting him off on that track, and me doing that is just another example of something or other.

Then Desi looks up at me, and he takes off his hat with one hand and I see that he doesn't have anything that looks like ears, really, just sort of a little dip on each side where ears might be. But that doesn't make him so odd. What's an ear mean, really? Having an ear or not having an ear won't get you to heaven, it seems to me. I look into Desi's big dark eyes and he blinks slow and then his other hand comes out from behind his back and he's got a flower for me that's got a bloom on it the color of I don't know what, a blue kind of, a red kind of, and I know this is a spaceflower of some sort and I take it from him and it weighs about as much as my Sunbeam Steam Iron, just this one flower.

He says, "I heard you sing for me," and he holds out his hand. If you want to know an exact count, there's eight fingers on each hand, I will end up counting them carefully later on our date, but for now there's still just a lot of fingers and I realize I'm not afraid of them anymore and I reach out to him and the little suckers latch on all over my hand, top and bottom, and it's like he's kissing me in eight different places there, over and over, they hold on to me and they pulse in each spot they touch, maybe with the beat of his heart. It's like that. And my eyes fill up with tears because this man's very finger tips are in love with me, I know.

And then he leads me to his flying saucer, which is pretty big but not as big as I imagined, not as big as all of Wal-Mart, certainly, maybe just the pharmacy and housewares departments put together. It's parked out in the empty field back of my trailer where they kept saying they'd put in a miniature golf course and they never did and you don't even see the saucer till you're right up against it, it blends in with the night, and you'd think if they can make this machine, they could get him a better suit. Then he says, "You are safe with me, Edna Bradshaw, daughter of Joseph R. Bradshaw and granddaughter of William D. Bradshaw."

It later turns out these family things are important where he's from but I say to him, "William D. is dead, I only have his favorite fountain pen in a drawer somewhere, it's very beautiful, it's gold and it looks like that Chrysler Building in New York, and you should forget about Joseph R. for the time being because I'm afraid you and my daddy aren't going to hit it off real well and I just as soon not think about that till I have to."

Then Desi smiles at me and it's because of all those words, and especially me talking so blunt about my daddy, and I guess also about my taking time to tell him about the beautiful fountain pen my granddaddy left for me, but there's reasons I talk like this, I guess, and Desi says he came to like me from hearing me talk.

Listen to me even now. I'm trying to tell this story of Desi and me and I can't help myself going on about every little thing. But the reasons are always the same, and it's true I'm lonely again. And it's true I'm scared again because I've been a fool.

Desi took me off in his spaceship and we went out past the moon and I barely had time to turn around and look back and I wanted to try to figure out where Bovary was but I hadn't even found the USA when everything got blurry and before you know it we were way out in the middle of nowhere, out in space, and I couldn't see the sun or the moon or anything close up, except all the stars were very bright, and I'm not sure whether we were moving or not because there was nothing close enough by to tell, but I think we were parked, like this was the spaceman's version of the dead end road to the rock quarry, where I kissed my first boy. I turned to Desi and he turned to me and I should've been scared but I wasn't. Desi's little suckers were kissing away at my hand and then we were kissing on the lips except he didn't have any but it didn't make any difference because his mouth was soft and warm and smelled sweet, like Binaca breath spray, and I wondered if he got that on earth or if it was something just like Binaca that they have on his planet as well.

Then he took me back to his little room on the spaceship and we sat on things like bean-bag chairs and we talked a long time about what life in Bovary is like and what life on his planet is like. Desi is a research scientist, you see. He thinks that the only way for our two peoples to learn about each other is to meet and to talk and so forth. There are others where he lives that think it's best just to use their machines to listen in and do their research like that, on the sly. There are even a bunch of guys back there who say forget the whole thing, leave them to hell alone. Let everybody stick to their own place. And I told Desi that my daddy would certainly agree with the leave-them-the-hell-alone guys from his planet, but I agreed with him.

It was all very interesting and very nice, but I was starting to get a little sad. Finally I said to Desi, "So is this thing we're doing here like research? You asked me out as part of a scientific study? I was called by the Gallup Poll people once and I don't remember what it was about but I answered 'none of the above' and 'other' to every question."

For all the honesty Desi said he admired in me, I sure know it wasn't anything to do with my answers to a Gallup Poll that was bothering me, but there I was, bogged down in all of that, and that's a kind of dishonesty, it seems to me now.

But he knew what I was worried about. "No, Edna," he says. "There are many on my planet who would be critical of me. They would say this is why we should have no contact at all with your world. Things like this might happen."

He pauses right there and as far as I know he doesn't have anything to translate and I swallow hard at the knot in my throat and I say, "Things like what?"

Then both his hands take both my hands and when you've got sixteen cute little suckers going at you, it's hard to make any real tough self-denying kind of decisions and that's when I end up with a bona fide spaceman lover. And enough said, as we like to end touchy conversations around the hairdressing parlor, except I will tell you that he was bald all over and it's true what they say about bald men.

Then he takes me to the place where he picked the flower. A moon of some planet or other and there's only these flowers growing as far as the eye can see in all directions and there are clouds in the sky and they are the color of Eddie's turds after a can of Nine Lives Crab and Tuna, which just goes to show that even in some far place in another solar system you can't have everything. But maybe Desi likes those clouds and maybe I'd see it that way too sometime, except I may not have that chance now, though I could've, it's my own damn fault, and if I've been sounding a little bit hit and miss and here and there in the way I've been telling all this, it's now you find out why.

Desi and I stand in that field of flowers for a long while, his little suckers going up and down my arm and all over my throat and chest, too, because I can tell you that a spaceman does too appreciate a woman who has some flesh on her, especially in the right places, but he also appreciates a woman who will speak her mind. And I was standing there wondering if I should tell him about those clouds or if I should just keep my eyes on the flowers and my mouth shut. Then he says, "Edna, it is time to go."

So he takes my hand and we go back into his spaceship and he's real quiet all the sudden and so am I because I know the night is coming to an end. Then before you know it, there's the earth right in front of me and it's looking, even out there, pretty good, pretty much like where I should be, like my own flower box and my own propane tank and my own front Dutch door look when I drive home at night from work.

Then we are in the field behind the house and it seems awful early in the evening for as much as we've done, and later on I discover it's like two weeks later and Desi had some other spaceman come and feed Eddie while we were gone, though he should have told me because I might've been in trouble at the hairdressing salon, except they believed me pretty quick when I said a spaceman had taken me off, because that's what they'd sort of come around to thinking themselves after my being gone without a trace for two weeks and they wanted me to tell the newspaper about it because I might get some money for it, though I'm not into anything for the money, though my daddy says it's only American to make money any way you can, but I'm not *that* American, it seems to me, especially if my daddy is right about what American is, which I suspect he's not.

What I'm trying to say is that Desi stopped in this other field with me, this planet-earth field with plowed up ground and witchgrass all around and the smell of early summer in Alabama, which is pretty nice, and the sound of cicadas sawing away in the trees and something like a kind of hum out on the horizon, a nighttime sound I listen to once in a while and it makes me feel like a train whistle in the distance makes me feel, which I also listen for, especially when I'm lying awake with my insomnia and Eddie is sleeping near me, and that hum out there in the distance is all the wide world going about its business and that's good but it makes me glad I'm in my little trailer in Bovary, Alabama, and I know every face I'll see on the street the next morning.

And in the middle of a field full of all that, what was I to say when Desi took my hand and asked me to go away with him? He said, "I have to return to my home planet now and after that go off to other worlds. I am being transferred and I will not be back here. But Edna, we feel love on my planet just like you do here. That is why I know it is right that we learn to speak to each other, your people and mine. And in conclusion, I love you, Edna Bradshaw. I want you to come away with me and be with me forever."

How many chances do you have to be happy? I didn't even want to go to Mobile, though I wasn't asked, that's true enough, and I wouldn't have been happy there anyway. So that doesn't count as a blown chance. But this one was different. How could I love a spaceman? How could I be happy in a distant galaxy? These were questions that I had to answer right away, out in the smell of an Alabama summer with my cat waiting for me, though I'm sure he could've gone with us, that wasn't the issue, and with my daddy living just on the other side of town, though, to tell the truth, I wouldn't miss him much, the good Lord forgive me for that sentiment, and I did love my spaceman, I knew that, and I still do,

I love his wiggly hairless shy courteous smart-as-a-whip self. But there's only so many new things a person can take in at once and I'd about reached my limit on that night.

So I heard myself say, "I love you too, Desi. But I can't leave the planet earth. I can't even leave Bovary."

That's about all I could say. And Desi didn't put up a fuss about it, didn't try to talk me out of it, though now I wish to God he'd tried, at least tried, and maybe he could've done it, cause I could hear myself saying these words like it wasn't me speaking, like I was standing off a ways just listening in. But my spaceman was shy from the first time I saw him. And I guess he just didn't have it in him to argue with me, once he felt I'd rejected him.

That's the way the girls at the hairdressing salon see it.

I guess they're right. I guess they're right, too, about telling the newspaper my story. Maybe some other spaceman would read it, somebody from Desi's planet, and maybe Desi's been talking about me and maybe he'll hear about how miserable I am now and maybe I can find him or he can find me.

Because I am miserable. I haven't even gone near my daddy for a few months now. I look around at the people in the streets of Bovary and I get real angry at them, for some reason. Still, I stay right where I am. I guess now it's because it's the only place he could ever find me, if he wanted to. I go out into the field back of my trailer at night and I walk all around it, over and over, each night, I walk around and around under the stars because a spaceship only comes in the night and you can't even see it until you get right up next to it.

Rodney Jones

Willows

These three eighth-graders
whispering down the hall
of the junior high school,
leaning on one another
and giggling into each other's ears,
resemble three willows
that ascend from a single root.
They keep one diary.
One bird darts among them
like the normal half-nervous
tremor of the thought
that next year will come
breasts and boys, but now
they radiate a sanguine health,
a preternatural closeness.
I do not know them well,
but I mark their shyness
and exclusive rectitude,
their light canopy and banter.
For part of one more year,
they will sway together
as ungainly trunks and limbs.
And then, a little eyeliner,
a dab of lipstick; just so,
no willow remains a willow forever.
I do not have to be
an ancient Greek to see
what they will become.
Happiness does not need
the future anymore than sorrow.
They do not need to study
leaves to know
they are already green.

Rodney Jones

The Swan

Once I might have written *suave potato* on a diner napkin
and left it without imagining that the waitress,
who weighed more than three hundred pounds
and called everyone honey in a fey, sugary voice,
would find it and mistake it for biography.
The week before a man who claimed to be Jesus
had leapt through the window of a cafeteria.
It was the year of omniscient, narcissistic martyrs,
the year I also might have written that a swan dipped in iodine
and infested with the prelapsarian dying cries of saints
had risen from the baling wire brain of a garbage dump
and purloined the secret codes of the holy church.
Forgive me. This was art for a few. These people
are with us. They understand things that we do not.
By day they might drive taxis or clerk at convenience marts.
By night they like to imagine Etruscan monks
translating moonlight into porcupine
or occult parodies of the thesaurus.
Others—realists, memoirists, identity philosophers—
believe this a silly, contemptuous sophistry.
To stand between the two, pelted on one side
with ordinary river stones, on the other
with zirconium umbrellas, is only to trip
with a dwarf, to flip upside-down underwater.
My grandmother complained to me
when the last stroke turned her briefly
into a disciple of Breton and Lautreaumont,
"They give me eyedrops intended for a dog."
It is possible to imagine that a swan brain
turning on bearings of scripture and felt
had cranked one of the engines that lift heaven
and that if a swan could express itself in human language,

it would say this very thing. It is possible to have a vision.
Though we do not live in an age in which a president
can readily admit that he has been guided by birds,
it is clear that the old ways go on, that the world is sad,
that it would be different if Willie Nelson were pope.

Beth Ann Fennelly

The River That Was My Father

I said, Again I step into the river that was my father.
He said, Again you step into the river that was your father.
I said, Again his thick college ring, its large purple eyeball.
He said, A river who drags his blankets rolling from bed.
I said, I thought of my father's knuckles and how he threw his head back when he laughed.
He said, A river like a language studied two languages ago.
A river without moorings.
I said, Knuckles, navy corduroy pants, ivory cuff links in a tray on a mahogany dresser.
Ravens fly upside down in this river, he said.
I said, Strict river of white parting his hair. Ivory seam in black marble.
He said, clocks swim in circles with their minute hands as rudders.
I said, Buttercups, arithmetic, wooden crutches. Cardboard coffin of red-hatted matches.
He said, The river will accept what you throw in.
But it asks for nothing.
I said, If only I could walk all the way under.
Letting the water's fingers splay the ends of your dark hair, he said.
I said, Teach me to drift in the eddies of clouds and willows.
Without this irascible grasping after meaning, he said.
I said, When I remember I'm swimming, I begin to start drowning.
He said, Yet this is the river of your desiring.
I said again, Teach me. I slip off my shoe named Conscience, its mate named My Tongue Keeps Flapping.
He said, Lower your lips to the water. Accept the coldest kiss.

Beth Ann Fennelly

Poem in the Ninth Month

Now that they've X-rayed
the mummified female crocodile
in the Egypt room in the British Museum
they've found a baby crocodile, mummified,
inserted far back in her throat.

Just so, little one,
we drift toward the next world.
Already, our days are numbered.

Strangers will catch your head,
will thumb your eyes back to zero,
will say *Welcome to the world,* not
the afterworld,

will peel away your caul like a bandage.

George Singleton

Fat Lighter

I'd gotten discouraged and pessimistic and irrational, to the point of hoping signs would show up in my dreams. Unfortunately, one of them kept recurring: It involved a talking raccoon, a buck so tall it dwarfed its mountaintop habitat, and two men in wetsuits who caught bass in their bare hands, then somehow sucked the breath out of them right there on the lake surface. Somewhere in the middle of this dream I taught a class in southern culture studies, but the administration made me use a memoir about a whiney, rich, private school teenager for the textbook. It always ended with that raccoon saying to me, "Get to the top now," in order to save my pregnant wife, who got head butted right off the world by the deer and tumbled in slow motion through space downward, repeating that she was all right, for me not to worry, that she was all right. More often than not I awoke at three or four in the morning, slipped out of bed, and walked down to the river, wondering if I should work it for rocks like my father did, like my grandfather did—if I should dredge out the usable flat stones and sell them to landscapers and do-it-yourself wall builders alike so that my own son could go forward, get an education, and become something useful and patriotic, like a psychiatrist, ecologist, or sniper.

"It doesn't take a week of Freud to interpret the stupid thing," Abby told me one morning at the kitchen table. I had finally confessed to what marred my sleep pattern. It might've been the twentieth dream I'd undergone—and to be honest I kind of looked forward to it before bedtime. The raccoon was soft, easy to cradle in the arms, and liked to lick my face. His name seemed to be Gus, or Clarence. I wished that it talked more. "You're at a crossroads, you're scared, and you don't want to let people down."

I didn't say, "Gee, do you think?" I didn't say, "Hotdamn—do you think that maybe I'm figuring out that I made a big mistake by enrolling in a low residency southern culture studies program down in Mississippi that, more than likely, is a scam; that when you called me up to say you were pregnant perhaps I first thought that it was someone else's child; that now that I know it's mine I'm obsessed with wanting nothing to go wrong; that since you can't take the weird job you got offered up at the Asheville TV station—and I wonder what they were thinking anyway seeing as you have the bizarre speech impediment—we might be in trouble financially?"

The sun rose outside on a clear, cold February morning. As I had done for the past month, I promised myself that I would get on the road and find someone to interview for a southern culture studies scholarly paper, suitable for my degree requirement. I would go down to the Unknown Branch of the Middle Saluda River and look at the homemade dredge again, and get no tangible work done. I said, "Maybe I'm supposed to be a trapper and that's why the raccoon keeps showing up. Or a cook."

Abby got up and fetched some cranberry juice out of the refrigerator. She said, "I think it's sweet. I mean, I hope that my floating off the Earth doesn't mean anything more than I'm out of this world in your subconscious."

I caught myself staring at the butcher knife on the countertop, and wondered what it was doing out. We'd eaten pancakes for supper, with blackberries I had picked and frozen myself back in August when I was supposed to be interviewing some old man about the exercise bicycles he'd transformed into ax grinders.

I said, "Everybody's already written about those guys who wrestle catfish. It's called 'noodling.' The dream can't be about *that* little weird sport."

My mentor and adviser had sent a three-page list of prompts, single-spaced, for me to respond to, write, and send back. He stressed that these were personal essays, not footnoted scholarly works, and all of them were wide-open. Number 13, which I skipped to immediately because I saw it as my lucky number, went, "Find an area that locals consider sacred due to superstition or legend. Describe the physical place, and interview people about experiences they've had there. Not like a place where the Virgin Mary showed up on a rock face or tree bark, you idiot."

"The mountaintop where the big deer lives—does it have trees?" Abby said. She picked up the knife and placed it in the sink. "When I'm tumbling down the mountain, do I hit treetops all the way down?"

I wanted bourbon in my coffee. I'd been awake for six hours. "I don't remember, Abby. I don't know."

"You're dreaming of Fat Lighter. The landscape you've described sounds like Fat Lighter, South Carolina."

I didn't get up and kiss my wife on the jaw, then down on her belly like I'd seen men do in movies and commercials for auto insurance. I pulled back from the kitchen table, went back to my study—which was only a taped off section of our arena-style log house—and picked up my backpack already filled with memo pads, pens, and a tape recorder. On my way out I said, "You want to go with me, honey?"

She rubbed her abdomen, which, by the way, didn't even protrude yet. She said, "I don't know that hanging out on moonscapes would be good for the baby. I haven't seen it written down officially in any of the literature I've read, but I'm thinking it can't be good. Plus the bumpy ride."

I made a point not to look down by the river, at the tools and machinery I'd let rust down there since abandoning Carolina Rocks. I thought about how we had enough money saved for about a year, and how I either needed to finish up the master's degree and get a job directly, or go back to raping the Unknown Branch of the Saluda River much like the entire Looper clan had done since the 1930's.

Or I could find the talking raccoon of my dreams and go on tour.

Here's the story with fat lighter: It's a piece of pine that's been down for years, and the resin has transformed into something this side of gunpowder. Some people call it fatwood. You take a piece of fat lighter, which will ignite when touched to an everyday paper match, and use it to start a fire of green oak. Fat lighter smells like turpentine, and the best way to harvest the stuff is to take a hatchet way out into some old growth woods, find a stump or fallen pine tree, hack into it, and inhale mightily. If what you gather olfactory reminds you of the two-by-four aisle at Lowe's, then keep going. If it smells like the inside of an obsessive-compulsive country mechanic's work shed who washes his hands over and over with turpentine, and you undergo visions of a possible hellfire explosion meant for only the worst of Republicans, then you've found fat lighter. Now take the hatchet and splinter off kindling-sized pieces.

Here's the story of Fat Lighter, the community: Somewhere off highway 288, up the mountain from Robertson's Berry Farm, between Pumpkintown and Traveler's Rest—not far from where Abby and I live, where my parents lived, where my paternal grandparents lived—is a manmade carp and catfish compound called lakes Laurel and Hardy. It was a resort, from what I understand, back in the 1940s. Airstreams once populated this area, and the summer shacks weren't so much shacks back then. If you drive past the lakes, which aren't much more than shallow four-acre indentions fed by the Saluda River, and drive until it's a one-lane asphalt road, then you're entering Fat Lighter. When the road ends, and there's a red cement block hunter's cabin with an outhouse thirty yards away, you're in Fat Lighter proper.

And it's not hard to miss, seeing as up until this point, there had been trees. Fat Lighter looks like the place timber companies send their blind loggers to practice. Pine tree stumps stand anywhere from six inches off the ground to six feet, and full thirty-foot pines rest haphazardly on needles turned to mulch. It's a land inhabited only by chiggers, red bugs, stupid hikers, escaped convicts, drunk men needing to hide from their wives, survivalists, xenophobes, and a federally protected plant known as the Ratface Touch-Me-Not. Fat Lighter takes up enough space to confuse satellite-imaging neophytes.

I drove my truck down to highway 288 and pulled over at a

place where men fished the Saluda. There I tried to scrape off the Phi Beta Kappa decal I made the mistake of gluing to my back window, and a square bumper sticker that showed a "W" with a line across it. One thing I'd learned—though not been able to write about yet—while working on my low residency master's degree in southern culture studies, and that was how it's easy to be labeled a troublemaker, misfit, rabble-rouser, traitor, heathen, freak, or homosexual just by having a couple stickers on your car. When I tried to interview the Modestine Duncans about their belief that printing the Book of Revelation on their mobile homes protected them, one woman came out and asked if I raised special Siamese Fighting fish, what with the "beta" she read. Another time when I tried to talk to some men I felt sure knew about a lynching that took place down by a barbecue stand, this edentate rib bone sucker came out and asked, "You a queer?" because of the supposed "W" I had with a cross through it. He thought it meant "No women." My wife had the same experience one time when she drove the truck, when a man asked if she was lesbian. But he ended up claiming dyslexia and read the crossed out "W" upside down.

I had not been out on highway 288 in a couple years, seeing as I liked going toward civilization, and because no one had thought to develop the area, which meant there was no need for rock walls, paths, ornamental ponds, and whatever else most sane people with too much money did with my family-operated flat river rock products. I passed a new breed of cow for these parts that looked like giant wooly worms, or Oreo cookies, or gene-altered pandas. I took a right turn at the Laurel and Hardy Lakes sign, which advertised both carp and catfish tournaments for a five dollar fee.

And then I went by No Trespassing signs nailed to leaning no-windowed shanties, imploded snailbacks, seared spots on the ground where sheds once stood. Outhouses. What I felt certain to be unmarked graves. But there was no smell of death in the air, seeing as, the closer I got, it smelled like a turpentine factory loomed right beyond the next ridge.

I turned on my tape recorder. I said to myself, like an idiot, "It's February ninth—oh, shit Valentine's Day is just around the corner and I better get Abby something or she'll say I take her for granted, et cetera—and I'm coming up on the area known as Fat Lighter here in northern South Carolina. I'm hoping to find some people nosing around up here who'll talk to me, though I imagine anyone with good stories won't be willing to tell them."

I rewound the tape and replayed it. I hit Stop, then Record again to say, "Valentine's Day. Don't forget Valentine's Day." I looked behind the seat to make sure that I had a pistol I'd not fired since my father made me shoot at some bluffs beyond our property, in order to loosen some rock that would eventually tumble downstream.

I parked at the end of the asphalt, in the overgrown dirt driveway of a trailer that had fallen in on itself, then walked up what looked like a forgotten logging road. It took only two slight inclines and one turn south before I hit Fat Lighter. Wisps of smoke extended down the slope. I scanned the area quickly, then slower. No one camped out in dome tents like I had imagined. There were no desperados entrenched into the hillside with ammo crossing their chests. No talking raccoons showed up to lead the way.

"I thought I heard a car come up," a voice said from off to the side, which made me jump. I looked over to find a man, maybe in his early seventies, crouched down by a fallen log. He wore leather boots to his knees and tucked his green work pants inside.

"How're you doing?" I said. My voice went a register or two too high. "I didn't expect anyone up here," I said, this time coming off like the bass in a barbershop quartet.

"Just me, I guess."

I walked over, holding the tape recorder. "Stet Looper," I said, extending my hand.

He held a yellow-handled Case knife open, shifted it to his left hand, and shook. "Howdy, Stet Looper. I'm Raymond. You ain't related to Loopers run the river rock business by any chance, are you?"

I didn't know what to say. In the past I didn't like giving up personal information while conducting an interview for a southern culture studies program. I said, "Yessir. My father and grandfather had the business. Now I do. Kind of. Well, to be honest, I'm probably going to give up the operation in order to finish up a master's degree, then go teach, I guess." Do not tell people you have an education. Do not tell people you have aspirations, I thought. "Or not."

"I knew your daddy and granddaddy." Raymond stood up. He might've been six foot six, I figured, which seemed tall for an older man. "This is killing my back."

"Listen," I said, pulling the tape recorder out of my pocket. "I came up here hoping to find out some truth about Fat Lighter. I was thinking that there'd be a bunch of people up here."

"Fat Lighter the place-name, or fat lighter the stove starter," Raymond said. "The only thing I can tell you about the place is this: We're standing at the very last mountain before the land flattens out into the piedmont. Tornadoes stop here." He stomped his right foot. "Tornadoes go all zigzagging down there, then kind of ricochet up against this area, tearing down all the pine. The pine goes down, and over the years the resin builds up—it's some kind of scientific chemistry explanation—and you get acre upon acre of fat lighter."

I said, "That's what I thought. There are all kinds of rumors, you know."

Raymond knelt back down. Scattered around his feet were wooden hearts, the size of fists. "Or: Yankees ran out of wood right after the Civil War, and some old soldiers remembered this place. They came back, chopped all the wood down with no plan whatsoever, and took it back north for their houses. Man like you in the river rock business should hate all men who build houses from wood."

I said, "We normally sell to landscape developers who build walls and walkways."

Raymond turned a knot of fat lighter in his hand, scraped at a place I couldn't see as needing anything, then dropped it back down on the ground. He got up and walked sideways down the slope, picked up a few pieces of fallen trees, kicked at a stump. He said, "Landscape developers. Hey, you interested in buying your valentine a hand-carved heart? What you do, you see, is you give them this here wooden heart, and then you set it out on the table next to a candle real close, and before you know it the heart ignites into flame. I thought it up myself."

I had to stand close to Raymond in order for the tape recorder to pick up his voice. For about a second I thought he might think I invaded his personal space, way up here with nothing but room to move around. I said, "What a great idea! Yes, yes, I'll buy one. I'll buy two or three! I have a wife, and a kid on the way!" I thought, If he knew my father and grandfather, then he knows where I live. I thought, Shut up.

Raymond said, "I don't know. I reckon I get anywhere's from five to twenty dollars apiece, depending. I believe I sell more of the things to people who just got out of a bad marriage. I'm not saying they use the hearts for voodoo purposes, you know, but I wouldn't be surprised none."

I said, "I wouldn't be surprised none," and reminded myself to listen better. I reminded myself to ask questions.

"You can tell me your last name if you want. That would make the paper I need to write about Fat Lighter that much more believable and authentic. Listen, how did you come across this area? Tell me about the first time you came up here. Have you ever come across people hiding out from the law? Is it true that sometimes old drunks come up here, running from their wives? I heard there were, at one time, a bunch of moonshine stills. I guess with all the fat lighter on the ground it would be easy to get a still fired up, you know."

Raymond looked at me and squinted. "I wear these high boots because lightning hits here often. When lightning hits, it causes some small fires. Keeps the ground warm. Has snakes confused as to the season. They don't know whether to hibernate, or come out of their holes and strike what's closest." He reached into his front pocket and pulled out a pack of Lucky Strikes. "Watch this." He struck a wooden match on his zipper, held it to a piece of fat lighter the size of a pencil, then lit his cigarette with the shard of pine. Raymond stuck the burning end of the fat lighter into the ground, counted to ten, then pulled it back out. It remained afire.

"They won't go out. They're like trick candles. My hearts are the same way." He pointed down the mountain. "Hate's down there. Fat lighter's all about love."

I couldn't tell if he meant the place, or the wood. I thought of Zarathustra coming down the mountain. I said, "Chemistry and science are two things I don't understand." I thought, *Finally*—a real, honest-to-goodness Old South man not encumbered or tainted or drawn to the New South, i.e., regular contemporary American thought patterns and capitalistic mindsets. I thought, I can write a low residency master's program-worthy paper on Raymond.

"Last name's Goss. First time I come up here was right about in high school, with a girl. Played a game I made up called 'Snake, or Dick?' She had to close her eyes, you know. The second time I come up here was to hide out, right after she told her daddy."

I couldn't tell if Raymond maybe spent too much time inhaling turpentine. I reached for my wallet, pulled out forty dollars, and asked what I could get.

Abby neared the end of her first trimester and, like most women I had read about undergoing the first twelve weeks of pregnancy, wanted her life back in regards to not running to the toilet sick to her stomach. I came home with three smooth, beautiful, though potent, Raymond Goss-carved hearts. He wouldn't sign the things, for he feared that when they burned it might work as bad luck on him. One heart looked like an actual heart pulled out of the chest cavity of a child—there were even little broken off branches from this particular knot, which seemed to represent the aorta, pulmonary artery, anterior and posterior vena cava, and so on—but was whittled down and sanded nicely. The second and third hearts looked like traditional Valentine's Day mementos, the image that Cupid aimed his arrow toward.

All of them stunk like all get-out.

I got out of the truck, walked beneath our outcropped front porch, picked up a bottle of bourbon, and then ascended the steps and walked in the house to find Abby splayed out on the couch.

She wore her aerobics outfit, and kept her feet propped up on a mini-trampoline. "Wow," she said. "I didn't expect you to come back in one piece. I figured I'd be getting a call from the police about right now. Or emergency room."

I walked up and kissed Abby on the forehead. "I didn't get a whole ton of information, but probably enough for a short paper. I'm thinking that Dr. Crowther will be happy. I know for a fact he hasn't ever heard of Fat Lighter."

"What the hell, Stet?" Abby got off the couch and race-walked to the bathroom. "What's that smell you brought in with you?" She immediately underwent a barrage of dry heaves. From the open living space where I stood it sounded like she called geese, or seals.

I called out to her, "I got you a Valentine's Day present, honey." I put the carved hearts to my nose and inhaled. They didn't seem to be dissipating whatsoever. If anything the three hearts gained strength. I had wanted to return home all sentimental and symbolic, of course, saying how we now had three hearts in the Looper family—even though Abby kept her maiden name and our child would have one of those weird hyphens that probably ended up being a pain in the ass when filling out forms—and then we could either place all three hearts on the fireplace mantle, or above the kitchen sink, or in the bedroom, or scattered around the house. When the worst winter of all time happened due to the current president's lack of an environmental policy, we could throw our hearts in the fireplace and help kindle a cord of wood, then whatever river rocks I threw in to radiate heat.

Between long, drawn-out, melodramatic wails Abby said, "Get out of the house and take what you brought in with you. Go bathe in the river before you come back in. Burn your clothes somewhere far away. What is that stench? I smell gin. Gin and passionflower and St. John's Wort. The inside of a dugout where a blind batter put on too much pine tar."

She went on. Abby shouldn't have said anything about the blind baseball player, for I would only think about playing "Snake, or Dick?" for the rest of the day. I said, "Okay. I'm out of here. Do you want me to spray some Lysol in the air before I go?"

The heaves that emanated from her inner core told me that her queasiness might be worse with such a quinella. I thought, Screw me for trying to be romantic. I thought, Fat Lighter's all about love, my ass.

Raymond Goss no longer had a wife. She died some thirty years earlier, of complications set on by a variety of lung ailments. "We used to heat with coal," he said when I came back up to Fat Lighter, my tape recorder at the ready. "Maybe that was it. But then we changed to a wood stove. She was sickly throughout her life, but it didn't affect her beauty. When I married her she had asthma, and then came on emphysema. In between was bronchitis. But she never smoked. This was back before all that talk of second-hand smoke came into the headlines. I blame myself nowadays. Right before she died was when I got the idea to carve her out a heart of fat lighter. It just came to me, you know. It's pretty much how I've made my living since Irvette passed. The mill closed directly after, and I kept carving. Never met another woman. Sometimes I'll be in the grocery store and hear a woman have a coughing fit two aisles over. I always find myself rolling my buggy that direction, expecting it to be Irvette."

I thought, Do not start crying. I thought, It is unprofessional for a prospective low residency southern culture studies master's degree student to become emotionally involved with his interviewee.

We sat crouched on opposing stumps. Raymond Goss carved another tiny heart. I couldn't understand how his knife slivered off tendrils of wood seeing as fat lighter's just this side of being petrified in terms of hardness. I said, "I came up here to buy some more hearts," which, of course, wasn't true. "My wife loved the first three so much, she wants more. She thinks they're good luck. She just has a feeling."

"Take your pick," Raymond said. He pointed his knife down toward his feet at what hearts lay there finished. "I don't charge as much up here. Hell, I've never had anyone come all the way up this way to buy one. Normally I sell them off Tuesdays and Fridays at the flea market over in Chesnee. And I got a contract out with one of the Buck woodstove distributors down in Greenville. They throw in a couple hearts to anyone who buys in February. And my hearts get sold at a number of specialty shops and boutiques down in Charleston, Savannah, Atlanta, and Asheville. Word is L.L. Bean's about to sign me on for their catalog. Another place called Plow and Hearth. My business manager takes care of all this stuff. Some outfit down Texas way called Neiman Marcus."

I thought, This is about the time the deer should come stand atop the mountain, when Abby should fly off because of a lack of gravity, when raccoons should nuzzle up to my ear and say, "Get out of here immediately." I felt myself nodding at Raymond Goss far longer than a normal person nodded. There was no way he could make up Neiman Marcus, I thought. No way he could let "L.L. Bean" fly out of his mouth without having to hesitate.

I said, "You're a millionaire, aren't you." I didn't say, "You're not worthy material for a low residency southern culture studies master's program essay."

Raymond Goss said, "I been thinking about carving out all the organs, all out of fat lighter. Liver. Spleen. Kidneys. Brain." He reached into his pocket, pulled out a cigarette, lit it. "Lungs. And then I could tie them all into a body-kind of shape, and you could start your fire with a whole human. Kind of like a mini-cremation, you know."

I tried not to think of my mother's makeshift cremation, some twenty years earlier. I thought, Do not cry. Do not give up. "Huh," I said. I thought, I need to get back home and cradle my wife from behind, hold her hair back, whisper in her ear that I'm sorry about all of my misdeeds, my odd ambitions, my lack of spirit in regards to manual labor. "Kind of like those kits you get as a kid to learn body parts and whatnot."

Raymond Goss stood up and stretched his back. "I'm going to take work back home." He leaned down, picked up what hearts he'd finished, and put them in his front pockets. "You say you want to buy some more?"

I'm not sure what changed my mind—maybe Goss's authenticity faded about the time he mentioned Plow and Hearth—but I said,

"I better hold off. I need to do some grocery shopping on the way back and I don't want to run out of money."

I thought, for the first time, How did he get up here? I didn't see a car or truck on the way up. Raymond Goss said, "I know what you mean. Well, if you're one to purchase from the catalogs, check out those places I mentioned. Or you can catch me up here, or at the flea market, like I said."

Then he picked up a stump, tucked it under his left armpit, and strode down Fat Lighter like a character out of a Tom Waits song, like Paul Bunyan's little-known brother. I stood alone atop Fat Lighter and looked way off toward flatter lands, where tornados danced throughout the year. There was no sound, no wind. No animals grazed below me, nor did birds fly by on their way to woods suitable for nests.

That night I would take my three hearts and throw them in the river, then wash my hands in the Unknown Branch of the Saluda. I would come back to Abby and announce that another southern cultures studies paper escaped me, and reiterate that I wanted to be a good father and husband. I would get out our three-county phone book, long after my wife fell asleep on our couch by the fire, and call every Goss listed, predicting that none of them would know of a rich and famous carver in their family trees.

Dean Paschal

Sautéing the Platygast

At nightfall we lit a lantern to begin our search. We do better with lanterns; they give a quieter, gentler light; I am convinced that the filament of a flashlight makes a sound. (Not much of a sound, mind you, but there are creatures out there that can hear it.) We were in particularly fertile territory now, the wild thickets below the bog. Still, I had my doubts about this; we seldom hunt as a family and we were making altogether too much noise. The ground was dry; nevertheless, within a week of a rain can be a dangerous time to hunt. My son and daughter were carrying the torches as well as a broom and shovel. My wife was staying close to me in the circle of light from the lantern. The dog was making most of the racket, pulling the cart behind us with the washtubs. I felt a foreboding and misgiving about all of it. I listened to the cicadas, to the frogs, to the resin in the crackling flames. The children had gotten somewhat ahead of us and I found myself watching the interesting shadows they cast. My daughter, especially, likes to carry a torch. "You *like* carrying a torch!" I said to her when we caught up again. But she is at a sullen age and I received (and expected) no reply. Whether she understands me or not, I could not say.

In addition to the lantern, I had my Luger and the newly modified prong, on which I have welded a sharpened, vee-shaped block so it won't slide so much on the vertebrae. The pockets of my jacket were stuffed with the egg cases of some *Stelacens*, the tense embryos nestled like pearls in the leathery pouches. I shelled a few of them out with my thumb as I walked. They are good to snack on: slick, vaguely iridescent, mainly skull but soft. Eaten alive they are almost gummy; floated in cream they remind one of blueberries; but best of all is the way I had prepared them tonight: toasted slightly, with butter and salt, the skin dried close to the bone[1] and giving a nut-like flavor.

I looked up at the new moon, the narrow rim as fragile as ice in the night sky. Inauspicious, it seemed to me. This was not a good time to be moving about; the air itself seemed to be holding out on us. I thought of those millennia past when the planet was lonely and the bulk of life was large, of the incredible saurians rumbling through this landscape, huddled against the emptiness and stars. It was an agony then, perfectly terrifying to be alive. Years ago, I used to tell my students:

"When you think of a *Tyrannosaurus rex*, gentlemen, nineteen feet tall and eight tons in weight. Think bluff, gentlemen! Think bluff!"

My son had stopped now and raised his hand for silence. "Bring the lantern, Frank," he said. (My children call me Frank.) He had found the first one. Then I saw it, too, at ground level, the silvered discs of its eyes reflecting.

What a night! We caught three washtubs full and afterward had to hurry home to put the corrugated covers on top of them. As the creatures around here warm up, they become more active and begin to gnaw and scratch at one another. In fact, we had hardly finished putting the covers in place when I began to hear their skins scraping against the galvanized zinc of the tubs.

Soon afterward, there was an intermittent fierce whacking (Whack! Whack! Whack!) from the third tub which left dents and protuberances in the metal that were sobering to look at. There is a slope behind the cabin and this particular tub suddenly began to nudge and slide down it. The animals seemed to be boiling inside.

---

[1] "Bone" is the correct word here (amazingly enough) not cartilage. Intramembranous ossification begins almost immediately in Stelaceiis—which, despite some superficial resemblances, are definitely not Elasmobranchii.

There was a great banging and rattling of the handles and I saw a couple of the smaller creatures slither out from under the corrugations of the tin. I shot twice with my Luger but missed both of them and watched their tails bumping out of the circle of light.

Then I tied the tub to a stake.

We have appetites, this family, but cook as fast as we could, we were four days getting to the third tub. I then found that we had made a terrible mistake. There was only one creature left inside, his body swollen like a tick, his skin so tight it seemed about to change color. He had evidently eaten every other animal. There was not one bone left, not one scrap of skin. He lifted his head toward us and opened his mouth wide. He had no shell but the way he maneuvered his body in rotation reminded me of a turtle.

I stuck the gig in and nudged him experimentally. He snapped the head of it clean off. (It was the old-style gig with the wooden handle.) Is this the whacker, I thought, or is this what ate the whacker?

I looked deep into his bloodshot and obdurate eyes. "Careful," I said.

The real tragedy was that we had not gotten a better look at the other animals inside. The wife took my place and kept the whacker distracted while I slipped around behind him. He moved forward slowly and pressed his claws against the metal. Then I managed to get him through the neck with the prong. I drove his throat against the wall of the tub and bent his head backwards over his spine. The pressure I was exerting began to smear his pig-like nose and awful wedge of a mouth. Then he twisted and began to buck on me. The wife stabilized him with another gig in the left leg while little-Frank ran to get the mallet. Meanwhile, I drove the prong steadily into his spinal column, the sweat plastering my shirt, my left arm beginning to spasm from the strain. Suddenly, the stake pulled loose and the tub began to slide on the smooth dirt. My great fear was that this guy might be able to jerk loose and flip out onto the ground. His huge mouth was open now and I could see his long recursive teeth and the glass-like ridge of his jaw.

"You're about to slip, Frank!" my son said.

He was right. Fortunately, this new prong won't slide. As I drove the final blows through the cord, the whacker's neck folded like a thick towel and he made a series of convulsive movements with his limbs. He seemed to smile at me upside down. It was perfectly obscene, this smile, more of a smirk I should say; it reminded me not so much of one of your standard animals, as one of those fat, triangular-headed kids that one sometimes sees in drugstores.

In hopes that he might have swallowed a few of the smaller creatures whole, we cut him open on the spot and turned his stomach inside out. But there was nothing identifiable inside, not a paw.

It was malicious the extent of this mastication.

We made haste to cook him immediately. Indeed, his eyes had scarcely glazed over when we began our prayers. Unfortunately, in our rush, we grabbed too small a pan and his legs, which overrode the rim, were charred rather badly in the flames.

Not bad, it was, this meat; and, despite some fibers, not really so tough either, a bit like pangolin or anteater. Unfortunately, my children are sloppy and stingy eaters. During the prayer itself my daughter grabbed all the claws.

"She got them last time!" little-Frank yelled. But before we could stop her, my daughter had put two of them in her mouth and was crunching them, bones and all. The others we could not pry out of her fingers. My wife said nothing but smiled with the corners of her eyes.

(It seems my daughter cannot get heavy enough to suit my wife.)

The problem with this "whacker"—a *Rhynochelon*, I ended up calling him—was that there was nothing appropriate to go with such a lean and fibrous meat. In addition, there wasn't nearly as much *to* him as one might have expected from the circumstances. At the end of the meal, none of us were truly full. What would have been nice would have been a skewer of scalatoids but I kept very quiet about that.

I watched as my daughter put her fork down and began looking at me from across the table. My wife and little-Frank soon did the same.

"How about a platter of *gills*?!" I said, getting up and taking my dishes to the sink. (*Scalatoids*, their eyes were saying and I didn't want to go through it again.)

My decision about the scalatoid matter is final, as far as I'm concerned—but the story, perhaps, bears repeating:

Scalatoids[2], though filling, are not really large. They are of a size with or perhaps slightly smaller than hedgehogs. Their appearance is considerably different, though. Looked at ventrally, they are very like platygasters (or platygasts as we call them, a very common little creature hereabouts) but the stomach is not nearly so flat and they are not as good for sautéing. I had given up cooking scalatoids years ago; there was far too much *fat* in the things which I found impossible to render out. But working secretly, and entirely on her own, my daughter discovered a way to prepare them. What she accomplished was a good deal more than a culinary miracle; it seemed to defy all reason. One afternoon, she allowed us to watch her at work. Even afterward, though, the mystery remained; there was no essential difference in her technique or spices. The difference in flavor was amazing.

(From the taste alone, I would have said it was a different animal.)

It took me some time to find out what she was doing. Scalatoids, you must understand, are nearly tongueless and incapable of making a noise. She was throwing them in a tub of water and letting them churn there for a week. They are by no means good swimmers, scalatoids; it was sheer desperation that was keeping them afloat. Hour after hour, day after day, they treaded in that water, silent, frantic, indomitable, constantly attempting to climb up on one another. I was in my daughter's room, one afternoon, looking for my razor, when I made the discovery of five of them in a washtub at the foot of her bed.

---

[2]Something of a common or popular name. (The teeth, though extremely tiny, are step-like.)

I hope never again in my life to see the like of what was in their eyes. It would be impossible to overestimate their fear of water and drowning. Scalatoids are vaguely globular creatures, full of surface and other tensions; and, forever after this, they seemed to me to be the embodiment of pure will.

(This, of course, was her way of burning up the excess fat.)

I put a stop to it immediately. Still, I must confess, I rather miss the things. There is no doubt about it: the struggle improved the flavor.

When we first moved to this area, it took me some time to realize that this is no ordinary place. Animals can be killed here but nothing dies naturally. It is a very special locus built on a confluence of singularities. The electric atmosphere plays subtle tricks of energy. On an otherwise bright day a bolt of lightning can *condense* itself out of the air. One can feel the static even in the soil itself, which has special properties. Part of the area may have been an island at one time, despite the largely sedimentary rock. There are signs, too, of a previous habitation (some fruit trees, for instance, not local to the area).

What is incredible is the extent the soil is layered and honeycombed with dormant animals. Having started from a slightly different angle, they have begun estivating through the millennia and running, somehow, parallel to death. They are tangled in places, clumped, like earthworms. In heavy storms they sometimes wash out of themselves. Fortunately, precious few of them are terribly large. The thought, though, of how they are layered here gravely bothers our occasional guests. My wife and I invariably hear them whisper to one another far into the night.

On first arrival, I paid little attention to the animals. I was so sick of academia, dazed and overrun that I did not want to expend any energy thinking. I ignored all implications and ate whatever was handy. I had worked too long and hard in a single line and it was as though I had wakened in the midst of a dream. Furthermore, much about these creatures was unfamiliar to me. Evidently there are evolutionary lines tangled here which did not proceed. I think there was a level at which I did not take them seriously; I expected them to fade, tooth and claw, at sunrise.

That was years ago. Now, I am fascinated once more. I have returned to my books and manuals and vowed never again to eat anything without a name.

Such persistent and single-minded endeavor is not without its dangers, however. One evening, not long ago, based on no more than intuition and a low mound, little-Frank and I discovered a large animal in the bog below the lake. We dug it out together. We were rather pleased with ourselves and each grabbed two of its legs in order to carry it back. *Little*-Frank, I persist in calling him, though at this point he is taller than I am. (In fact, the whole way home he complained that he had most of the weight.)

I was anxious to flip it over to see what was going on with its reproductive system; but by the time we got to the basement we were both too exhausted.

(It had three eyes and I knew it had to be a rather early specimen.)

Our basement gets very cold at night and I figured it would be safe there till morning. I couldn't begin to decide what to call it. This was the first one I'd ever caught and, in my ignorance of its strength, I looped a chain around its neck of scarcely more than half-inch links.

When I went upstairs, the wife was already in bed. The windows were shut and the lamps were lit. We augment our illumination with kerosene lamps. In fact, we keep one lit at the foot of the bed at all times. Our electricity is not reliable and I feel it is best to have a bit of light instantly available, being as what we are surrounded by out here. "Honey..." I said, but lost my train of thought.

I began wiping my feet together over the side of the bed. I couldn't get the thing out of my mind; it seemed to have scales; it definitely had claws; I was not altogether happy about it. The lamp on the nightstand had just been extinguished and there was a pale glow of red from the wick.

"It might not be a reptile," I said.

At three in the morning, I woke up. It sounded like there was something in the basement swacking around with a four-by-four. I got out of bed immediately. But my son was already in the room. He turned up the lamp till it smoked. The light was swinging, the whole cabin shuddering at each blow.

"Frank, it's loose!" he said.

"What?"

(I began fumbling around on the night table for my glasses.)

"It's *loose*, Frank!"

I slipped on boots, got my Luger out of the closet, grabbed the prong and the gig and went out the back way, tripping on the stairs. I ran around to have a look in through a basement window.

I have a workshop at one end. The creature had dragged through the tools for that, tangled himself in the cables for the arc welder and begun chewing on the vise. A piece of the chain was still attached to his neck. I got around to the closest window, broke out the pane, and, using the flashlight, began firing down through all the orbital foramina. The dog was barking hysterically. I reloaded the Luger five times and emptied the entire last clip down its throat.

Then I stopped and waited.

My daughter stood by, watching.

It took two full days for all motion to cease; the meat, when cut up, would not lie flat or lose its muscle tone. Even after being cooked, it seemed to positively creep on the plate. Never have I so underestimated a metabolism.

We got a total of seven pounds of thyroid tissue out of the thing, most of which, admittedly, may not have been active. The entire gland was goitrous and cystic and took a lot of chewing to get through.

"Always room in this world for surprises!" I said, somewhat lamely, when it was over, though nothing truly big is ever getting inside this house again in one piece.

The experience was terrifying, though the animal itself was, on the whole, rather straightforward. Not like everything we find here. Consider the one I discovered some years ago while planting the fig tree: He was about a yard long, completely legless, with a distinctly submarine-like shape and something of a beaver-like tail (the tail turned vertically, though). He had two close-set eyes and a single upturned nostril.

(The nostril, in fact, was the part of him I came upon first.)

The problem was that there was no way he could be placed on the ground that he would either balance or sit level. I kept playing with his cold body in the cold sand but he kept tilting or rolling over on me. Finally, I became frustrated and tossed him, end-over-end (he was as stiff as a log) into the lake. I thought no more about him. But, two years later, I found what was evidently the same guy, very much alive, placidly sculling around in the backwaters, keeping that single nostril above the surface of the water.

"Blah!" I said, suddenly very disappointed in myself.

(I felt then, as I do now, that his aquatic nature should have been obvious.)

The truth is, were that lake drained, that creature would not be the most interesting thing in it. My feeling is that the denizens of its depths must scarcely eat anymore. It contains a virtual stew of life-forms which have been coasting through that liquor for millennia. Such a collection is marvelously edifying, of course, though truthfully, what one has here, as in all evolution, is variety more than improvement.

(I have eaten plenty of the modern animals and they simply don't taste any better.)

Occasionally, I go fishing in the lake, most often with the wife or little-Frank, though at the last outing it was my daughter that wanted to accompany me. We keep a small steam launch at the end of the dock. My daughter insisted on riding in the very back of it and adorned herself, perfectly inappropriately, in a flowing dress and a straw hat with purple ribbons. (So that's it, I thought, she wants to wear her new hat.) It took her some time to arrange her body on the cushions in the stern. We went chugging out slowly, with my doing all the stoking of coal and adjusting of valves. I locked the tiller and busied myself screwing down grease cups, the vapor and smoke settling around us on the black water. There was a disquieting calm within the lake and in the huge trees that overhung it. Every time I looked back at her, I found my daughter watching me, those purple ribbons trailing behind.

(Some of her proclivities I worry about.)

We—or rather I—fished all day but caught nothing interesting: a dozen catfish, a few trout, and a small amphibian which resembled a hellbender. While chugging back, the pump to the condenser broke which put us another forty-five minutes behind. It was nearly sunset when we got home. It was then that I found we had only one fish in our tank. I was furious considering the total effort expended and demanded to know what had happened to the rest of them. Surprisingly enough, my daughter did not hesitate to say:

She had been poking their eyes out with her hat pin and releasing them into the water.

We walked to the cabin with a dreadful silence between us. I didn't know what to say. The worrisome thing about my daughter is that she will do anything she thinks of. This is a trait she gets from her mother, who, when she is in a bad mood, has been known to clean an animal alive. Our pathetic catch—one short and rather fat catfish—I carried in myself, holding it by the tail. I was disgusted and didn't even bother to kill or clean it. My wife has a tin-lined copper pot which holds eight gallons. When placed on the stove (which is where I put it) the pot appears huge and overlaps two burners. I filled the bottom of it with water and watched my fish swim in circles inside. I sliced some wedges of lemon (two of which it gobbled whole). Then it began to nibble at a third. Afterward, the fish seemed to notice some shadow of itself reflected in the bright tin and thereupon began to make what seemed to be threatening, territorial gestures toward it.

"Blab!" I said, slicing another lemon. "The fruit of our labors!"

The fish circled and returned to its illusory companion. I watched it more carefully. The movements began again. Perhaps they were not territorial at all; perhaps they were gestures of courtship.

"Who knows?" I said, lighting both of the burners.

The anger and fire in the eyes of animals is not unrelated to the motion of the body. If one holds them perfectly still, there is a vulnerability which appears in the pupils that one can look deeply into. We found this out largely by accident thanks to a method we sometimes use to marinade creatures while they are still alive. (We bind them with ropes to wooden boards and platters.) Even in the most vicious the look will be there. In the mammals it is very obvious; in others, it can be obscured by a surface glitter. I have come to think of the pupil as a two-way mirror, a dark portal both reflecting and opaque. I know not what the brain behind it makes of us, but always before I make ready the pots and sever the cord, I bow down at the point of focus and offer myself as if to a god.

The endless dying with so little visible birth contributes to the melancholy atmosphere in this place. We have cold and snow, heat and rain; but no winter or spring, no face to the seasons here. Far more than the times are out of joint; there seems to be some fundamental dislocation to life itself.

I find myself wondering on occasion, "Why isn't there any central *trunk* anymore? Why is everything out on a limb?" Sometimes in my despair, I will turn to the invertebrates, gaze at a cluster of eyes on stalks and ask: "Where did we go wrong?"

In our den I have started a museum of sorts of a taxidermic nature. I spend much time in the basement, too, rubbing arsenic into skins. In order that nothing go unappreciated, I have been working on a book with some recipes. My wife thinks this an egregious waste of time. However, it was thanks to this particular endeavor that I discovered the possibilities of the thip-lo.

"Gentlemen!" I used to tell my students. "Never underestimate the principles involved! Most of life has nothing to do with living!"

(Cooking is but chemistry, after all. Here is what I found.)

The thip-lo[3] is quite a local animal, dull grey, and reminiscent

---

[3]Popular name. Sold in baitshops locally. Difficult to classify but almost assuredly amphibian.

of a tadpole. It is limited to four ponds nearby which are scarcely larger than mud puddles. Thip-loes are naturally sluggish but when placed in fingerbowls of wine they begin to move faster and afterward become very active in the light. The alcohol doesn't seem to harm them; they swim in loops, it is true, but the motion itself is colorful in its way. They dress up a table, like parsley. As individuals, they are curious-looking, with a single median eye, lidless, in the pineal area, though there are also vestigial rudiments of other eyes, appearing like tiny warts in front. (Thus there is a sort of pseudo-face on their anterior aspect.) The mouth is very ventral so that, like skates and rays, they can't really see what they are eating. They are toothless but this is perhaps a degenerate state as they seem to have well-developed little gums. Though very limited in their habitat, they nevertheless reproduce surprisingly rapidly. (Indeed, they always seem to be interested in one another.)

As an experiment, I kept several in cold water and out of the light over the length of a summer. Under such conditions, they can grow to a hideous size. They are tougher then, somewhat stringy, a double handful: much more slimy, too, and rather difficult to catch.

Far more interesting, though, is another change:

When small, I would not say thip-loes are *cute*, exactly, but there is a definite sadness to them. If ever there was an animal completely "at the mercy..." The change that comes with increased size is not alone of dimensions but of character: something *evil* seems to come out in them.

I consigned my bloated experiments to the furnace, dropping the heavy iron lid on their noiseless writhing in the flue. Thip-loes make mainly passive sounds in flames, a vicious bubbling and hiss. Nevertheless, the whole experience was disturbing to me. I felt very much like the alchemists of old at morning: haggard and sleepless.

There can be no catharsis in work doomed mostly to fail.

Fortunately, none of this affected my appetite for the smaller form. One can toss a dozen in a huge brandy snifter of an evening and let them loop for hours in the yellow wine. I hope it is not blasphemous to say so, but very Godlike I feel with a bowl of thip-loes by the fire. Even a small snack gives much to chew upon. How quickly they exit the living state! They make a distinct pop when chewed, not unlike caviar, and are best, I think, with a good thick cheese dip which keeps them from flipping about so much. Occasionally, I will find myself turning one so it can see me—or what is *eating* it, as the case may be. No more than a bubble, it seems, a rubbery pop.

But I suppose the least of the dead know the secrets of death.

Sometimes, I think a good part of what I have is akin to an archaeological interest. I imagine myself in Pompeii or Crete and the first to find an ancient mosaic on a floor. A sweep with my broom will reveal a ridge of horny scales or skin, the curve of a tail, possibly an eye, which after being uncovered will begin to look about.

"Gentlemen! (as I used to say) What you are truly trapping in field-biology, is *perspective*, not consciousness!"

One must always separate the creatures from the soil. They can't be reliably killed in situ. Indeed, it is often difficult to know when they are dead. Many of the animals have to be pried up with a crowbar and I cannot sufficiently emphasize the importance of trying to estimate the full extent of the perimeter and account for all appendages before beginning to lift one out.

(The animals are often mud-colored themselves and it's easy to be misled by a close-set pair of eyes.)

Altogether, our days are not unpleasant; life is not fundamentally different in this place, only more concentrated. What is most interesting is that the hierarchy within our lake doesn't work out as advertised. Of course it is probably unfair to have all the animals in the same pot, so to speak, at the same time. Still, it is sobering to see how quickly one of your stupid old crossopterygians can chew up a teleost.

The black water of the lake and the slick calm of its surface belie how much one can learn within and around it. Every day is a discovery and an experiment. I am no longer certain that it is only in humans that the religious practices can become part of the life cycle. There seems to be a great *piety* in the shallows here among the diplocauli with their upturned eyes. The truth is quite a few of the early creatures look very worshipful to me.

It is children that are inherently irreverent.

I must confess that, lately, I have been thinking along that line. Babies may exhaust a woman but they keep her from being moody. And there is no doubt my wife has been cantankerous recently. Just last week, we were digging near the bog with a hoe and potato rake. Despite the cold we were doing rather well, working on our second wheelbarrow-full, when suddenly she said she was not going to clean all these things. (She *would* wait till I had found a vein of them.) I was down on my knees now, yanking them loose from each other and the dirt. Where their skins abutted they were wet and slick as salamanders. I lost patience and began yelling at her:

"It's not just *food* we're after! We're completing the fossil record!"

(I heard nothing in response. After a while, I stood up and turned.)

She had thrown down her hoe and stormed off.

It was anger that had made me speak thus. In truth I know the record cannot be completed.

"Gentlemen! (as I would say, of old) There is *nothing* in between! It is like an organ pipe! Only certain modes can be supported! An ascending tone is not music! And what you see in the animals is the equivalent of chords!"

The truth is, I don't miss any of it. It was all too cumbersome and slow. How much of evolution is given over to the correct spacing of eyes?

Nevertheless, I can still reel off the lectures in my mind:

"Gentlemen! The environment's role is akin to tuning a *circuit*! It is akin to adding acid to precipitate something out of solution! The animal must be made *uncomfortable* in nonexistence!"

Gentlemen! Gentlemen!

Blah.

My wife is disgusted with me.

Sometimes I think we have no right to eat anything; that the goal of a good man should be to become a good skeleton, to have one's silent bones swept, disarticulate, amongst the rocks and minerals. In the meantime, I persevere; I am convinced of the importance of it all. With my gloved hands, I rub in arsenic in order to preserve some trace of the skins. I feel that the pursuit of knowledge is not incompatible with appetite. I look deeply into the eyes of the creatures we are preparing to kill, pray constantly, and arrange around us the food we have eaten. I work, perhaps, in the spirit of the great Wallace who ate blue macaws for breakfast. I don't know who will appreciate all of this. The truth is visitors are horrified by our den and by the leftovers in our refrigerator. They reproach us, I know.

What they think, I cannot imagine.

Still, I keep up my spirits as best I can.

My book of recipes is a major consolation. "Leviticus, Too," I plan to call it. When demoralized, I think of it as a discreet series of challenges. About the other (the paranoia, I mean) I really should not complain.

I suppose I am not the first father to feel his family is in conspiracy against him.

In order to get away from them, I began digging a new cistern. Day after day I worked at it, finding enormous relief in the sheer physical activity. To my surprise, I found absolutely nothing in the way of creatures. Then, at a depth of maybe twelve feet, my shovel struck something soft.

What I had hit, I seemed to have hit near the tail. I began to uncover the animal quickly, then afterward more carefully and finally at the full length of my broom and shovel. I could not bring myself to look at what I was doing. With what became a sudden appreciation of a great fear, I scrambled out of the hole and did the rest of my looking *down* at it. I had never seen the likes of the thing. It was huge by our usual standards, buried deeper, too, perfectly stupefied with age. Fully exposed, it was almost too nauseous to contemplate; it rattled my faith in everything I have ever believed in. There seemed to be flippers; there seemed to be claws; the five eyes were disturbingly arranged.

The creature looked frankly incomplete.

(If it were organized at all, it was in ways I never dreamed possible.)

I dug into the side of the cistern and fixed boards in a steep ramp to drag it out onto a tarpaulin with a block and tackle. It was nearly sunset and I was hesitant to leave it uncovered. I had my Luger, of course, but it does absolutely no good here to shoot anything until it moves. There was hardly any wind but the air was getting cold. It was supposed to snow during the night, so I hung the tarp on a rope between two trees.

Then I looked down again:

The eyes, which were not closed, were fixed forward, blankly. There was no obvious pupil to them. They resembled balls of granite.

The earth itself might have been staring up at me.

I returned to the house very slowly, lost in thought. It was true my academic era was over; still, in my heart I knew I was making daily what were great discoveries. I could not shake an abiding suspicion that I had been eating for years what I should have published. I saw, too, that what I had taken previously to be an occasional ugliness in animals was a complete illusion; I had vastly underestimated the power of symmetry.

"Gentlemen," I said (of a sudden, to an imaginary classroom in my mind), "we are not bowing *low* enough! We have prayed overlong to a two-handed God!"

I slept fitfully, if at all. Nevertheless, by morning I thought I knew the answer. True, this creature was odd to begin with, but what it is is *dead*; what it is is *dead* and partially decomposed. At such a level, the character of the soil may be somewhat different.

(Still, I reasoned, the meat itself might be good.)

I went outside. The air was bitterly cold and indeed it had snowed in the night. In my musings, I had almost passed the trees when I noticed that the tarpaulin I had hung up yesterday evening was missing. I looked around now and became much more hesitant. Then I went forward to the pit, crunching in the snow.

No, I thought.

The tarpaulin was in disarray at the bottom.

The animal was *not* dead. Evidently, it was a female, too, possibly of some vaguely mammalian inclinations. She had done her very best with the tarpaulin and her awkward flippers and claws to protect her babies from the cold. I could see them suckling in long rows beneath her, their thin skin almost translucent in the grey dawn. The blue ice had caught alike in the folds and ridges of canvas and their lidless and vulnerable eyes.

The snow of centuries would fall upon them now.

I looked down for some time. Then I returned to my bedroom. I brought out a blanket and took it to the pit, and, with a long stick, arranged it so that it wrapped and sheltered all of them. I cannot know whether the creature herself saw or understood me but she made no effort to move.

I walked back silently, very deep in meditation. "This can destroy us," I thought.

In front of the cabin, my daughter was working on a huge form in the snow. "Hoo!" she said, when she saw me. She is a little too old to be making snow creatures. Moreover, her sense of proportion is flawed. There are some that would say it's because my daughter herself is fat. That is no matter; it will not be long now; she is some two years older than our son.

As I walked, I thought of the creatures sleeping beneath my feet, and how these were being shown unto us and how pleased we were with them. A more bountiful cornucopia could not exist. I cannot hope to understand what brought our little family to the midst of such plenty. It is more than I can do just to name these animals.

My wife was by herself in the house. It seems the two of us, alone, were to share a late breakfast. As she moved about the kitchen, I watched her smiling eyes, slightly yellow in the light. Evidently I am forgiven. She is in an amorous mood. We must have some more children soon. She had sautéed a platygast and stuffed it with raisins and slices of apple. I poured the syrup over the thin and purple-looking skin and, like a wave, an unexpected happiness came over me. Verily I say unto you, I have never been more content. I made a joyful noise and bowed my head in prayer:

"Bless this food, oh Lord. Bless all food, living or dead. Bless our children and the metamorphic world in which they live. Forget us not in our strange homes and forgive us our curious prayers, for in our souls we know the one point behind the eyes is central to all. Allow some considered share of thine infinite blessings to fall gently upon this house. This we ask in thy name, oh Lord, and in the name of whatever love or wisdom beats within the vastness of thy three-chambered heart."

"Amen," I added, picking up my fork.

Pinckney Benedict

Pig Helmet & The Wall of Life

Pig Helmet needed to see the Wall of Life. I call him Pig Helmet because he's the sort of fellow that, in olden times, you'd have been one of the Civilized People trying like hell, with fire and boiling oil and molten lead and such, to keep him and his kind out, and he'd have been one of the dreaded barbarians, he'd have been the lead barbarian in fact, climbing over your city walls by means of an improvised ladder, with his snarling face painted a furious blue, and something large and heavy and sharp-edged clutched in his massive fist, and wearing a pig for a hat. The head and hide of a boar, thick and knobby and naturally tough, hardened further by curing and the cunning attachment of metal plates and studs and rings, with the great toothy maw of the feral hog sloping down over his heavy brow, its tusks like upthrust sabers and its dead piggy eyes glinting dully above his own. Pig Helmet.

Pig Helmet is a cop. He's employed by the county sheriff's department, and he lives down at the end of my road with his diminutive, pretty wife. Before that he was a "contractor" in Iraq and Afghanistan, where the money was good and the action was better, but his wife worried too much with him away. We tried to look after her as much as possible, my own wife and I, but we were no substitute for the ministrations of Pig Helmet, as you can imagine. He's a dutiful and attentive husband. Before that work, he was a bail bondsman, a bounty hunter (he hates that term, silly movie bullshit he calls it), and one time a guy that had jumped bail threw acid in his face, trying to blind him, to avoid capture.

The acid missed his eyes but crisped him pretty good otherwise, and the left side of his head is kind of a nightmare. The teeth show through permanently on that side, and the flesh is rippled and brown like old melted candlewax. He keeps pretty much to himself, does Pig Helmet, has some acreage and a few animals like we all do around here, following his hobbies in his off-hours, hand-loading cartridges and felling trees on his place and then turning the stumps into sawdust with his stump grinder.

He loves the stump grinder. When I cut down a tree, he'll bring the stump grinder over to my place and grind the stump into the ground, leaving nothing but a hole and a few roots and a mound of soft, warm sawdust. He'll grind stumps for hours with apparent satisfaction. Sometimes in the fall he'll bring over the loin from a deer he's shot, and that's good eating. His wife's vegetable garden always produces plenty of tomatoes for them and for us.

Pig Helmet is not a fellow much given to self-pity, as you can imagine, or even to much at all in the way of self-regard, but he had recently been through a bad experience, and he was feeling down and lost and deeply in need of an encounter with Life that would restore him to a proper sense of himself, which is to say, no particular sense of himself at all, except for a kind of exuberant well-being of the sort that would allow him, as of old, to grind a stump or love his wife or swing a truncheon with a deep-seated sense of pleasure.

The bad experience that he underwent can briefly be described as follows: OxyContin addict, alcohol, family Monopoly game gone bad, shotgun deployed, multiple homicide. Topped off with suicide-by-cop. When Pig Helmet arrived in his cruiser at this lonely place to which he had been called, way out in the wilds of the western end of the county, the OxyContin addict was sitting shirtless and blood-spattered on the porch of the little frame house where he had just killed his brother, a cousin, his grandmother (can you imagine?) and an uncle. The house wasn't an unpleasant-looking place, a neatly tended bungalow, with a pretty trumpet vine twining around the porch railing. The door stood wide open behind the OxyContin addict, the screen door too, the room behind it black as pitch; and he still had the scattergun in one hand, wouldn't turn it loose no matter how loudly Pig Helmet yelled for him to do so. Most people, people even marginally in their right minds, do what Pig Helmet tells them to do when he raises his voice at them.

This guy just smoked his cigarette down to the filter and then kind of lazily (this is how Pig Helmet described it to me) stood up and swung the muzzle of the gun around to cover Pig Helmet. So Pig Helmet took him down, double-tapped him right in the center of his chest with the .45 caliber service pistol he carries, and the guy sat down again, hand still wrapped around the stock of the shotgun, and he died right there on the porch. Pig Helmet wouldn't have felt bad about shooting the guy, he said, if there had been some utility in it; but the people beyond that open door were already dead as it turned out, and so there was nobody to rescue. There weren't even any shells in the shotgun anymore. The OxyContin addict had used them all up on his Monopoly opponents and the grandmother, who hadn't even, to all appearances, been involved in the game at all.

"Fucking mess," Pig Helmet said, and I believe him.

So when he saw the sign for the Wall of Life down at the county fairgrounds, he was in the mood. He didn't anticipate any trouble on account of the shooting, because the homicides in the bungalow had been so brutal, and everybody agreed that the OxyContin addict had needed killing. It was a good shoot. Being on administrative leave pending a formal inquiry, Pig Helmet had the leisure to do what he wanted, and he didn't feel much like hand-loading any ammunition, and he didn't feel like grinding stumps, and he knew that his wife's sympathy and worry, while affectionately meant (she's an affectionate woman, with Pig Helmet at least, though cripplingly shy around others, even those of us who have known her for years) would just make him feel worse. So he took himself off to see what the Wall of Life was all about.

Pig Helmet on duty, wearing his Nomex gloves and his bulky body armor and his brown sheriff's office uniform with its broad Sam Browne belt across his barrel body and his thick utility belt (flex cuffs, pepper spray, billy club, taser on the left side, service pistol on the right, plus radio and tactical flashlight and knife and other assorted gadgetry), can be a pretty unsettling sight. He's a big fellow, as I say, a man mountain, well over six feet tall, two hundred fifty pounds if he's an ounce, with a head shaved bald and gleaming and broad as the Dome of the Rock in Jerusalem. And he's got that nasty confusion of his face on the left side, which a person can grow used to, and even fond of, but not in a short period of time.

Now, you know what the Wall of Life is, even if you don't think you do. It's just like the Wall of Death, the county fair attraction where a rider on an old motorbike roars around the inside of a big wooden cylinder, centrifugal force sticking him perpendicular to the sides. The crowd stands on a catwalk at the top of the cylinder, looking in while the guy on the sputtering motorbike apparently defies gravity below them.

At the bigger, better shows, there are a couple, maybe even three motorbikes on the wall at one time, crossing one another's paths, cutting down toward the bottom of the cylinder and then shooting back up to the top again, to cause the crowd to draw back in alarm, fearful that the biker will shoot out onto the catwalk and knock them over and kill them. Sometimes a pretty girl will stand at the bottom of the cylinder, in its center, gesturing toward the motorcyclists as they circle above her head, showing her faith in them, that they will not come unstuck from the walls and crash down on top of her. That's the Wall of Death.

The Wall of Life was just like that, only it was an evangelical preacher and his family who did the riding, and it was the preacher's daughter who stood in the bottom. The Wall of Life was this preacher's ministry, like an old time tent revival meeting but on motorcycles, and he went from town to town, fairground to fairground, setting up the Wall, running for a couple three days until the crowds let down, preaching at the people that came to see him ride and shout.

When his work in one place was done, he and his family would tear down the Wall of Life into a series of short arcs that stacked neatly one inside the next, and stow them aboard the aged Fruehauf tractor-trailer his ministry moved in. There was a huge portrait of the Wall on the side of the trailer, the great wooden cylinder and crude human figures speeding along on motorcycles inside, with a giant Jesus stretching his hands out on either side, like he wanted to catch the little riders if they flew out. After he packed up his stuff, the preacher and his family would shove off for the next place he felt called to.

Pig Helmet wasn't a particularly religious man. Like most of the rest of us he grew up in a Baptist household, and he had been saved at a certain point in his boyhood because it was expected of him, and he had given testimony at various times for much the same reason, but none of it—as he has told me—touched his heart very much. As soon as he moved out of his parents' house, he stopped going to church, more through indifference than any animosity toward the institution. When he met and started courting the pretty girl who would become his wife, he took up going again, because it was what she wanted, it was one of the few places where she came out of her shyness a little and felt at ease among people; and her beauty and kindness and gentleness toward him did touch his heart, and so he went.

Pig Helmet has told me about a tribe of savage Germans whom he particularly admires, that lived back in Roman times. These Germans, it seems, were converted to Christianity sometime after the reign of the Emperor Constantine. This is the sort of thing Pig Helmet knows about, though to look at him—the truculent set of his jaw, the heavy forehead, the glittering left eye that peers out from within the folds of scar tissue—you would never expect it. He reads a lot of nonfiction books about obscure tidbits and peculiarities of history, and other books about the oddities scattered throughout the galaxy: singularities and quarks and quantum theory and gravitons and the like. He says these things just naturally catch his interest.

In the book about Christianity, when these great big hairy Teutonic warriors were baptized, when the Roman priests led them down into the cold rushing water of the river that ran near their home village up in the Black Forest, they willingly pledged themselves to Christ and dunked themselves under. All except their sword arms. Their right hands, palms horny and hard with callus from years of wielding their long blades, those they kept dry above the fast-flowing current. The rest of them might belong to gentle Jesus, but their strength and their killing skills—they still belonged to the god of battle.

Pig Helmet told me that was what he always felt like: some kind of a half-breed monster, a chimera, part one thing and part another and nothing that was whole. He had felt that other piece of him—the sword arm, held up above the current—when the OxyContin addict brought the shotgun to bear, the muzzle yawning wide and dark, and when Pig Helmet, without so much as thinking or deciding, sent a pair of 230-grain Speer Gold Dot jacketed hollowpoints into the guy's chest at nine hundred feet per second.

He had stood there for a moment, pistol in his hand, the pistol reports so closely spaced they might have been a single sound, echoing off the clapboard side of the tidy bungalow. He'd been around death plenty of times, working for the creepy little bail bondsman in Craig County, in the Middle East, and while serving mental hygiene warrants and issuing subpoenas and such for the sheriff's office; and he could sense it now, boiling off the punctured corpse of the mutt with his shotgun, percolating out of the dark doorway of the bungalow behind the slumped body.

Death dwelt in the house, he knew, and probably had for years, for decades, just waiting on this day, on this combination of drugs and rage and cheating, to take down everyone inside. He could tell it was there, crouched inside the doorway like a lurking beast, but he couldn't see it.

He said he might as well have been naked out there in that little yard, with a couple of dusty chickens pecking in the thin grass around his feet, and the branches of the trees creaking and talking in the light wind that had sprung up. That empty doorway, with its moronic dead guardian, it called to him. It yearned for him. All of his body armor, his pistol and his taser and his years of training—worth nothing. He knew that if he walked into that place alone, he was finished. When backup arrived, he would be gone. He could cross the yard and step over the OxyContin addict and past the threshold and on into the dark. He even took a step or two in that direction.

And then—this is his take on it—a miracle happened. A woman

called his name. At the time, he thought it was his wife. It was definitely a woman's voice. And it wasn't his regular name that she called, it was his secret name, a name no one knew him by. It was a name that he himself didn't know he owned, or that owned him, until the second he heard the woman's voice speak it. He wouldn't tell me what it was, no man should know that about another man, but he said the moment he heard it, he knew it as inescapably his. It was like she was saying it into his ear. He imagined that his wife must be praying for him, a thing she did regularly throughout the day when he was on duty, and that her prayer was what halted his progress toward the door of the bungalow. He imagined that the name she called him was how she referred to him when she spoke with God.

So he found himself at the Wall of Life. After the search of the bungalow revealed the extent of the slaughter (Pig Helmet couldn't bring himself to go inside even after other units from the sheriff's office arrived), after the arrival and departure of the county coroner, after the ambulances had borne the body bags away—after all that, as he drove homeward, he passed the county fairground, and he saw the tractor-trailer with its garish illustration on the side, and beyond that the squat cylinder of the Wall of Life itself. That word, *Life*, written in letters of orange flame on both the semi-trailer and the Wall, captured and held his eye. Death clung to him. It was on his clothes, his hands, in his nostrils. *Life*.

He pulled the cruiser into the near-empty parking lot, paid the old lady at the foot of the stairs that led to the catwalk along the top edge of the Wall. As he handed her his money, he thought briefly of the grandmother who had died, cowering in one of the narrow back rooms, her hands held up beseechingly before her. The other deputies had described her to him in almost loving detail. "The show's already in progress," the old lady at the Wall told him in a voice like the chirp of a bird, and he nodded at her. The board stairs under his feet trembled with the unmuffled roar of the motorcycles, and the entire Wall shook with their passing.

There were maybe half a dozen spectators atop the Wall. It was the first show of the day, a light crowd. In the evening, under the unearthly glow of the sizzling sodium lamps, there would be more. The few who were there at the catwalk's railing drew back when they caught sight of Pig Helmet ascending the stairs. He was used to that reaction to his size and his marred face and his uniform, so he hardly noticed. A couple of the people held dollar bills out over the void, so that the motorcycle riders would come up near the edge of the Wall and snatch them. With Pig Helmet's arrival, the dollars and the riders were forgotten. Pig Helmet strode to the edge of the platform and looked down.

Easy enough to imagine what he saw as he looked into the well, which was poorly lighted, just a few strings of dingy Christmas bulbs clinging to the safety railing against which Pig Helmet leaned his weight. What else could a man like Pig Helmet see? The stench of exhaust flooded his nose, but it seemed to him to be the smell of burning cordite. He was looking into the muzzle of a great gun. It was the muzzle of the OxyContin addict's shotgun. It was the muzzle of every gun he had ever stared down. It was the muzzle of his own service pistol, pointed straight at his face.

Easy enough to imagine, too, what it was like for the preacher and his people, his family, when Pig Helmet appeared above them, his Neanderthal head silhouetted against the light of the lowering sky, his exposed teeth gritted, his expression (what they could see of it in the dim light) filled with mortal terror, the other spectators on the catwalk drawing back from him, their offerings suddenly out of reach.

Near catastrophe as one motorcyclist, flames crackling from the straight exhaust pipe of his aging Indian bike, dove unexpectedly low on the Wall, nearly colliding with his younger brother, while their father, the preacher, fought to avoid running over them both. The preacher was shouting out above the roar of the engines the text of the gospel of James—he had just gotten to "There is one lawgiver, who is able to save and to destroy. Who art thou that judgest another?"—and he lost his place momentarily, dread and fascination drawing his attention upward to Pig Helmet's looming head and shoulders, the gleam of his shaved skull, the puckered flesh of his scars. His speed dropped as he braked to avoid his boys, his bike wobbled nauseously, and he nearly toppled off the Wall and to the floor.

Pig Helmet's vision quickly adjusted to the changed light. Now he saw more clearly. In white letters two feet high, just below the lip of the wall all the way around, ran the legend "In my name shall they cast out devils. They shall speak with new tongues. They shall take up serpents." Pig Helmet was standing just opposite the word *serpents*, so he could only see the end and the beginning of the quote, *...shall take up serpents. In my name they shall...*, but he was a good enough student of the gospels from his youth up to know what was hidden from his gaze. The floor of the well seemed to be alive. It was moving, shifting, shining in the blasts of fire from the motorcycle exhausts: iridescent scales, eyes, flickering tongues. It was a snake pit. Adders, vipers, harmless bright green ribbon snakes like blades of grass, the undulating lozenge pattern of diamondback rattlesnakes, the warning sizzle of their tails drowned out in the cacophony of the bikes.

Standing in the midst of the snakes, ankle deep in them, her feet bare, was a young girl, her face turned upward toward Pig Helmet, her expression delighted as though she was glad to see him. In each of her small, pale hands she grasped, just below the spearpoint head, a struggling pit viper. Her eyes were wide and bright, and Pig Helmet realized that she was not looking at him at all. She was gazing past him at something just over his shoulder with that rapturous look on her face.

Her eyes weren't unfocused or dazed. They had the concentrated aspect of the eyes of someone who has caught sight of something precious and vanishing—a lover who has spotted the ghost of a long-dead darling; a sniper to whom a target has just offered himself up for a head shot—and who can hardly bear the intensity of the vision, but who doesn't dare to look away lest it be lost forever. There was something behind him, above him, Pig Helmet knew, but he couldn't bring himself to turn around to see what it was. The girl was seeing it enough for both of them.

The men on the motorcycles, the preacher and his sons, had speedily recovered their composure, and they swung back into rhythm, racing their bikes in swift ellipses around the interior of the well, now at the top, now at the bottom, weaving across one another's paths at measured intervals, as though they were performing an intricate dance. They were a handsome family, fine-boned and slender, their faces similar, old, young, younger, like the same man appearing in a series of photographs taken through the years. The preacher found his voice again, this time calling on the psalms, as though perhaps to ward off Pig Helmet with his perpetual unintended sneer, whom the preacher might have suspected of being not altogether human, not altogether benign. "Yea, though I walk through the valley of the shadow of death, I will fear no evil," he called out to the crowd on the catwalk.

Pig Helmet saw that the girl wasn't quite as young as he had first taken her to be. She was exquisite, her head tilted, her hair light as silk, her back slightly arched, her breasts pressing against the thin white cotton of her shirt. From his vantage point above her, Pig Helmet could see down into the neck of her blouse, could see the small hollow at the base of her throat, the sheen of perspiration that collected there. He could see the soft swelling of her breasts, the lacy edges of her bra. He loved his wife very much. And, in that instant, he wanted simultaneously to protect the girl in the snakepit from all the death that was in the world and to screw her silly. Her lips were moving, revealing glimpses of her healthy gums, her small even teeth, her glistening tongue. He couldn't hear her voice, but he knew that she must be praying. He wondered what her prayer was.

The preacher's voice was still audible, and the crowd had begun offering their dollar bills again. "Thou preparest a table before me in the presence of mine enemies," the old man declared. Pig Helmet had a couple of dollars in his wallet, and he thought about holding them out so that one of the riders would snatch them from his hand, and perhaps his fingers would brush against Pig Helmet's fingers, and in that brief contact Pig Helmet would feel what he needed to feel, would know what he wanted to know. *Life.*

It occurred to him that he might even, under the guise of holding out his offering, grab a passing motorcyclist by the wrist. Who among us, faced with that moment of failed equilibrium, the man teetering on the edge of the icy step, the woman the heel of whose shoe has caught in a steel grating, hasn't entertained, however temporarily, that temptation to reach out and, gently, almost lovingly, *push*? Just to see the expression on the face of the one who might have been rescued but who has been doomed instead. Pig Helmet told me it was like that feeling. Would the rider be jerked from his bike and swing there, dangling by the wrist in Pig Helmet's grasp until Pig Helmet dropped him into the writhing snakes? Would the weight of the man and the hurtling bike jerk Pig Helmet's shoulder clean out of its socket; might he be dragged bodily off the catwalk and into the well?

The motorcycles were running in unison, stacked like the rungs of a ladder as they raced around the Wall, and the girl had begun singing, her voice a thin piping that barely reached Pig Helmet's ears. A woman near him on the catwalk had begun clapping her hands together and shouting "Hallelujah" while the men beside her looked slightly chagrined. The boards thrummed like a vast heart beneath Pig Helmet's feet, and the voice of the preacher, in constant flux from the Doppler effect as he came near and went past and away again, beat at Pig Helmet's ears. "I shall dwell in the house of the Lord forever," he called. The snakes flopped and coiled at the girl's feet.

Pig Helmet no longer felt as though he was looking down, into the cylinder. He suddenly knew himself to be looking up. It came to him that he was staring into the barrel of an incalculably large telescope, one with greater power even than the ones they mount on the high ridges, far from the cities and their polluting lights. He knew himself to be watching through it something distant and ancient, something akin to the circuit of the planets, old, young, younger, near, far, farther, around and around in their endless courses; and the weak little Christmas lights were the surrounding stars; and the girl, the infinitely desirable girl clad in white at the very center of it all, singing and praying, and now she's even laughing, laughing breathlessly, her mouth wide with joy, her eyes half-closed, her nostrils flared, a viper grasped tight in each hand, her feet sunk in the unfathomable twinings of the serpents—At what is she laughing?

At him. At Pig Helmet. He's speaking, he's crying out in the command voice he's been taught to use on suspects, in the irresistible voice with which he directed the OxyContin addict to put down the shotgun. He doesn't understand the words he's saying. They're bubbling out of him like water from a busted spigot. The woman next to him is swaying, gaping at him worshipfully, shouting "Hallelujah! Hallelujah!" for all she's worth.

They're the girl's words that pour out of him, Pig Helmet knows, the words she was speaking earlier but that he couldn't hear. The words of her prayer. Her body is shivering and shaking, pulsing like a quasar in one of Pig Helmet's peculiar books, a quasar at the far distant end of the universe. The girl in the pit, the stout woman on the catwalk beside him, they're dancing the same dance, binary suns, quivering as though they're demented with some awful fever. Pig Helmet's hands are spread wide. He cannot understand the words of the prayer, but in the midst of them he hears her say, once, clear as a bell, his secret name. It was not his wife at all who called him. He tries to make it be his wife, who has known him in his most intimate moments, and who wants nothing more in the world than to save him, to keep him safe and beside her forever. But no matter how hard he tries, it is this girl who knows the name, who calls to him in his most secret places.

"Put down the weapon." It was a prayer, what he had said to the OxyContin addict. He knew that. "Lay down on the ground." It was a prayer. There was no way for the OxyContin addict to divine what Pig Helmet truly wanted. Pig Helmet didn't hold the key to his understanding. The words of Pig Helmet's heart must have sounded like gibberish in his ears, and it didn't matter how loudly Pig Helmet spoke them, or how beseechingly he meant them. He couldn't imagine the OxyContin addict's secret name; he couldn't save him. We are so distant from one another, impossible to know. "Don't make me shoot you." An unheard prayer.

Pig Helmet's hands are open. The motorcycles continue to circle above him, hanging precariously over his head—who knows what astonishing force keeps them there?—but the screaming of their engines is muted, it no longer reaches his ears, his brain. He speaks in tongues, and spittle flecks his fleshy lips.

He's reaching outward, upward, straining toward the whirling constellation of men, motorbikes, snakes, voices. He's reaching for the girl who knows his name, and she has stopped dancing. She stretches out her slender arms toward him, her skin shining with sweat. She stands on tiptoe among the snakes. He's a tall man, but she's far away. Faster and faster the motorcycles go, and her prayer rises continuously from his lips, unmediated. The Wall of Life is an intricate machine built by men to show him this girl at the other end of space. The door of the little bungalow yawns behind him, and the slain OxyContin addict is the doorman, he's the concierge with the disconcerting smile, holding the portal wide, gesturing Pig Helmet inside with a generous sweep of the scattergun. It's an easy door to enter, the door to that house.

What lies before Pig Helmet's eyes is likewise a door, a hard entrance, a long narrow tunnel of infinite length. Pig Helmet thrusts his killing hand, his unbaptized hand, out toward the girl. She is far away and getting farther, but she extends her hand toward him as well, and her lips shape his true name. If Pig Helmet is strong enough, if he strains far enough, if the motorcycles spin fast enough, and if he keeps stretching out his unclean hand forever, he will reach her.

Katie Estill

The Drinking Gourd

In the spring I began to see dead people in the yard. The first time it was a tea party, a gathering of women in long dresses and sunbonnets, sitting beneath the great old oak in front of our house, and I saw the girl I would later call Stellaria. The dead were most often present on those moody days before my periods when I was beset by headaches and bloat. That period of days before bleeding when a woman's consciousness opens to the other side and if she is receptive she may feel emanations, intuitions that are beyond her grasp during the more stable times of the month. And so the dead arrived like a migraine headache and a feeling of butterflies deep in the lower intestines. I did not tell my husband about the dead who were wandering in our yard. There are some things about a woman's menstrual cycle that he doesn't need to know.

I knew they were dead because there were so many of them, and our cats walked among them without fear or begging to be petted where their tails met their hips. Furthermore, I discovered I could pass my hand through their bodies, split their torsos with my palm without causing them the least disturbance or indigestion. And then there was their lack of solidity, wherein they seemed both whole and transparent, wraithlike, real but of a different time. Boys in breeches pitching marbles on the hill, a man in a straw hat tending the vineyards of the terrace, which are no more and have not graced this hillside since the 1920's.

My husband and I lived on an acre lot in a small, Ozark town, in a house whose age was unknown, but granted to be the oldest in the neighborhood. The title to the property went back to 1856, when a woman named America Curry owned this land and the entire hill. America had three children who survived, and three husbands who did not. I know for I have often walked alongside her grave, two blocks from our house.

It did not surprise me so much that the dead are still alive. Didn't Faulkner say as much? And so did the Greeks. When I witnessed them, I reacted as I often do to the unexpected or the upsetting. I became very quiet and still. I observed.

After a while it seemed obvious to me that they were unaware of my existence. I wondered how it was possible for me to see them while I remained invisible, in a future century that had yet to unwind for them. I bargained with my condition. If I took my fish oil on a more regular basis, might I not hold them at bay, or simply admit that I'd been daydreaming like I hadn't done since I was a child? As a child my waking dreams had seemed so real that I chattered like a bird to imaginary friends.

I recognized that I might be disturbed, but I preferred the other story, the one about moons and mysterious cycles, all that stuff about seeing to the other side. I preferred to accept the fact that periodically I became a secret gorgon with writhing snakes for hair, whose look could freeze my husband's heart for a second when a glass leaped from the kitchen counter and shattered beside the salad bowl, shards possibly scattering among the greens, and I served him the salad, anyway.

"How many times have you tried to kill me?" he murmured, philosophically.

America Curry, the grand dame of this land, had gone through three husbands, and I began to feel that she must have prodded at least one of them more quickly toward the grave.

Then one day the dead saw me. Winter had sunk back into the ground and the earth was sprouting a healthy hair of wild greens. At noon I went out into the yard, determined to eat well. Most women I knew ate pot herb, especially in the spring when our bodies are craving living nutrients. So I walked down the broken cement stairs beside the terraced gardens where once the grapevines thrived. In my hands a colander and a small paring knife. Under my tenancy the ruined terraces had been briefly subdued to raise crops, but it all became too much like house cleaning, so I permitted wildness to return to the terraces—red clover, dandelion, dock, poke. I was letting it all go and calling the disorder an experiment to see what would take over this space. I stooped with the paring knife and collected some dandelion greens, so helpful with the bloat and the swelling of knees and knuckles at certain times of the month, then I headed over to the hillside behind two derelict tin sheds, for here the dirt was black and a profusion of chickweed and henbit blanketed the hillside.

The sight of this hill in springtime always gave me a little thrill. Here, without the least bit of help from my human hand, grew a hillside of food—nature's garden wherein there are no weeds, but only a variety of nourishment. I always felt like a wealthy woman studying her bank account when I walked about my wild land in the center of town. I liked the idea that I would cut them from the ground and eat them while they were still alive.

The religious fundamentalists in our hills believe the End times have begun; the environmentalists say the earth is dying, and the ex-hippies who settled here believe that civilization may soon pass from our lives. But I would be feeding my husband pot herb for a long time, for the wild plants returned to us perennially, and would even sprout repeatedly in the course of a single season, just by giving them a good hair cut.

So I climbed part way up the hill, surrounded by my wealth and retirement plan, and kneeled on the thick carpeting of chickweed with their tiny heart-shaped leaves that grew in thick mats. And it was then, as I grabbed hold of a fistful of chickweed (Stellaria media) and readied the knife, that she rose out of the hillside, a blond child, a girl, her thick curly hair in my fist, and for the first time the dead saw me. It seemed as though I pulled her from the hillside, her eyes wide with fear as she came out of the earth like a root being pulled from the ground. The two of us shrieked at the sight of the other, and I rolled away to escape, and, in doing so, grabbed the nearest clump of henbit to stabilize my purchase on the hill. Just as I grasped henbit, a member of the mint family, I pulled another head from the ground, a young African American with a broken front tooth. My shock at retrieving another dead one was compounded by his dark face, for these days there are very few African Americans in our small town, our town fathers having driven them out over sixty years ago by bulldozing the neighborhood that once was called "Nigger Hill." Today if you see a young black man in our town, you cannot be blamed for wondering if he is a member of the college basketball team, but this dead man seemed just as startled to see me.

"My lord," I said. To whom was I speaking? Anachronisms always leapt from my mouth in a moment of duress. Good grief. Mother of pearl. He was wearing a ragged shirt and seemed to be stuck in the earth at the waist.

He placed his palms upon the clumps of henbit and pushed to leverage his lower half from the hold of earth. He strained and pressed against the hillside but he did not come out as easily as the girl, and I thought: he is more like burdock or poke or possibly has a giant taproot. He seemed stuck, as it were.

"Who you?" His eyes wide in alarm. A simple question, but at that moment I could not have said who I was or who or what any of us was.

"I have to write something down," I said, but I had not brought my tiny notebook that fit inside a shirt pocket, and I seemed to have lost the mastery of my limbs.

"You the conductor?" he said.

The girl I came to call Stellaria had collected herself and was sitting upright on the hill, her legs stretched out in front of her, as she smoothed her long skirt over her ankles. She wore curious high top boots of another century or two and clutched in her right hand what looked to be a corncob doll. Stellaria gazed at her peer in death who could not get loose of the hill. "She ain't no conductor. My mama is. My papa is. And I can be if I want. I don't recognize her. She looks strange."

"She armed," he said, giving a nod to the paring knife that was still clutched in my fist.

"I'm—I'm not really armed. I was just getting lunch and you came out."

"*What*?"

"Dinner," I said, remembering that the noonday meal was always called dinner, and the evening meal was supper to them. "I was collecting greens. Pot herbs."

"I could eat a mess 'o greens," he said, "but I find myself in a predicament."

"Yes," I agreed. "I can see. I can see you both. That's a predicament for me, too." I turned to the girl and asked, "Should we try to help him out?"

"Some would. Some not."

It seemed to me that I should help him, a dead African American stuck fast like a root in the earth. As I moved toward him I thought more of his race than of the fact that he was dead, and it seemed that my town had behaved so despicably toward the African Americans once living here that the least I could do was to give him a hand. But as I crawled toward him and reached for his arm, which I saw was scarred as though he'd been flayed, his deadness suddenly became more prominent than any other fact, and then I was scrambling down the hill, racing around the rusty metal sheds and loping up the stairway on the hill, for the safety of the house.

Later that afternoon I had to return to the chickweed hill to retrieve the colander, for we were having spaghetti that night. I found my colander at the bottom of the hill, sitting upright, the paring knife laid upon the dandelion greens that had wilted in the afternoon heat. I did not mention to my husband my encounter with the dead. He doesn't even eat pot herbs, and frankly, come to think of it, there are many aspects of our domestic life together that he doesn't want to know about. How socks get in drawers. The mechanics of the dishwasher, or when exactly the garbage has to be placed out on the curb. He has no particular interest in the details of our domestic life. He's a focused man. He knows the sound of the mail truck, the way our cats recognize the sound of our cars and know they will soon be fed.

The next month brought a repairman into the house. The dishwasher had blocked up, sending a stream of water across the kitchen floor. There was something fundamentally wrong about the plumbing in our old house, the pipes installed, it appeared, by various owners with an incurable sense of optimism about new pipes that failed to take into full account the laws of gravity. The pipes that flushed the gray water from the house were slanted uphill. We would need a pump to keep things moving, the plumber said. No one could find the pipes that ran outside of the house but we knew they ran down hill in some fashion and across an adjacent lawn that must have once been a part of America's property, an interesting detail we discovered when dye tests proved that our sewage was ending up on the bathroom floor of the neighboring rental house. The plumbers explained that the neighbors had simply attached their outflowing pipes to our sewer line. This month's plumber, a blond young man with an open country smile, was occupied in our basement, and when he finished installing the pump he approached me solemnly and said, "Do you know the story about this house?"

"No. What story?"

"I always wanted to get inside this house, and study the basement. There's a cave, they say, that you could access from the basement, but the entrance has been closed. My grandfather told me this house was a part of the underground railway. There's a big cave under this hill, and the house was built to use the cave to help the slaves who were running north."

Being a reliable magnet for repairmen, our old house attracted a carpenter the following month. I can't remember what he was fixing, but he was extremely impressed by the heft of the oak beams in the basement, and, before leaving, he took me to the west porch and knocked the cement floor with the rungs of a metal porch chair, and said with satisfaction, "You hear that? It's hollow. Must be an old cistern down there."

What followed next could only be blamed on fluctuating hormones and a domestic irascibility that could not be appeased by mere exercise. What I required was a grand exercise. Something that would demolish walls and take me to the other side. I had not seen any dead people in weeks, and maybe I was just missing them. They had remained inside of the earth. I told myself that I was not possessed by delusions but of the spirit of scientific inquiry. I was quite sure what wall to begin demolishing (the west side, of course, under the porch, where the carpenter believed he had found the hollow space of an abandoned cistern).

Nevertheless, I wished to keep this ambitious project to myself, and so I waited until my husband left the house before I got a mattock from the shed and started whaling at the basement wall. Nothing more than stones and river concrete separated me from the hollow space beneath the western porch. This month no mere daydreaming, but the assertion of muscle and sweat.

The wall was stubborn and did not give. The thud of the mattock against stone sent aches into shoulders and back, but there was something thrilling about destroying the wall between me and the cave, and not just any cave, but one that had been used for righteous purposes. "Let it breathe!" I said, and swung the mattock and hit mortar that gave away in crumbles and bits. Eventually the first rock tumbled to the floor, and I discovered that the west wall was more than one layer of rock, which convinced me I was on the right trail, for why else would Ozarkers have built anything so solidly, except to hide a secret from the world?

My progress was slow because my husband is a writer and therefore rarely leaves the house. The mailbox doesn't count, and the post office is just an extension of the mail box, and such trips do not provide enough time for excavations. But with subtle feminine encouragement and entreaties I prodded him from his lair and repeatedly sent him into the world. Perhaps I was guilty of rationalizing my desire for secrecy, but my husband had never been fond of home improvements, so I felt it was unnecessary to mention my activities. I knew full well that unless he actually heard the thudding of a mattock, he would never enter that distant room in the basement and notice that I was digging out.

I broke through into darkness the following month, during that two weeks when the sweetness of my being receded into my spleen. My little world changed with the falling of one stone. Freed of mortar, I pushed and it fell backwards with a deep, loud thud. I pressed my face to the resulting hole and smelled the cool dankness of one of the earth's interior rooms. Here, this black hole and dank air, was the proof that I was indeed quite sane. I felt certain that the dead I had met on the hillside were a part of whatever lay behind this basement wall. That much was obvious. Stellaria must have once lived in this house, her parents: conductors on the underground railroad, a loose network of religious folk and abolitionists, who had quietly protested the laws of slavery by helping slaves escape. And the young man who'd been stuck at the hips in the hillside, whose arms were scarred by lashing, was a secret traveler who had risked life and limb to head north to Canada.

But why were they still here? I thought. Why had they clung to this bit of earth? My musings were cut short by the sound of our Ford Taurus pulling up to the front of the house, and I heard my husband slam the car door. Three days passed before I had sufficient time to enlarge the hole enough to climb into it. Again and again I tantalized myself by shining a flashlight into the gloom, and the tunnel before me looked tall enough for me to stand inside.

The thudding sounds of a boxing match on TV reverberated through the living room floor above my head, and I knew my husband would remain incurious for a good two hours, each of us mesmerized by myths of our own genders. Into the hole I climbed, armed with the kitchen flashlight. Upstairs on the other side of the hardwood floors, my husband's adrenalin soared as men punched each other in the face and were cursed for low blows to the testicles, but at the end of the match there would be a fair win, unless the judges had been bought. In this world the outsider always had to beat the frontrunner by knockout if he wanted to win in the favorite's town, a lesson my husband saw repeated in the world at large.

I crawled into the darkness of the earth's womb and left behind the muted noise of pugilism for the profound quiet beneath the skin of the earth where the sound of my soles on the ground resounded eerily. I was under the porch, a slab of cement overhead, my flashlight sending poles of light. The passage here was low and I had to bend to crawl through the entrance, but not for long. The sound of my feet began to echo and then the passage, like a hallway in a house, opened into a large dome-shaped room. My flashlight beam flit like a bug over the cave ceiling and walls, alighting on tiny sparkling crystals in the rock. My stars, I thought, an exclamation my grandmother would have used, for here was the underside of our hill, and what passed for solid ground from above was, from below, an overturned bowl.

The house we called ours had been saving people for a long, long time and had been built with a purpose that went beyond itself. Sometimes you could feel the spirit of the house, as if stone and wood emanated kindness into a room. This was where they hid the runaway slaves, I thought. They must have used this room like a barn, but underground.

I half expected to see old crockery or fragments of moldering leather, lead spoons or the broken handle of a knife, but whoever had closed off the cave from the house had picked it clean of artifacts, at least to the naked eye. All that remained were the emotions that clung to the place. The waiting. The threads of fear and uncertainty. A strong sense of will emanated from the cave, then I felt the faintest draft across my cheek, a welcome movement of air. I turned to find the source with my flashlight beam, and it was then I discovered that the trail led on like a giant vein in the earth's flesh.

I began to follow the path that other feet had walked. I felt like a trespasser from another time, but it occurred to me that all explorers are really trespassers. I guessed the tunnel would end beneath a nearby house on Poplar Street that was reported to have two acres and a spring.

Underground, time passes differently. There are no markers of an hour transpiring, no sign from the sky as the moon travels, no signal from the clock on the wall, and since I was one of those persons who disdained wearing a watch, I was without temporal guidance. I continued until the tunnel split and followed the larger vein off to the left. When I next had to make a decision I took the right path, again following what I believed to be the main channel. Time passed. It could have been thirty minutes or an hour and a half when my flashlight began to flicker.

When was the last time I had changed the batteries? Well, no matter, I told myself. I can feel my way back if the light goes out, and since darkness was imminent I turned around.

When the light failed, I could not express the utter blackness that enfolded me. I had never experienced such a complete darkness, such silence, such encasement like a tomb. I thought of the bells they used to rig from a buried coffin up to the surface, so that, should the dead awaken to find they had been buried alive, they could pull the string and alert the night watchman of a grave error. I had a growing sense of what it was like to be buried alive. The utter horror and helplessness. *Breathe deeply*, I told myself. I was still alive, and there was a very good chance that I could retrace my steps and find the light from my hole in the basement. The thing was not to lose your head.

I felt my way along in the dark, my palms and fingers reading the rough tunnel walls like a form of earthen braille. It was not so difficult until I came to a fork and had to make another decision. By then I could no longer remember what choices had led me to this point, but finally I decided it didn't matter which passage I took. The passage would end or lead back to my house.

Eventually, I confessed that I should have reached the house if I was on the right trail. My hands felt raw and scraped and I'd bumped my head a couple of times and felt a painful knot rising on my temple. Surely, the boxing match was over now. My husband would come looking for me. But the more I thought of it, the less certain of rescue I was. The basement was the last place he would look. It could be weeks before he noticed that the lights were on in the basement and there was a hole in the basement wall.

I tried to trace the steps his reasoning would take—entirely logical, but useless in this case. I often took a walk around the grounds at night, stalking the boundaries of our yard along with the cats. He would naturally think I'd gone into the yard and go searching for me there, calling me, and, when I didn't answer, he'd become consumed by irritation as a masking of his fear.

Part of him always feared I would get into a stranger's car one day and never be seen again. I was not sufficiently suspicious of the outside world. By now he had envisioned that I'd been whisked away by a carful of drunken men, or the stranger who stopped in the dark to ask for directions and grabbed me from the yard. I was hogtied in the trunk with duct tape over my mouth, and they were driving somewhere far into the woods where they could take their time with me before they chopped me into little pieces and fed me to the pigs. But maybe they were lazy when it came to cutting me up, so they'd dump my naked body beside a logging road and cover me with a slab of linoleum, and come deer season some hunter or his dog would find me, and, at least then, my husband would know what had become of me. I never even told him that everyone in my family gets cremated. I wondered if he'd think of that.

Oh, shit, if I die down here, I won't even need burying. I'm already more than six feet under. I was, I realized, hopelessly lost. How I longed for water. I sank down and began to cry.

By now he'll have called the police, I thought. But what good would that do? How many days do you have to be gone before they call you a missing person? If you were a slave, a quarter of an hour would be long enough, but a free person has free will to exercise and the law assumes you are using it, until enough time has passed that the hogs have been well fed.

Sometime after tears I noticed a heaviness sliding down in my lower abdomen, and I realized I was starting to bleed. *Well, that's just great*. But then I started to think about the benefits of menstruation. If they ever discovered the basement hole, maybe the scent of blood would bring the dogs more rapidly. A more ominous thought occurred to me then. Would a woman keep bleeding after she died? I succumbed to another wailing. I felt a terrible loss for the things I might yet have done with my husband. And I cried for my husband. How was he going to manage the finances? He didn't even know where the passbook was. I should have left a trail about the finances, but it had always seemed like a morbid endeavor.

It was then, as I lifted my head from my hands, that the dead sat with me again. I shuddered and wondered if I too had died, but surely sufficient time had not yet passed. Dark as it was down there, a pearly light surrounded the heads of the blond girl I called Stellaria, and Henbit, the former slave, at her side.

"Are you the conductors?" I asked.

Maybe they were my guides to the other side of life, which was to say I would not die alone.

Henbit said, “Do I look like I reached the promised land?”

“He died down here,” the girl explained. “We had to bury him.”

“Bury him?”

“In one of the passages that ends.”

“They buried me standing up.”

“Walled you in?”

“With stones and dirt. We couldn’t take the chance to bring him out.”

“I lives here now. So many years. Never reached the other side. I rattle around these rooms beneath the ground.” He leaned forward and looked me in the eye. “You never heard me once?”

“Maybe. Maybe,” I said, “when the house is quiet in the middle of the night and I can’t sleep, I go to the sitting room that overlooks the big oak to the north, and I sense the other ones who gazed out those same windows. I thought you were a train.” He had, I realized, a thoughtful, intelligent face, and I was ashamed it took me this long to ask, “What is your name?”

“I’m called dead. But the name they gave me once was James Durban, on account I belonged to the Durban farm in the delta lands.”

I asked the girl, “Have I lost my mind?”

“You have lost the way,” she agreed, “and you’d better keep your head. That’s what my mama always said: don’t go losing your head.”

“Who were your parents?”

“My mother is called America.”

“America Curry?”

“She is my mama.” Stellaria primly smoothed her long skirt. “How do you know her?”

“From the land title. From her headstone in the cemetery a couple of blocks from our house. She had three husbands.”

“She did. The first was my own papa; he died of cholera. The second one was going to talk, and he lost his head. The third one came after the war. That man did not spare the rod and one night he lost his head, as well.”

I did not believe in angels, but the shimmery light that surrounded James Durban’s dark head made him look like a saint in a Medieval church fresco. It seemed his eyes knew the depth of human sorrow. The girl had a serious little face with a pointed chin and a spattering of freckles across her cheeks. A gauzy light suffused her golden hair. She looked up at me and said, "Influenza cut me down. But I know the way. Whenever Mama took sick I led the way."

She stood up then and gave a shake to her curls. "Remember, when you leave us, follow the drinking gourd."

She began to lope down the tunnel. If I had lost my mind, I did not care. I was just glad not to be mad and alone, for the girl and James Durban lent a comforting glow to the tunnel. I quickly fell behind. Sometimes they would turn a corner and be lost to me. "Wait! What is your name?" I called after her.

"Margaret."

"Please stop, Margaret, I feel dizzy. There's not much air down here."

"They've closed her off," Margaret said. "Blocked her openings."

"Let me catch my breath," I said. "You're young."

"We're dead. Don't tarry!" she ordered in her stern little girl voice, then off she fled like a young deer, James Durban and I trailing behind. Durban, I saw, had a limp and dragged one leg as he scurried off-kilter. My breathing became more labored and then James Durban loped ahead of me, and I trailed behind, holding myself upright by feeling along the tunnel walls. In the distance the two of them were small bouncing golden lights. I was no longer rational. I was remembering the gown I wore to the London Film Festival the year one of my husband's novels was made into a film. What a lovely shimmer of bronze. I wept during the film and throughout the standing ovation. Afterward, in the VIP room, we were drinking champagne, and Emma Thompson turned to me, six months pregnant, absolutely stunning and swelling out a cranberry velvet gown. "Your husband is brilliant," she said. Then I was in the dark again, feeling quite dizzy, and the glow of my guides grew faint and small as fairy lights. *That was a nice one, Cinderella.*

I ran after those fading lights with what strength was left in me. I chased their evanescence. I watched them fade to dark. "No!"

"Follow the gourd!" A thin thread of the girl's voice rippled over me and was gone.

I heard my feet bounding along the passage. Somehow I made a turn in the dark without banging my head, and I chased after them, desperate for their light, desperate for their company. I hated the darkness then. I ran for what was coming next. If it was death then I ran to it, ready to drink it down.

Once again the tunnel turned, and then I beheld the light. A pure white shaft of light streaming down to the cave floor. I raced to it, thinking: so, it's true, there is a God, and when you're dead you see the light. I ran toward whatever it was, feeling my consciousness ebbing away like a receding tide. "I loved you," I said. "Remember that."

Then I stood inside that beautiful, silvery light, and tilted my head to look up at God, and what I saw was a hole in the ground. Shafts of moonlight came down from the heavens through what looked to be the roots of a tree where the dirt had fallen through. I grabbed one of those bare roots like a bar on a jungle gym and hoisted my head through the ground. Eye level with the grass, I drank in the air with a joyous, raspy honk. Then I looked up. I saw the Big Dipper in the sky.

"The drinking gourd..." I whispered to the blades of grass. The Big Dipper... that's what she had meant. You could never be entirely lost at night, even if you were terrified and running for your life with the blood hounds yelping in the distance. If you followed the two stars at the bottom of the gourd to Polaris, the last star in the handle of the Little Dipper, you had your compass north.

I had to dig at the dirt clinging to the roots, until I had a hole large enough to pull myself through. I climbed out, almost getting stuck like James Durban had when he came out of the hillside that day among the weeds. What had become of them? Did they fly out of this hole or were they still inside the earth?

I crawled across the wet grass and collapsed. I had been saved by a full moon. There was a God, and it was the first night of my period. I was so thirsty I ran my tongue over the dew that clung to the blades of grass.

There are awkward moments in a marriage when no amount of

explaining will do. You simply have to suffer through an emerging recognition of how strange you really are. You have to sit beside your oddness as I sat beside the dead.

Don't be afraid. Why do any of us meet?

By tomorrow I would be on a more regular frequency. In all probability no dead people in the yard, and sitting beside my husband would be paradise. All my pores were drinking in the night. I was heading south again across the broad lawn of the Lunk mansion. My house, my paradise, was on a terraced hill just below the part of the gourd where you put your mouth to drink.

Tonight, my husband, death did not take me, but I am beginning to know the residents.

Benjamin Percy

Swans

Weekends, Drew bicycled to Huntington Lake, where the Murfreesboro cheerleaders gathered to sunbathe and swim and dive off the high sandstone cliffs. He liked watching them, when they didn't know they were being watched, at the sandy cove where they spread their neon beach towels and oiled their bodies and drank rum and Pepsi.

Nobody knew about the cove, really—not about the deer that drank from it, dampening their hooves, nor the crawdads that slept in its beds of warm mud, nor the many panfish shining beneath its water like precious stones—nobody except Drew, his friend Kenny, and the cheerleaders.

Nobody knew about it because a storm brought some logs down the Harpeth River and into the lake where they settled at the mouth of the cove, camouflaging it, and Drew, making a nice shady spot for the water moccasins and the black bullhead catfish to doze.

Here he floated, among the logs and the slippery creatures, his eyes just above the surface, like an alligator, watching so long his skin got wrinkled and the catfish considered him just another part of the lake, something to nuzzle and chew, to rub with their whiskers, and occasionally, when they wrapped their sharp sucking mouths around his feet and tasted them, he wanted to move but didn't. He rarely moved—not even when the powerboats ripped by and shifted the logs and disturbed the snakes—and he never made a sound, never moaned, never screamed I-love-yous at the girls.

Though he wanted to.

He loved them with everything he had. He loved them more than anything in the world. The water was warm and he floated there, pretending the girls belonged to him, like dolls, and if he wanted to kiss them or hold them or anything else—anything at all—they would gladly succumb to it.

Sometimes Drew brought along his friend Kenny. Kenny was tiny and fine-boned and got thrown in garbage cans a lot. He could swallow an entire banana and bring it back up. It was spooky. He liked the cheerleaders, too, but feared the snakes and snappers and Drew always worried he might suffer a screaming attack and ruin everything.

Sometimes—bobbing in the water, algae clinging to his bald cheeks—Kenny whispered all the unbelievable things he wanted to do to the cheerleaders, his voice accelerating into a quivery pressure-cooker hiss that bothered Drew.

It made him feel grotesque. Like he had been caught doing something embarrassing. It made him feel fat and fifteen, which he was, with hair only beginning to bud in his armpits.

You keep quiet and listen to your fantasies—Drew thought—and it sounds like God is talking to you. You say them out loud, you expose them to the air, and you *ruin* them, as it is with copper.

Drew preferred the sound of the cicadas humming in the forest, the lakewater softly popping against the logs, the girls laughing. He preferred to forget who he was, even where he was, his eyes tearing from the sunlight on the water, making everything glittery, like the best kind of dreams, where you are never afraid and everything turns out for the best.

Around noon, when the sun burned away all the clouds, when the air just trembled with humidity—making the girls look like some mirage you prayed was real—they ate their tiny lunches of baby carrots and yogurt and tortilla chips before climbing the nearby hill, through the hardwood forest, and assembling at the jumping place, the sandstone cornice that jutted above the water, maybe fifty feet above it.

There was never any wind—Drew could hear everything they said—which was how he learned her name was Jessica.

She was the most beautiful among them—her hair as brown as her belly, as brown as a bean—and maybe her beauty gave her bravery, because she always jumped first—her legs tight together,

her feet pointed down—screaming ya-ya-ya until the lake swallowed her with a *ploosh*.

A bubbling curl of water lingered where she broke it.

This was Drew's favorite part, when he adjusted his goggles and took big gulps of air and dove down among the catfish, flapping his arms, palms up, so that he might remain submerged long enough to see her bikini torn away when she struck the lake, revealing her breasts, so pale against her brown body, surrounded by the grayish green nowhere of underwater.

Never was anything so beautiful as she was then, her hair swirling, her bikini twisted around her neck, her eyes closed, her mouth open in an oval, savoring the casual danger of the jump, the elastic acceptance of the water.

She made you want to cry, just seeing her.

When she scissored her legs—so smooth and innocent to all the evil things that lurked beneath—when she kicked her way to the surface, the water rippled and bubbled, the bubbles rolling off her skin to form a shiny ribbon, twisting in her wake, soon vanishing.

Drew wondered what the water felt like to Jessica—and what it would feel like to be the water, cleaning her, embracing her, finding his way into her every crevice.

Here is what it would feel like to seep between her legs—he decided—it would feel like the lake mud feels when it swallows your foot to the ankle, a warm obliging pull.

Drew lived in Overall. Overall is just outside Murfreesboro.

Everybody who lived in Overall wished they lived in Murfreesboro and everybody who lived in Murfreesboro knew this and reveled in it.

Here, in Overall, five stoplights swayed over the wide empty streets. Here, in blocky black and red letters, billboards advertised Budweiser, Marlboro, and Lynyrd Skynyrd playing at the Rutherford County Fair.

Here a dusty Dairy Queen sign read, "OVERALL. WE LIKE WHO WE ARE."

Here a deer crossed the highway and hurdled a barbed-wire fence, rolls of alfalfa moldered in the fields, a farmer chased palomino horses with his pickup. Here was the Feed and Seed, the First Baptist Church, the Piggly Wiggly, the Pinch Penny Tavern, the Old Hickory Trailer Park, hidden among the pines, where the shadows gathered in bluer shades, as if trapped deep underwater.

That was Overall.

A rifle shot's distance and you were past it, you were going to Murfreesboro, where they had a Cineplex and a Wal-Mart Supercenter and beautiful cheerleaders who did high kicks and somersaults and flashed their clean white panties, where—as Drew saw it—life seemed a better thing.

Every Friday night was the same old story.

Around eight o'clock, when the bats and the owls and a deep purplish color rose from the forest and filled the sky, the Murfreesboro footballers paid Overall a visit. Everyone gathered on the sidewalks and on their lawns, in lawn chairs, as you would for a parade, with cold cans of Bud Light tucked into Amoco cozies, with bags of jerky balanced on their thighs, waiting for the footballers to come.

And then they came.

Their tricked-out Cameros and El Caminos and cherry-red Chevy pickups with the Cummins diesel engines made a collective noise that started as a barely perceptible whine—you could hear it a long way off—and rose to a grumbling shout that rolled into Overall like a deeply gray thunderhead.

Probably they went a hundred-miles-per-hour—that was what people said—but who could know for sure. They were so fast, they were their own kind of fast. Their speed was such that it ruffled Drew's hair and popped his ears. Their speed made him jealous, like: I wish I had the guts. They tore through the streets and parking lots and slammed their brakes and cranked their steering wheels so hard they spun around corners, tires smoking, blistering, melting, leaving behind swirling rubber designs for Overall to remember them by, until next Friday.

Of course the cops chased them.

Overall had two cops whose singular duty, it seemed, was to chase the footballers while everyone watched, not cheering like maybe you'd expect, just watching, for the spectacle, knowing the cops didn't really want to catch anybody, and even if they did, they would never be fast or brave enough.

The footballers hurled eggs and crumpled beer cans, they tooted their horns, they did donuts in the park and screamed mostly unintelligible screams about your mother, before zooming back to Murfreesboro and leaving Drew, trembling, slightly dizzy, with their noise still in his head.

They had done this for years. It was their custom, as it was Overall's to watch, afraid and panicked and excited at once, not really understanding why they sat around and let the footballers beat them, only knowing it was horribly entertaining, somehow.

Drew's father, Marty, called himself the fish czar. Which sounded a lot better than Rutherford County's senior fisheries biologist. He spent his days in waders, catching striped bass and northern pike and yellow perch and measuring and tagging them, collecting scales, classifying and reclassifying trout streams on their ability to support good trout habitat, that kind of thing.

Sometimes he gutted fish and examined their spiralized guts and made marks in his little black notebook. Sometimes he gathered their eggs, as crisp and yellow as corn kernels, to look at under a microscope.

And sometimes he caught fish so big they scared him.

The man had energy. Of that Drew was certain. Forever clapping his hands and smiling and jumping from the sofa to answer the phone with a *yello*. No matter how early, when Drew woke in the morning, there his father was, at the kitchen table, spreading marmalade across wheat toast, never drinking coffee or Coca-Cola, claiming he didn't need it, apparently drawing his energy from a source deep inside, some warm mineral spring of a source that Drew often wished he could pour in a pitcher and drink.

Though Drew sometimes wondered, was that an all-over smile,

when his father showered so long the house filled with steam, when late at night wet choking sounds fluttered down the hall, seeping through the crack under the door to wake Drew and make him wonder.

Marty handled so many fish, their smell crept into his skin and followed him around and stayed behind to introduce him. It was a sharp oily smell, something you might find at the bottom of a well. Drew didn't mind it except when the kids at school said he smelled not good, as in funny, *spermy*.

The two of them didn't have much to talk about—"That was great," Drew would say when they finished a movie or a meal, and Marty would say, "Wasn't it?"—but they loved each other. They loved each other a lot, in the unsaid brutish way that fathers and sons acknowledge such a thing, with slugs to the shoulder, wrestling matches.

Fishing away their afternoons on a skiff.

When they fished, they wrapped peanut butter balls around their hooks and plopped them in the water and hung bells from their lines, so that they might nap, together, with their caps pulled low, sometimes so startled by the bell's ringing they screamed and grabbed each other.

Then they reeled in what was oftentimes a largemouth bass, sometimes a bluegill, and removed the hook and tossed the fish back in the water because they didn't enjoy killing. It wasn't in their hearts. Both of them were tender in this way—a certain combination of bruised and gentle—no thanks to *her*.

She left them to marry Shane Harvey, a.k.a. Donut, the former Overall High defensive coach, whose early retirement led to an offensively lopsided football team led to a series of chronic and devastating losses led to the Friday night troubles with Murfreesboro.

She and Donut went north, to Wisconsin, to escape the humidity, they claimed.

Wisconsin was a place Drew never wanted to go.

Sometimes he forgot what she looked like. Like everyday her memory sank deeper inside, where it was slowly digested, broken down into little particles that cried their way out of him late at night when he buried his face in his pillow. And soon there would be nothing left? How could he resent what he couldn't remember? Sometimes he wanted to chew grass like a sick dog and throw her back up.

And sometimes he dug through the closet and wiped the dust from the wedding album and saw her and his father, happy and hopeful and running down the aisle.

"That bitch," Drew wanted to say, "that fucking bitch!" Though he kept quiet, keeping his anger for his mother as he kept his love for the cheerleaders, nested inside him, like a seed.

Drew went down, beneath the water lilies and logs, past the black bullheads that nipped playfully at his shorts and toes—five, ten, twenty feet—until he reached the lake's muddy bottom, until the blood pulsing in his head matched that in his groin.

Down was a good place to be.

Below him were bird and fish bones tangled in the roots of silky grasses. Above him were the black silhouettes of catfish, lazily whipping their tails back and forth, and beyond them, a rippling sky, colored white and orange and blue, like an enormous church window forever reorganizing itself into little crescents and diamonds, sparkling.

There was nothing else. There was nothing to say and nothing to hear—no powerboats, no airplanes, no cicadas, no Kenny whispering his hunger for the cheerleaders—nothing to do except resist the alternate gravity that took hold of his fat and tugged upward.

He embraced a slimy boulder and held tight. Here his mind was single. Here he plugged into his pulse and yielded to it. A yellow perch brushed past him, its scales the brightest thing in the water until the girls crashed through the ceiling of the lake, every one of them beautiful, with their breasts bared and their arms wide open.

He could hold his breath a long time—he practiced at home and at school, sometimes gasping in the back row and making everyone turn around and laugh—and so he waited for Jessica.

Even when black and red spots danced across his retinal screen, he waited.

When she finally appeared above him, surrounded by a white column of bubbles, as if she were boiling hot, the blood came rushing to his face and bordered on causing an aneurysm, struck as he was by the misery that was his desire. Earlier that day he found himself suddenly aroused and in a pinch ended up jerking off not into his own hand or sock—that would be pathetic enough—but into his mother's bedroom slipper, the one shaped like a bear claw, which she left behind and which they had not bothered to throw away.

Now, among the black leeches and crawdads, he felt the impulse to grab her ankles and drag her down, swallow her with his arms, *squeeze*, until they both lost their breath and perished, thrilled and doomed.

But together.

And this was April, when the swans came.

The Murfreesboro footballers—who played baseball now but who fundamentally remained footballers, swinging at every pitch, swinging with everything they had, sometimes forgetting to drop the bat and charging first base with it tucked in the crook of their arm, other times tackling a runner to make certain he was *out*—they won their sixth straight game and the cheerleaders celebrated this by drinking their way deep into a rum drunk.

At the cove they skipped stones and practiced their cheers and their human pyramid and when it collapsed they laughed so hard they cried, their nearly naked bodies tangled together in the sand. Then, after they sunbathed and ate some lunch and jumped off the cliffs, forwards, backwards, hand-in-hand, Jessica pulled a hatchet from her backpack and announced they would build a raft.

It was a hot day full of flies that tasted their sweat when they took turns with the hatchet, in their bikinis. There was just enough fat on their bodies so that when they swung, when they chopped at the dogwood trees, they jiggled. It was erotic, somehow. They put their hair in ponytails and wiped their faces with their forearms and bound the logs with rope, the sap sticking to their skin, the sand sticking to the sap, and together they dragged the raft to the lake. When they discovered it floated, kind of, they celebrated with more rum and collapsed on their towels and fell asleep.

Drew and Kenny watched all this all day and into the early evening, their chins and cheeks glistening from where the water touched them, their hands pale and wrinkled with strange hieroglyphic designs.

If you could read the designs they might say something about being alone and being in love.

Owls called. Bats swooped down and seized mayflies and moths off the logs, making Kenny nervous. He said, "Maybe we should go," and Drew didn't say anything but shook his head, *no*. The sun eased toward the horizon, into the forest, setting the black oak and blue ash and dogwood aflame, their tops haloed with a light red light that slowly darkened to clay's redness.

Out of this came the swans.

There were about twenty of them altogether, all flapping and honking and making a very big noise when they circled the lake, flying together but not like geese do, a tangled white cloud that descended on the cove, their wings breezing silvery ripples on the water when they slowed and settled there.

The cheerleaders woke up and made high sounds of appreciation when they raced down the beach and into the lake. Here they laughed and tasted rum from their Styrofoam cups and said, "Pretty," and "Would you look at that? Would you just *look* at that?" and "Can you believe those are swans. I mean, *swans*, for Christ's sake."

They waded until the water came to their thighs, a short distance from the swans, approaching the flock as they approached the jumping place, with Jessica leading them, unafraid, innocent to the awfulness of nature.

The sunset flared and for a moment you could see every shadow and broken feature of the land, and the swans seemed to glow a phosphorescent white, white like you wouldn't believe.

They were fat—off cattails and duckweed and water moss—and they wanted to get fatter. They were hungry. Drew wondered where they had been and what they had seen that made them so hungry when they dunked their heads in the water, searching for something to eat, and finding it. One swan withdrew a crawdad and chewed it until it cracked, pleasuring in its soft gray muscle and sour green guts.

The air darkened to a purplish color and as if on cue the swans moved toward the girls without appearing to move, gliding, like ghosts, with little collars of foam trailing behind them. The girls watched them come, with their arms wrapped casually around each other's waists and shoulders, with Jessica asking, "Do we got any bread? I bet they want bread."

Then the swans opened their six-foot wingspans and lowered their heads and straightened their necks and a tremendous hiss filled the air, a noise associated with snakes and flat tires, with imminent danger, a noise that told the girls to run.

So they ran. They splashed their way to shore and ran along the beach, squealing with frightened pleasure, the sand sticking to their feet. And the swans followed. Their great white shapes lifted from the water as if drawn by invisible wires, gracefully, effortlessly, honking and hissing and striking the girls with the big blocks of airs that came rolling out from under their wings.

Drew wanted to help. But it was easier to watch.

Some of the girls screamed, others tripped in their drunkenness and scrambled forward on all fours and began to cry in panicky gulps when claws raked red lines across their butts and backs. They abandoned their towels and coolers and crashed off into the brushwood where they could be heard for a long time, wailing like sirens, branches snapping, leaves sizzling beneath their bare feet so you would have thought the whole forest was pulling up its skirt to dance.

Kenny said, "Cool."

Drew said, "I'm worried about this."

The next weekend Drew and Kenny visited the cove and found the swans there, roosting on the beach and on the raft, bobbing in the water, coiling their necks—necks as long and slender as a woman's arm—into positions that made you question the existence of the bone within them.

The boys entered the cove from the small lakeside inlet, plunging deep before swimming forward, to avoid the water moccasins that gathered in nests that looked like twisting balls. Once underwater Drew heard that sound—the one everyone heard—the pulsing of a heart, but when he surfaced it was gone, lost among the cicadas' noise.

Where are they? he wondered. Where is *she*?

He pictured a town, Murfreesboro, a house, hers. Probably she lived in the same kind of house everyone lived in around here, ranch-style with a brick exterior, with white gutters and white trim surrounding the windows and doors. Probably she just stepped from the shower, he thought, and now stood opposite the bathroom mirror, combing her hair with a horsehair brush, her breasts flattened by the neon towel wrapped around her body. Surely she thought about the lake, the jumping place, the rush of wind when the water rose to meet her. Surely she would come.

He felt a pounding in his chest and in his groin. He tried to calm it, imagining it as aligned with the breaking of the water against the logs, a vision ruined by a catfish slipping its mouth around his foot, a moistly violent sensation just obscene enough to stroke him all over.

When Kenny said, "Maybe they aren't—" Drew put a finger to his lips that told him to be quiet.

Finally she came, along with the rest, but only to retrieve their towels and coolers, which the swans had ravaged and shit upon, thoroughly.

The girls stood where the beach met the trees, shading their eyes, watching the swans nap with their heads tucked under their wings, and from a distance—with their scooped backs—the swans looked like enormous molars and the lake looked like a lake full of teeth.

Whereas the other girls darted forward and snatched their things and hurried back to the safety of the trees, Jessica sauntered out and stood with her legs apart and yelled, "Hey!" The swans paid her no attention. "Hey, fuckers," she said and picked up a rock and hurled it at a nearby swan, striking its back. The swan released a surprised honk before uncurling its neck and sighting Jessica and departing the water with one determined snap of its wings.

She had a wild happy look on her face when she lifted her hands to accept its body and together they crashed to the sand.

She fought in a way that reminded Drew of dancing—swirling, crouching, leaping, sometimes closing her eyes when she found a steady rhythm—and she did this as she did everything, with abandon. There was no turning back—and so even if she bled, even if she fell in a tangle now and then, she would right herself, she would lean forward at the waist and move her arms and legs and continue to fight.

The swans gathered on one side, the cheerleaders on the other, each voicing their encouragement with honks, screams, each scurrying forward and then back, as if eager and afraid to join the violence.

A perspective Drew understood completely when he swam from his hiding place and dashed along the beach and joined the girls—who paid him no attention—soon followed by Kenny.

Her lip curled back in a snarl, her muscles jumped beneath her skin, her hands needed no instruction, knowing what to do, where to go, a left hook to the wing, a chop to the neck, even as the swan snapped its beak, pinching her chest and arms, hissing.

It was a beautiful thing to watch.

Then, in exhaustion, she wrapped her arms around the swan and the swan curled its neck around hers, so that they seemed but one fantastic creature that eventually broke apart—and when she and the swan retreated to the woods and to the lake, each of them breathing in asthmatic bursts that revealed how badly they hurt, Drew imagined approaching Jessica.

The girls would part before him, zipper-style, and there she would be, bleeding and hurting but putting on a big show, giving him the thumbs-up when he asked was she okay, did she need anything, *any*thing at all? "No," she would say, "nothing," and he would brush from her face a damp strand of hair and she would close her eyes a moment, savoring his touch, still panting from the fight, looking both fierce and vulnerable. "You're worried about me," she would say. "That's sweet." And then they would bring their mouths together, hard, making blood. Hers would be sweet, like maraschino cherries, and the cheerleaders would murmur all around them.

I should totally do that, Drew thought. I should kiss her and carry her home. That would be brave. That's what I'm going to do *right now*.

But he didn't—and the girls disappeared between the trees, touching Jessica and following her to where the clay game-trail turned to the gravel path turned to the asphalt road that led to the highway, and after that, Murfreesboro.

Friday night came and so did the footballers. They entered Overall en masse—ten Camaros, three pickups, and a salmon-colored El Camino, all with their mufflers drilled to make their noise bigger, all with faces leering and hollering through their open windows—and then they split apart, some of them blazing along the main strip, others diving down side streets.

From all corners of the town they squealed their tires and honked their horns, like birds answering each other. Police sirens joined their noise and the effect was strangely musical, not something you could tap your foot to, but nice.

Drew watched all this from the sidewalk, along with his father and Kenny and the rest of Overall, watching like you would watch a sporting event, jealous of and awed by the players' upsetting power. He drank from a glass bottle of root beer that sweated in his hand. He kept the bottle to his lips when a Camaro came tearing by, its wheels rising on one side when it took the corner, followed by a cop car.

Marty was being Marty. He was being happy. Except to say *duck*, he ignored the beer cans thrown in their direction. Instead he pointed out the footballers when they zoomed past, saying *hey*, that's so-and-so, who broke the Rutherford County rushing record.

Like everyone else he paid careful attention to Murfreesboro, subscribing to their newspaper, *The Mondo Times*, sometimes reading it twice in one sitting, holding it close to his face, studying names and scores and obituaries, as if they were the most important things.

"Man," he said, his voice a joyful shout you would not use unless imitating joy. "Holy smokes, did you see that? He drives as fast as he runs."

A couple Boy Scouts walked by selling popcorn and Marty bought a bag off them. He passed it to Drew and said, "Isn't this great, guys? Drew?"

Drew didn't say anything. For some reason he felt bothered by his father, the way he clapped his hands, the way he smiled so big the corners of his mouth twitched slightly. He saw him as if for the first time, and it was like something thrown at you when you weren't looking. It was annoying and it was shocking. His father's face remained an old familiar happy thing but beneath it he seemed sick.

Drew could smell the fish smell puffing off his father and though it had never bothered him, it bothered him now as a smell that partnered a fever, a bad one, one that keeps you up all night, sweating. Like a lover.

He tried concentrating on his popcorn, which made him thirsty, so he guzzled his root beer down, only to spit a mouthful out his nose, hacking for breath when one of the pickups rocketed past with a blonde cheerleader hanging out its window, giving him the finger, her face painted blue, orange and white, *their* colors. From the open bed three more girls—*his* girls—shook their pom-poms and cheered, "Murfreesboro!" while the wind knocked their hair every which way.

"Oh, great," Kenny said. "Now they're in on it, too." He lifted his thin arms and let them fall. "Wonderful."

Marty said, "Pretty sure that was Hank Haines. Heck of a quarterback, that guy."

Drew now studied the window of every passing car. He sought her face and hoped he would not find it. He hoped she was better than this. He drank more root beer and his throat moved up and down as if something was trapped there.

Then the El Camino fishtailed around the corner and came to a sliding stop, and though Drew didn't recognize her at first—with her face painted blue on one side, white on the other—this was her, this was Jessica, the girl he wanted to know in so many ways. She sat on the passenger side, the side facing him, and he wondered was she *with* the dumb ape behind the steering wheel? He hoped not.

She looked at Drew and he liked being looked at. *She sees me!* he thought. *We are having a moment.* He interpreted the moment as one exchanged between two strangers who meet unexpectedly, in the forest, at the mall, and develop in one lingering glance that weird kind of closeness people get when they know zero about each other but *feel* a deep connection. Then she smiled at he didn't know what, and he wondered what she saw, a fat boy or something else.

He raised a hand to her: she copied the gesture.

And an egg, launched from her hand, struck his face, oozing into his eyes and mouth. With equal effect she might have punched him in the guts. He felt all the hope knocked black from his body—though the longing was still there.

She laughed, her mouth wide open and holding a shadow, and the El Camino took off and she was gone, so elusive, yet lingering, like the pain that wakes you from a dream and ends up belonging to the dream.

Kenny laughed, too, before choking it back, knowing better but still smiling.

Drew didn't bother wiping away the egg. Instead he held his head in his hands as if it were something separate from him. He could hear the anger mounting in his breathing.

Marty said, "Are you okay? Are you okay?" He looked emotional enough to kiss Drew on the mouth. To prevent this from happening Drew took another root beer from the cooler and drank it in one long gurgling swallow that foamed a belch up his throat that took longer to get out than the root beer took to get in. He kept the bottle against his lips and when his father asked again, was he okay, he said, "I'm fine."

The words dropped in the bottle and broke.

Sometimes—not very often but *some*times—when Drew and Marty were out on the skiff, sucking the peanut butter off their thumbs and waiting for the bells to ring, they talked. Marty would talk about the nurse shark he landed at Beverly Beach, Oregon, how it took him an entire afternoon, and how the shark kept biting at the air, at nothing, long after it died. He would talk about the Labrador puppy he once found inside a catfish's stomach, whole, with its tiny pink tongue stuck out. And he would talk about women. The girls he dated in high school and in college. But never—not ever—did he talk about *her*.

At times like these Drew felt more like a friend than a son of any sort, his father seeming at once younger than him and like an old man who remembered life sweeter than it honestly was.

So Marty talked and Drew listened and they laughed when zipping up and down Rutherford County's lakes and reservoirs—so impossibly blue—and along the streams that sometimes petered out into salty marshes crowded with mosquitoes and snapping turtles and cypress trees, the middle of nowhere.

Marty knew where to find the fish. Sometimes they would be where two rivers converged, feeding in the eddies, hungry for the swirling larvae. Other times they would be where the willows hung off the banks or where the logs piled up, hiding in the shade, which seemed to Drew a good place to go. Where the fish were depended on the time of day, the time of year, but Marty knew where to find them.

On one of these trips he showed Drew the most amazing thing.

At the time he was working on a study that estimated the striped bass' annual growth and reproduction cycles. For this he used a mini-boom shocker, a small device with a generator the size of a microwave and a rod he lowered from the skiff into the water, applying 400 volts that first drew toward the anode every fish within a hundred feet, and then, with a simple twist of the output settings, effectively paralyzed them, so that the surface of the water suddenly filled with convulsing fish you could pluck from the water with your hands.

Drew noticed how Marty smiled the whole time. He always smiled, sure, but right then, when the fish rose and tremored and gaped in pain, he looked *truly* happy. He looked like the footballers looked when they terrorized Overall, like Jessica looked when she dove off the cliffs, like his mother looked when she walked out the door with a suitcase in each hand. He looked like he felt good.

Drew knew what he needed to do. When his father showered and the house filled with steam, he stole from the skiff the mini-boom shocker and with bungee cords strapped it between the handlebars of his bicycle.

It was noon and it was hot when he arrived at the cove. The swans napped with their heads tucked away. Flies buzzed around them. The raft had run aground and he carried the shocker there. The logs were slick with guano. With not a little effort he shoved off the raft and climbed halfway onto it, legs kicking, propelling him toward where the swans waited, now awake and yawning and stretching like people.

Near the middle of the cove he crawled all the way onto the raft and held his breath when the swans inched toward him, fanning out to surround the raft, shifting nervously, cocking their heads, opening and closing their wings to pound the water. One of them showed its sharp pink tongue and hissed and the hissing quickly spread among the other swans, drowning out the cicadas, so loud and terrifying that it became the only thing.

For a second Drew didn't know what to do—hugging himself, he felt lost—but only for a second. He reached for the rod and lowered it into the water and knobbed on the power to 400 volts, like his father showed him.

Their hisses transformed to shrieks. It was a sound Drew never imagined he might cause—it sounded like women in pain or in sexual climax—but he did not stop and neither did they—they continued to move toward him—and so he upped the voltage.

Beneath their screams was an *under*sound, the sound of the mini-boom, an angry buzzing as electric currents crackled into the water, currents whose yellow fingers snapped and popped and took hold of the perch and the catfish and the eels and leeches and drew them to the raft so that the water gradually darkened and stirred with their presence.

So many creatures broke the surface, seizuring, rolling over and over, showing their pale bellies, that the cove just shook, just boiled. The swans crawled more than swam toward the raft. The smell of fish was everywhere. Next to the raft a black bullhead rose, its muddy eyes rolling back in its head, its broad ugly face gaping in silent agony, and then, as if its pain belonged to him, Drew began to weep in the open way men normally avoid. He couldn't help it. He cried as he had never cried before. He cried over everything and nothing

Never had he felt so powerful and repulsive and so awfully *good.*

The swans were nearly upon him when he switched the output settings from an alternating current to a direct current—a switch that caused muscle paralysis and illuminated the water with flashes of light—and the buzzing sound vanished, replaced a heavy arterial pulsing that Drew recognized.

The swans went quiet and limp, their necks collapsing, their wings unfolding, so that they just floated there, among the fish, not dead, but not wholly alive. Still sobbing, Drew switched off the mini-boom and picked them from the water, stacking their trembling bodies on the raft to put elsewhere so that the girls might return to him, falling from the sky with their arms wide open, their faces beautiful.

Brad Vice

The Bear Bryant Funeral Train

"Mickey Mouse is the most miserable ideal ever revealed . . . . Down with Mickey Mouse! Wear the Swastika Cross!"

—Newspaper article, Pomerania, Germany, mid-1930's, as quoted in Art Spiegelman's *Maus II*

Bryant always told his quarterbacks that if they had five yards of running room, take it, even if a receiver was open downfield. "Someone in the stands with a rifle might shoot the receiver," he said.

—Mickey Herskowitz, *The Legend of Bear Bryant*

Today one of the secretaries brought out a little white cake with candles and my name written on it. Then she got over the intercom and led the whole Vance Mercedes factory in a rendition of "For He's a Jolly Good Fellow." The song, like my retirement, was a bit forced. But some of my engineering friends brought gifts.

"How about this!" cried Doogie Sims, brandishing a stainless steel Sabatier meat cleaver high in the air. I pretended to cringe in fear, then we laughed. Cleve Weathers brought me a bottle of Laugavulin Scotch with a red bow tied to the cork. "I thought they'd have to drag you out of the labs in a body bag." Everyone laughed.

The guys on the assembly line got together and framed a poster of the 1934 Crimson Tide team at the Rose Bowl, the one with the dapper young Paul Bryant standing in the third row. Later Bryant would grow up to be the winningest college football coach of the twentieth century. These were gifts tailored to my enthusiasms.

"Gee guys, I don't know what to say." Handshakes went all round. In one of them the new kid, Uva, slipped me something, a small disk. Uva was a prematurely balding twenty-four-year-old Kraut, with a stiff new BAMA baseball cap and a metallurgy degree from Hamburg. "What's this?" I asked.

"I heard you are a Beatles fan."

I nodded.

"It's a bootleg I burned for you, digitally remastered tracks from Sergeant Pepper."

He gave me a wink as I slipped it into my pocket.

Here is a secret about the future. One day we will live in our cars. One set of keys for both home and automobile. I know because I design them: cars, buses, the shadowy tractor-trailers that hover for a mile or two in your blind spot and inexplicably disappear. I design them to run, not only on electricity and polonium, but on whims, dreams, states–of-mind. I pay special attention to spatial relations, ergonomics, the marriage of mood and structure. Five days a week, nine to five, I alone descend into the depths of the inner sanctum of the CAD labs like an ancient and learned abbot, down the catacombs of the factory where there is hidden an otherwise secret and forbidden library. There I sift much forgotten lore and arcana in hopes of recovering something useful or important to the collective spiritual imagination of my people—Alabamaians, Southerners, Americans, in that order or reverse—good consumers one and all. Within the confines of the Vance factory, I am the engineer with the highest level of for-your-eyes only security clearance—clearance to knowledge that can open your mind, your heart, your pocket book. I make cars, and my cars make you feel like you're driving a cathedral.

Picture this. It begins on a cold day in my hometown, Tuscaloosa, Alabama, near the banks of the Black Warrior River. It is cold even for January, an unnatural mechanical cold. There is a thin rime of black ice on the roads and the air carries with it the bitter freon chill of an old refrigerator running itself into a state of absolute despair. As the mute rhetoric of the super-8 reveals, the Bear Bryant Funeral Train is over ten miles long and at its maximum width spans the latitude of eight lumbering Pace Arrow recreation vehicles. The Bear Bryant Funeral Train is not a real document. It is a computer-generated film made to look like a document. I have given the film the grainy look and feel of celluloid to make the events that are to follow more or less plausible. Even though my movie is based on a true story, the truth is not enough. The super-8 makes it more true—more real. Without the convention of the super-8 you may not be able to believe that this many people actually came to one funeral, but they did.

The camera opens up to a sixty-mile stretch of road that is literally packed with mourners. They stand in the misting rain, shoulder to breast, waiting for a glimpse of the hearse that carries the most important man of their generation. For those of you too young to remember the Bear Bryant funeral, the setting is the year nineteen hundred and eighty-three, in the old petrol age—anno domini as we used to say in school.

The trouble all started a couple of months ago when my boss Hans called me into his office. By then most of the work on the Bear Bryant Funeral Train Project was done.

"Sorry, Sonny," said Hans. "But it's time for the old dead to make room for the new dead."

I have spent most of my life working as an engineer for Daimler-Chrysler in the Vance factory on the edge of Tuscaloosa. When I first began working here fresh out of college, we made SUV's, the M-class, and later on the more eco-friendly hydrogen cell M-80 and M-81 models. I've made a lot of money for the Germans over the years. But when Hans told me it was time for me to fade, I didn't kick. I had a multimillion dollar 401K filled with company stock and it was clear Hans had troubles.

"Hans . . .you don't think it was me, do you?" There had been some recent problems with corporate theft. Designs for the new solar tractors had turned up missing. And on top of that, someone was tampering with top-secret files from the CAD labs. Protocol mandated that heads had to roll. "You know it's those bastards at Disney again?" I said.

Hans was a little pink man with pale blue eyes and a white crew cut that gave one the impression he had been bred for the express purpose of a laboratory experiment. "Shhhh." Hans held his fingers to his lips. "The walls have mice."

Hans walked over to the mini-executive stereo system that was shaped like an early twentieth-century victrola. He whispered "Wagner," his activation word, into the bell. Mysterious waves of dance music filled the room from all directions.

"I've always meant to ask you, what do you say if you actually want to listen to Wagner?"

Hans just grinned mischievously. "Louder" He ordered the victrola. The machine obeyed. Then he put his arm around me and began to whisper in my ear.

Really the cars are just part of my job. My real passion is for trains. I used to collect them, first electric model replicas like the *Dixie Flyer* and the *Silver Eagle Express*, then the digital choo-choo's I downloaded into the wallpaper of my workstation. In college, I took a degree in electrical engineering at the University of Alabama, and when I got the job here at the Vance factory I was sent to Germany for six months to be trained in their new interdisciplinary architecture program. There we learned how to use the CAD graphics systems to sculpt new automotive designs. We used digital trains all the time to rearrange information in artistic ways. One of our first assignments was to take a medieval diagram of the great chain of being, lay it on its side, and rearrange its links. You could let the whole story of creation unfold like a Mardi Gras parade: it was a grand march of ass-shaking seraphim and garden slugs, cabbages and kings, bears and men.

⊷

When I was very young, my parents did their parental duty and took me to Orlando to visit Disney World, which for them was kind of like making a pilgrimage to Mecca. In those days, Orlando was the holy city of the middle class.

I was waiting in line for tickets to Space Mountain when it happened. A man just getting off the ride had a heart attack. He wasn't an old man, maybe forty, but I noticed his face was kind of green as he lumbered out of the darkness of the subterranean roller coaster. I thought he was simply going to vomit as he staggered toward one of the overflowing garbage cans. His left arm fluttered up as he leaned on the trash barrel for support. Then all of a sudden, as if he had been gunned down by a sniper, the man lurched forward and fell over, spilling discarded Cokes and funnel cakes everywhere.

When the paramedics arrived, one of them ripped open the man's buttondown. The paramedic placed his ear to his chest. He turned to his partner and shouted, "Massive MI! What if he doesn't make it?"

His partner was already rubbing the paddles of the defibrillator together. "You know the rules. That can't happen. Not inside the park." Then they shocked him and the victim of the roller coaster's body arched with electricity.

Around them a crowd had gathered.

Snow White and Goofy looked on in horror.

⊷

CAD is an acronym for computer-aided-design and it is a friend to architects, engineers, and landscapers everywhere. In the seventeenth-century, Descartes developed analytic geometry, which holds that any point on a plane can be specified by a pair of numbers, what are now called coordinates. Points, lines, and arcs could be described by mathematical equations expressed in terms of X and Y. Then in the middle of the twentieth century, the American military funded the development of several guidance systems for rockets and other such weapons. These guidance systems became the models for early computers built by IBM. In 1959, IBM and GM set out to build a series of computers that could help them design cars, and in 1961, engineers working on this collaborative project discovered how to create crosshairs on the monitor.

Later that day I stormed into Hans's office. This time he kept the music off.

"You can't just run me out like this."

"It's not just you, Sonny. We are changing all the personnel in the CAD labs. It's become too dangerous for you there. You're better off puttering around on a golf course."

"I'm agoraphobic."

"Don't make this hard on me."

Since the end of the second World War, the brass at Disney had held a grudge against the Germans. The Nazi propaganda machine had attacked Walt & company as products of a sick American society that glorified vermin, and Disney responded by funneling millions of entertainment dollars into the American war machine and providing American G.I.'s with Mickey Mouse wristwatches with which to synchronize their missions.

Daimler-Benz merged with Chrysler years ago, and now that Mercedes was as American as apple pie, these grudges were no longer supposed to exist. But there were old men in smoke-filled rooms in Pomerania and Uruguay, kept alive with gene therapy and artificial hearts, whose memories stretched deep into the past. A few years ago when Chrysler-Benz bought out Anheuser-Busch, owner of Busch Gardens and Six-Flags, we were making it clear to Disney we were ready to compete with them on their own turf. Many people like me, adept at designing mood-altering rides, were set to work building theoretical roller-coasters, concepts for theme park attractions.

"Be honest, Hans, the mice are gunning for something in the architecture office?"

"Are you still working on your Funeral Train project?"

I nodded. Then I remembered to say, "Yes." Somewhere out there those large ears were listening. Hans had a plan. A draw play.

"Kill it."

For sure, the Bear Bryant Funeral Train surpassed the jangling military cavalcade that escorted Jeff Davis into the netherworld. The Davis Train started on the steps of the New Orleans City Hall and ended at his sarcophagus, which lay within the gates of the Metarie Cemetery. That was a mere four-mile procession. Many in the parade carried floral arrangements woven into images of cannons, Confederate battle flags, and sabers. But it was hot that summer. No matter how pretty the flowers, their sweet perfume could not hide the stench of Davis's putrefaction.

In the Bryant era, ours was a time less of pomp and circumstance and more of heroic joy. No longer did we live within the dispensation of the lost cause. When we put the old man Bryant into the ground, we did it in the epic spirit of Vikings.

The last track on the disk Uva had given me turned out to be a simple video reel, a film of the Bear Bryant funeral procession. I had probably seen this material a hundreds of times: on the news, spliced into heart-warming and motivational movies, run on a continuous loop at the University of Alabama's Dionysian homecoming pep rallies where one watched the footage on a huge screen placed between the Denny Chimes clock tower and a raging bonfire. These pep rallies had all the mystery and magic of a midnight book burning, the air charged with the smell of sweat, sex, and smoke as we burned the visiting team's mascot in effigy and watched the funeral procession of our greatest coach on the big screen. The kid knew that this stock footage was the original template for my Funeral Train; now he wanted me to give him the disk with the finished story.

"What are you going to do when you retire?" Uva asked me in his dead, flat, perfect English.

Often in daydreams I have pondered what I would have done with my life if I didn't spend all my time in the lab testing the structural integrity of the latest DC hydrogen cells and solar tractors on my network station. "With my first pension check, I am going to put a down payment on a vintage Airstream trailer with a 300-semillon gas combustion engine and 1.7 gallon flush toilet and follow the Crimson Tide to all the great cities of the SEC. I will visit the General Neyland dogwood orchards of Knoxville, the celestial Huey P. Long Stadium in Baton Rouge. I want to go to Georgia and see the obelisk of Bobby Dodd. Old fart kind of stuff."

"You know you have other options."

That's when the kid laid it on me. The offer included wealth, nubile women, and asylum within the walls of the Magic Kingdom. He even hinted that immortality was not out of the question.

The crosshairs changed everything. All of a sudden it was possible to make countless modifications on a single design, whether it be on a car, house, assembly line, or a rose garden. One could build a virtual bridge on the computer and know exactly how much weight it could support, exactly how much wind resistance it could withstand, and so on.

Now we can design a car and never build an expensive prototype, just press a button and send it directly into mass production. On the other hand, it's now also cost- effective to make customized cars specifically tailored for your personality, your lifestyle, your idiosyncrasies. I can design that special car to make a stylish exit from your high school graduation, or that perfect pearly white land cruiser to get you from the wedding chapel to Niagara Falls. I can even design a car for when you leave this life. Think of it—a special hearse, just for you.

"My father cried," I told Uva. "When I was invited to be part of the Bryant funeral, he was so proud." Up until that time, my father had never had much use for me. I was a fastidious little blue-eyed snot with precious blond curls. At the age of nine, all I wanted to do was play with my choo-choos. But it was my presence the Governor requested in the funeral, and I was henceforth transformed in my father's estimation. "The state needed children to act as mutes, like in a Dickens novel." I was given a little black suit. It had crushed black velvet lapels and a top hat onto which a long black bow had been fixed to the band in the back. "The sleeves were too long, but I loved it. A funeral makes you feel so dignified, especially when you're a kid."

When Uva comes for the exchange, I lead him into the labyrinth of the inner sanctum of the CAD labs, one dark corridor stretches into the next in a spider's web of increasing narrow hallways—off limits to all but a select few. Finally we reach my private office, a little nook in the heart of the factory no bigger than the janitor's closet, only the walls are decorated with vintage sports paraphernalia—several pennants reading "BAMA vs Sewanee" and dozens of handbills with rosy Norman Rockwellseque boys and girls eating Golden Flake potato chips and drinking Coca-cola as they enjoy the game.

Uva looks around the room, eyes wet with wonder and ambition.

"Watch," I tell him. I load my version of the Funeral Train into my workstation. There is a cut in the film. The film reopens. The lens focuses on a mighty team of mules, each standing twenty hands high. They have been exported from a farm in Chattanooga to pull a green cotton wagon behind the hooded Appalachian sin eaters. From the look of them, these mules are monsters, ears flat, milky black-blue eyes, vapor pouring from their near-perfect round nostrils. The green cotton wagon contains several old women. Even though it's freezing, they wave LO, I KNOCK AT THE DOOR church fans in front of their faces.

It is the lack of sound that captures it all so perfectly. The withered lips mouthing the Fa, So, La notes to Amazing Grace.

"Who are these women?" asks Uva.

"The wagon full of old women represents Bryant's childhood among the hardworking and religious," I say. "It is a little known fact that Bryant's mother never attended any of his games because they were too worldly, not even when he played high school ball in Arkansas."

"The train works on an allegorical level?"

"Allegorical, anagogical, literal. Like an epic poem, they all collapse into one point at the end."

"Ah, you would call this closure."

"Something like that."

It is the lack of music that makes these women beautiful. It is the same power exerted over us from ancient ruins or Roman statues with missing heads. I wish Uva were somewhere else and I was alone in the cloister of the labs. Silence. Sometimes I wish I could write a poem of nothing else.

For over a year now, the Funeral Train has played in a continuous loop on my CAD station. Downloaded and refined in the circuits, in some otherworldly distillation process, the train is in constant flux, always revising itself. I have loaded all the images from The Beatles' S*ergeant Pepper's Lonely Hearts Club Band* album cover and added them into the matrix of randomly selected mourners.

"Until I moved here, I had never heard of this Bryant. Why is he so important? Why choose him as the vehicle for your mood coaster?" Uva wants to know what he is buying.

"Up until 1983, Coach Bryant's was the largest funeral procession the postbellum South had ever seen."

"Bigger than Martin Luther King?

"Oh yes."

"Than Elvis?"

"Without a doubt." What Uva failed to understand was this: Coach Bryant lived in the pre-merger era. He was a demagogue, and he carried a cult-of-personality aura similar to that of Hitler and Gandhi. He was our patriarch and we revered him as a sort of superlative invention of the South. He was our Nietzsche in houndstooth, wielding his grid-iron will-to-power like an ax-handle. Walking tall, redneck *ubermensch.* "When he was alive, his very presence inspired . . . terror and joy."

"As does the film."

"Maybe. I think of the film more like Greek tragedy. A poetic re-creation of the mythic past."

"Pity and fear, then?"

"Maybe. Maybe just fear."

In the old days, no one in Tuscaloosa drove a Mercedes except for maybe a few divorce lawyers. These were dark times before the sports utility vehicle. Tuscaloosa had no smiling, bilingual executives like Hans or Uva, no need for Montessori daycare or Starbucks. "In this town, up until the death of the Bear, all we needed was football to be happy." I felt myself getting a little misty with nostalgia.

"Oh how we had loved to watch our beautiful sons smash into one another, crushing knuckles and breaking ribs." We were fascinated with the elusive quality of youth. I cried out, suddenly, "And the cheerleaders, what angels."

In my mind I summoned up a picture of a blond in a crimson skirt, a crimson A on her breast, her arms raised in victorious salute, pits shaved smooth as a pane of glass, and then I pictured what she might look like if inserted into the Train.

Uva looked startled. "We wouldn't use the Train to hurt anyone, you know. We want to use it to help us build a new coaster. That's what you want, isn't it? You don't want Hans to kill it, do you?"

I thought about the man dying in the mouth of Space Mountain, the unholy crowd gawking around him, doing nothing, waiting for the paramedics to shock him back to life.

After the retirement party's cokes and cake, I had gone back to my cubicle where I proceeded to test the wind resistance on one of our electromagnetically refrigerated transport trucks. Only I could hear Doogie Sims talking to Uva, in whispers. I could tell there was a general sense of agreement in their murmurs. Was Doogie in on it? A double agent?

"Did you ask him if it were true, about the Funeral Train?"

"What?"

"You know he was there. When he was a kid."

"At the funeral?"

"In the funeral," said Doogie.

"A participant?"

The film begins again on the steps of the First Methodist Church of Tuscaloosa, with a group of stalwart looking pallbearers, former linemen, loading the mahogany coffin into a mammoth hearse with long black fins. There are little black curtains on the doors, and on the side a window unit air-conditioner. The Bear had loved air conditioning.

"As I recall, there had been no elaborate funeral oration within the church before we buried him in Birmingham." No eulogizing. No choir. Only a few tears and a little organ music that wafted from the corners of the packed church. Closed circuit TV cameras recorded this part of the funeral, as many other mourners paid their respects at nearby churches and watched the service on wide-screen TVs.

"Why bury him in Birmingham?"

"His wife, Mary Harmon, her family was from there." But the real funeral wasn't in Birmingham or in the church but outside on the streets. The eulogy was the unfolding parade itself, a living Bayeaux tapestry unfurled down University Boulevard. A wreath was hung on the Cadillac's back door as we began our long slow journey into the city.

Behind the hearse stands a congregation of Appalachian sin eaters in black cassocks. Like many Southern demagogues such as Wallace and Long, the Bear had a taste for strong drink and fast women. It was the job of the sin eaters to consume these paltry sins along with the more formidable transgressions caused by pride. The names of these sins have been written down on little slips of paper and baked in several pans of cornbread, which the sin eaters will feast upon as they commit Bryant's body to the grave. These sin eaters are broad stout men, well-fed on the weakness of others.

"It was their job to carry us, all the little mutes, on their shoulders. That's me right there." I point toward the edge of the screen at a little boy, blond hair stuffed under the black top hat.

Uva nods as if he understands what I am talking about. But how could he?

There is a cut in the super-8 and for a moment the terminal goes black.

The Bear Bryant Funeral Train moved with the quiet dignity displayed at all great obsequies. Martin Luther King's hundred thousand mourners in Atlanta showed no more meek and humble reverence when they lowered their leader into the earth. The Bryant procession was much bigger and grander than even the glitzy, white Cadillac flotilla that carried Elvis through the chartered streets of Memphis. There were no food vendors or T-shirt salesmen in the Bryant Train. Certainly there were no florists along the highway, only the fans, nine hundred thousand of them holding signs that read "We miss you Coach."

As a reporter from the *Tuscaloosa News* wrote the next day, "The Bear Bryant funeral train was a cheerless tailgate party, with no food or libation to warm the crowd."

* * *

The next car in the train tells how the Bear won his name. A grizzly, on loan from the Birmingham Zoo, sits next to a farm boy in overalls, who holds the bear firmly on a leash.

"Bryant earned his name in 1925 at the Lyric Theater. He agreed to wrestle a carnival bear for his hometown's entertainment. Secretly I think he was trying to impress a girl."

"And he won?"

The grizzly rides its parade float calmly, almost sleepily, next to the serious farm boy.

"When it looked like the boy was going to beat the old, frazzled bear, the owner jerked off its muzzle and it mauled him."

* * *

After the boy and bear comes the University of Alabama's Million Dollar Band.

"I think I remember them playing a New Orleans dirge."

"Dirge?"

"A funeral song. Something they must have picked up from one of their trips to the Sugar Bowl."

The drum major is dressed as a voodoo priest, the faces of his band mates painted like skeletons. Then the parade floats decorated by the fraternities and sororities. Huge crepe paper elephants roll along the asphalt, each carrying flags reading "Roll Tide Roll" in their trunks.

* * *

Here comes the march of teams, car after car of aged football players, players from Maryland and Kentucky, players from Texas A&M. Finally the players from the Crimson Tide. Over forty teams in all, most of them wearing red jerseys. Those too fat to fit into their uniforms carry them under their arms. Here comes the march of heroes. Here comes Bart Starr and Big John Hannah. Here comes the "Italian Stallion" Johnny Musso and "Mr. Tackle" Billy Neighbors. Here comes Ken "Snake" Stabler. Here comes Joe

"Willie" Namath with his wobbly weak knees and his black aviator shades to hide the tears.

Championship teams carry banners. So many of them pass by, after a while it seems as if they are all the same team marching forward down the road, as well as backward through time, getting younger and younger as they progress forward. It looks as if the super-8 is moving in both fast forward and reverse; the faces of the athletes glow with a sheen of ruined youth that has long since fallen away. Behind them the majorettes twirl flaming batons. They seem to hover a millimeter or so above the spinning earth. Then come the fans in their vans, RVs, and mobile homes.

Behind the parade of fans comes the motorcade of foreign ambassadors: parliamentarians from The Hague, senators from the Kineset, Politburo members. There is at least one Chinese field marshal. There is a caravan of oil sheiks from Yemen with fine barbered beards and almond eyes. The choleric Soviet Prime Minister Andropov is there, clearly drunk, and so is the black-bearded writer Solzhenitsyn down from Vermont. Idi Amin in a sky blue El Dorado convertible with leopard skin interior waves at the crowd. From the Sergeant Pepper matrix of mourners, only John Lennon and Johnny Weismuller wave back.

The eldest son of Ho Chi Min, Ben Pheu, rides near the end of the train. He has come to America to research Civil War reenactments at Gettysburg and Antietam and has stumbled upon a most impressive ceremony.

I point Ben Pheu out to Uva. "When Ho died, his funeral was just like this."

"Here on the caboose of the train," I tell Uva, "is the greatest football fan in the world at the time. In his own country he was something of a God, where he was revered and worshiped."

There is a look of fearful recognition on Uva's face. I whisper a song of menace in his ear: "M-I-C . . .K-E-Y ."

Of course Uva had offered me a bribe. Just as Hans had said he would. And I accepted, just as Hans had instructed.

Several barbarous dwarves in Ray Ban sunglasses run alongside the last convertible, one hand held to the transistor radios in their ears. The car's diplomatic flag flutters in the wind.

There is something majestic about it, even now, especially since I already know what is about to happen. Even Uva knows what is about to happen, though he hopes it will not.

Muddied sunlight reflects off the hood of the car, momentarily blinding the camera.

The massive dignified head tips to the side, his ears as big as satellite dishes; the unwavering plastic smile is now almost vertical. The official concubine can't stop waving. She is not as solemn as the rest of the funeral train, in her polka dots and pink pillbox hat.

The camera shakes, turns sideways, rights itself.

The crowd scatters. The concubine clutches the string of pearls at her throat.

Did he scream behind the smile when the first bullet pierced his wrist and smashed into his pelvis?

Mothers fall on children.

Husbands on wives.

Aleister Crowley falls on top of the Vargas Girl.

Duck and cover.

The dwarves draw their Walthers, pointing them in all directions. Only there isn't enough time to discern that the shots are coming from the clock tower, from the carillion on the quadrangle, Denny Chimes.

Another shot and the entire train begins to fall like a row of dominos toward the hearse, which by now is halfway to Birmingham.

The driver of the hearse hits his brakes and the Bear's coffin spills out the back door and slides along the slick black ice. The team of demonic mules attempts to run in different directions, toppling the old women out of the green cotton wagon and splitting the yoke apart.

"Halt!" Just at that moment, Hans's security team bursts into the room making an awful racket in their jackboots.

Uva screams, "No please . . . I don't know how . . ." But the captain of the guard smashes him in the face with a billy club, and the poor metallurgist falls to the ground like a rag doll. From this point on, things won't go well for Uva.

The third slug from the bolt action is the head shot. This is the part that becomes more unbelievable each time I watch it. The massive mouse skull splits apart like a plaster cast, leaving exactly one half of the unwavering smile. I stop the film, roll the counter back a few seconds and then call up the crosshairs on the monitor to lock the XY coordinates on the skull.

"Watch this," I tell Hans. "I added a little fuck you here at the end."

Hans beams. "Fine job, Sonny." He pats me on the back.

I can retire in peace now. I can retire The Train too, having accomplished its true purpose. I have drawn out the mole, killed the mouse, kept Tuscaloosa safe from the encroaching tendrils of the Magic Kingdom for another day.

I hit play as the security guards drag Uva's limp body into the elevator. I am hoping to pinpoint the very instant that everything changes. Everything that came before this moment must be reconfigured in our imagination as leading up to this event. Everything that happens after can only be perceived as a result of this taking place.

We watch as the mouse's skull splits apart again. Even though we both know the Bear Bryant Funeral Train is merely a dream-like hoax, neither Hans nor I can turn away.

The camera jerks back and to the left.

Back and to the left.

Jacinda Townsend

Night

"My," said Amiya, when I turned my flashlight on her face. She clicked hers on Celestin.

"Love," he said, and Amiya clicked off.

"Has," said Ephialo, when Celestin's light shone on him. He threw his beam back to Amiya.

"Big," she said, giggling now. She shone her flashlight on me.

"Wings," I said, finishing off the sentence, hardly the best we'd formed.

We were starting our third round of Camel, and Celestin poured hot water from the kettle into the little glass jiggers to wash them between rounds. Between her words, Amiya fanned the coals at the edge of the porch to keep them hot for later tea. The night had borne a round, full moon, and the sky was so clear we could see the moon's mouth smiling down at us; we could faintly trace the craters on its cheeks. The moon shone so bright it eclipsed the stars and made visible the people when they came walking down the path. We could see the power lines strung through utility poles that had been erected eight years earlier, when there was talk of bringing electricity to the village: now, the lines fell slack to the ground, juiceless. That night was so like day that we had no need of flashlights, which made the village elders sitting out in front of their huts angry at us for wasting batteries.

"Mon amour a les ailes grands," I said. I shone my flashlight on Ephialo's face.

"I think you're making people angry," he said.

"What?" I turned my flashlight on him. "What is it?" I asked.

"The wall," he said.

I was deep into my second year in the village. The brick frame of the school stood at the edge of Sahuble, an expectant shell waiting for strong hands to work it into further being. I had made many friends and no enemies, though I realized that the village's cooperation came partially from the pleasure of accomplishing something behind Barouan's back. My only interactions with Barouan happened in the canned goods store in Guedi, where he continued to badger me for a cadeau. He managed to get about sixty thousand CFA out of me altogether, and by my second Christmas there his daughter rode around Guedi on a new bicycle, taunting the other children. I tried to ignore him and her as best I could.

The wall would be my last project. Most trash in the country was foodstuff, eaten by goats, but every piece of plastic brought into the village never really left it: what the village couldn't digest according to the old ways, it spit out. Plastic didn't burn well, so mostly it appeared as an outcropping on the land. The wall would stand between this trash in the center of the village and a stream where people bathed in public view. I had hired a mason from Guedi to come survey the land. Just after he left, Ndele Aka, an older woman in the next hut, had come to me and asked me who he was.

"He's going to build a wall there," I'd reported brightly. "You can visit the stream without looking at the trash. And you can bathe without being seen.

She had said nothing, just chewed, spat, and nodded. That night of the full moon, Ephialo became the first person to mention it since.

"What are you talking about? The wall will make someone mad?" I asked him.

"It is a sacred spot, that," said Amiya.

I clicked my flashlight on Ephialo's face, but he was looking at his feet. I rolled my eyes, unsure they could see me do it in the moonlight. "They'll get over it," I said in English.

The next day the mason came again from Guedi. I rose not with the sun, but later, with the short, loud bicycle horn blasts of the man who sold French bread in the villages. I had just started shaking the dust from my bedding when someone knocked on my front door.

"Who is there?" I yelled. Sometimes children came, asking for money, and I told them to come back with a good school report first.

"*C'est moi. Ephialo.*"

I let him in, and went about my business. Ephialo's routine was to go over to the bookshelf and turn the dials on my radio for four or five minutes, after which he would speak, leaving me with the most important piece of village gossip I would hear all day. True to form, he fiddled with my radio while I swept dust out my back door.

"When is the man coming to make the wall?" he finally asked.

"Tomorrow," I yelled at him from my bedroom.

I was smashing all the mosquitoes that had trapped themselves in my bednet and eaten me all night long. Too drunk on blood to move, they sat immobile as I gathered two folds of the net around each one and clapped it dead. Each morning, the net got more stained with mosquitoes. It was proof of some sort of victory, though I wasn't sure whose. I never bothered washing the net. I took doxycycline religiously.

"It's not good," Ephialo said. "People are upset."

I came out of the bedroom and sat down in the chair across from him. "Who is upset?" I sounded angrier than I meant to.

"The feticheur," he said.

I had seen the diviner around the village. He was a thin man in his middle forties who wore blue jeans and t-shirts but who had on his face the ritual pattern—three long scars on either side of the nose—that we in Peace Corps had jokingly dubbed "Adidas."

"Why hasn't he come to me directly if he has a problem with the wall?"

Ephialo just blinked at me.

"Wait here."

I went out to the well and dipped the rope down three times to fill by bucket, and then took it back up the path to my latrine, which had an adjacent concrete enclosure roofed with wood that served as a bath space. I took off my clothes, picked my soap out of the morning's cobwebs, and washed off the night's sour sweat. The soap burned the sores of mosquito bites scratched raw. I rinsed off, put my sleeping costume back on, and went back in the house. While I changed clothes in the bedroom, I asked Ephialo again, "Why hasn't the feticheur come to me?"

"He knows Americans don't believe."

I came out of the bedroom, jabbed his elbow. "Let's go."

We took the road towards Guedi. On a Wednesday we had no reliable transport, so we had to walk the six miles unless someone happened by along the way. I was still wearing socks with my flip-flops in order to nurse a blister on my heel, and every once in a while I asked Ephialo to stop so I could pull up the sock that had wriggled its way down my ankle. This, and my walking with my right foot slightly on tiptoe to avoid the pain of my heel, made our route longer. No one happened by along the way.

We got to Guedi just before noon, when the morning's yellow ball of sun had already stretched to an amorphous white sheet on the sky. I had never before felt such thirst, that if I didn't get water I might actually die. Ephialo went off to find his Burkinabe with the cigarettes, and I went into the canned goods store and asked for an orange soda, *bien glacée*, as they said in town. The baby-faced Mauritanian reached into the freezer and popped the cap.

"*Cent francs*."

I paid him, drained the bottle in five swallows, and gave it back to him for his deposit. "*Merci bien*," I said. He grinned his baby-faced grin. Dead sexy.

I always created my shopping list on the six mile walk to Guedi, and committed it to memory by keeping track of the exact number of things I needed to buy, in alphabetical order. Then, at the store, only the number eight presented itself, so I went next door to the telephone cabin to finish other business while I remembered. "*Abidjan*?" asked the woman slumped over the metal desk.

"Fixed," I told her, "*Etats-Unis*." She handed me the land line, and slumped back over her desk while I dialed my mother.

"*Bonjour, maman*," I said into the transatlantic delay, the peculiar digital lip of time between spoken and heard words, third world and first.

"Amy!" she squealed. The last I had seen her she was up and well, healthy and happy, but what I remembered was us all praying over her bed, me and Sharon and the gossipy women from the mosque, while she lay thin in pink pajamas and a red flannel gown, recovering from ovarian cancer, all her thick curly hair lost to chemo.

Ma, I made it to my village, I'd told her when I first arrived in Sahuble. *Well, of course you did. I didn't raise no fools*, she'd said. She had been my biggest cheerleader, the person I called when I was down and out and haunted by insects and vermin, a lack of hot water and conversation in my own language. *Stick it out*, she'd told me. *It's like being in the army. Your tour will be over soon, and you'll be proud.*

Now, she told me she'd seen Sam. "I told him you were doing so well over there," she said. "I tell everyone I see, the women at the mosque and Marthajean at the mall and everybody." In her lexicon, the women at the mosque and Marthajean at the mall were gods—why would she need tell anyone else?

"Ma, what did Sam say?"

"He said to tell you hello."

Generic. It was clear she'd already forgotten what Sam said.

"Okay, Ma, this is costing a fortune. Love you."

"Be very careful, Amy. Always be very careful."

The woman in the telephone cabin woke up and fanned flies away from her face as she took my money. As I left for the Mauritanian's, she slumped back over in sleep. All one could do in that heat.

The people in Guedi had never quite gotten over the habit of following me around the store to examine my purchases, and even now an old woman wrapped in layers of cloth came to peer at the can of corn I held in my hand. When I picked up a tin of sardines she walked away, satisfied, but then a teenaged boy began to follow me around the store while I picked out mosquito coils and toilet paper. I moved over to the end of the counter, where lay toothbrushes, deodorant, and aspirin. I picked up a box of sanitary napkins. *Serviettes hygéiniques!* I said, wheeling around to show them to him. He screamed and ran out of the store.

Oignie the mason came back to Sahuble with me that afternoon and laid the foundation for the wall. Unlike any other African man I knew, he was downright stocky. He teased and joked with me all day, and at sunset, when I gave him 5000 CFA, he bowed and practically ran back along the dirt road to Guedi. The following day he didn't come. Two days after that, a little boy came to tell me he was dying.

"Pardon?" I asked. "Oignie is sick?"

"*Il va mourrir*," the little boy repeated.

With the skipping little boy I again limped the six miles to Guedi with a band-aid on my heel. The little boy insisted on holding my hand the entire way, even though he was skipping, and when I let go to wipe the sweat of my palm against my pants, he grabbed onto my shirttail. He led me off the main road to a dirt path, in the middle of which lay a broken pitcher. Under the cracked pieces, the dirt was still muddy with the liquid that had long since spilled out of it.

"Why did someone throw out such a nice pitcher?" I asked the boy.

"The feticheur in Guedi said to do this so Oignie might be well."

He led me down the path to a group of thatched roof huts. At the door of one of them, Oignie lay on a mat under a printed cloth. His eyes were closed against the sun, and flies buzzed around his mouth. He was much thinner than I remembered.

"Oignie?" I whispered, leaning closer to him.

He didn't move. A woman came out of the hut where he lay and began speaking to me rapidly and angrily in her language, and the little boy soon reappeared.

"What is she saying?" I asked.

"She says you didn't tell him about the feticheur's warning. She says you are killing him."

"Tell her I am sorry."

The little boy spoke to the woman, after which she sucked on her teeth and spat on the ground in front of me. She went back in her hut. I handed the boy a 10,000 CFA bill.

"This is what he would have earned for two days' work," I said. "If there is anything else I can do to help—"

But the woman, who had been watching from inside the hut, ran out, snatched the bill from the little boy, came over to me and took my hands. She bowed slightly and said something.

"Thank you, auntie," the little boy translated. "Thank you."

"Has he been to a doctor?" I asked.

"The feticheur has been by," the little boy said, impatiently.

"But a regular doctor?"

"Yes, I told you. The feticheur has been here. He has seen him."

I hadn't thought to bring *Where There Is No Doctor*. Just looking at Oignie, lying on his mat in front of the hut, I couldn't determine what his symptoms might be. And getting anything but superstition out of the little boy would be impossible. I left, followed to the end of the path by the little boy and his mother, who kept repeating one word. *Thank you*, the boy translated each time she said it, so that it became syncopated with our footsteps along the path. At the edge of their settlement, the boy spoke to his mother, and they held back and watched me as I walked back to the main road. I walked the six miles back to Sahuble, and decided to go back on market day and telephone a doctor I knew in Man. When Ephialo came that night, I told him the story.

"I told you," he said, shaking his head.

"Look, Ephialo, we are talking about people who think the devil runs the electric plant."

"It is true. When they first got electricity in Guedi, the chickens slept all day and pecked around in the night like they were crazy."

"And then they stopped, right? Now they sleep at night, huh."

Ephialo didn't answer. Instead he went inside and ran a finger along the spines of the books on my shelf. We had, without saying so, decided not to discuss the wall. Later in the night, I picked up *Where There Is No Doctor*. Oignie's symptoms—rapid weight loss and dehydration—were the symptoms of a thousand tropical diseases: I got no answers. But for the first time I noticed the very first illness addressed in the book, under the heading WITCHCRAFT—BLACK MAGIC—AND THE EVIL EYE. Next to an illustration of an old woman sticking a doll with a pin, the text read, *If a person believes strongly enough that someone has the power to harm him, he may actually become ill.* I knew already that the feticheur had real power in the village: he cured, he solved crimes, he fixed marriages, he made sons love their fathers again. His hold on the village seemed more powerful than simple belief.

I had two visitors the next day. The first was old Bekrou, who walked in with her spirit husband and handed him to me. "For you," she said, grinning. "I want you to keep him company for me."

"But Bekrou—"

"I am pregnant," she said. "Finally pregnant. I have no need of him anymore." It would be big news in the village, since Bekrou wasn't even married, or even permanently attached. "Look here—" she said, rubbing the lobes of the wooden man's oversized ears. "My husband in the other world is a good listener. Maybe you can talk to him and find a husband here in the village. Many good men here," she said. "Many good men."

How to explain that I'd already found the perfect man right at home in America, the man who'd guessed my idea of a perfect first date, the man with cocoa skin whose hair curled tight and lush in humidity, the man whose feet never smelled unless he'd been shooting hoops with me, the man who, when I moved into his apartment, always left enough orange juice in the carton for me to have one last glass, the man who solved math problems in his head and recalled baseball statistics during sex so that he could wait for me, the man whose memory, like a friendly ghost, was sustaining me through this hard time alone in the village. How to explain? I couldn't. Bekrou handed me the spirit husband, whose arms were now worn smooth where she had handled him. His big ears seemed to flare; his downturned eyes still wore sorrow.

"Thank you, Bekrou. Who knows? Before long I may even be pregnant like you."

She took both my hands in hers and gave me a serene, final smile, and then she walked out my front door and off across the tall grass towards her hut.

My second visitor was Amiya, who came walking slowly from the road through the low grass, her shoulders swayed back like a beauty queen's.

"You have bandages for me?" she said when she came to my door, and she let herself in, a bold move by her standards. I had been sitting on the porch; I followed this woman into my own house, where she plopped herself down on the couch.

"What do *you* need bandages for?" I asked, crossing my arms in a mock show of disbelief.

In answer to my question, she stood up and untied her pagne at her waist and opened it up, baring her lower body. She had a white paste between her thighs that spread all the way to the middle of her pubic hair. She sat down again and spread her legs, showing me that her labia were gone. Her vagina, lacking its fleshy folds, looked like the bottom of a fruit, a lemon or an orange. I whistled, low. She smiled.

"I'll get you some peroxide," I said, but a washing away didn't seem called for. Instead, I got down on my knees and smoothed Neosporin on the area around her vagina. She flinched at first, but didn't look away. Instead she smiled, and envy surged through me like a poison. She probably hadn't experienced more pain than someone getting a prison tattoo. But she was poised now, and knew things I never would. She lived in a world I wasn't party to. She wouldn't be coming back with Celestin and Ephialo to visit in the evenings; to her I would thereafter be a young American blofué, unworthy of her attentions. I didn't put on as much Neosporin as I had squeezed out of the tube. I smeared what was left on my shorts. I didn't want to interfere with whatever Amiya had become.

On market day, the little boy from Guedi knocked on my door before the bread seller had even ridden past on his bicycle.

"What is it?" I said sharply, not recognizing his voice.

"My father is dead," he said.

I let him in and poured orange soda for both of us as he climbed onto the couch. His feet didn't even touch the floor. At first he just sipped a little soda from the edge of his glass but once he had tasted it, he gulped it down and asked for more. I poured him three glasses before I spoke.

"I am sorry," I said. I took a 10,000 CFA bill from the table and gave it to him. He then got up to leave. "Wait," I said. "I'm going back with you."

I gathered my backpack and we made the long walk back to Guedi. This time the boy did not hold my hand. We walked to the back road and finally came upon a tent that had been set up in the path. People sat in plastic chairs talking excitedly and fanning themselves, and a plate of rice and fried plantain sat on a tattered, yellow tablecloth. Flies buzzed near the food but it was too hot for them to light.

The boy's mother, Oignie's wife, came out of her hut and took both my hands, just as she had after I had given her the money, and she kissed my cheeks three times—right, left, right.

"I'm sorry," I said in English. She understood, and nodded slowly towards Oignie's body, which was lying on the same mat as it had three days earlier, alongside the wall of the hut. Cloth lay draped elaborately around his body. Someone had shaved his head, and he was much thinner than he had been, even on Friday. His face had worn down so gaunt it was hardly recognizable. A tiny fly, a baby, buzzed near his ear. "I'm very sorry," I said again. I was crying, and I had to wipe my nose with the back of my hand. The woman nodded again, and she showed me to the outside where a dozen others sat. A portable radio blared music. Someone brought *koutoukou* in a ceramic mug. It burned my insides when I swallowed, and my head started to ache.

The crowd changed throughout the day, as people came and went with 500 CFA notes and plates of rice and sauce. I stayed, rooted to the spot by my palm wine stupor, listening to conversations in a language I'd never heard. At dusk, people began to bring mats, and again the crowd changed. We lay on the mats all night, though no one slept save me. The radio blared and the foreign conversation continued, and every once in a while I would wake to the clattering of new plates of food that had been brought and set on the table. It was silence that woke me for the last time.

Everyone else had finally gone to sleep, and the night sky was just beginning to lighten into royal blue. I took all the money I had out of my backpack. 30,000 CFA. Forty American dollars. More than the average villager made in three months. I left it under the corner of the mat under Oignie's head.

The business end of my latrine had a white enamel plate nailed over an eight-foot-deep hole in the ground. The plate was perfectly square, with two raised, gridded places on either side for positioning the feet, though the foot grips were spaced for someone much tinier than me. I put my feet on the outside of the plate and squatted, but after two years I was still making a mess of things. To "flush," I had a bucket of bleach water, which I poured down the hold to the sloshings of two years' worth of the prior volunteer's waste, so that every time I went to the latrine, I felt like I knew him intimately. Afterwards, I usually poured the bucket over my feet, which were often sprinkled with drops of my own urine. After a year, I had decided to stop drinking so much water.

I usually waited until the moment of my last available sanity to go to the latrine, but the day after Oignie's funeral, I had gone five times by the noon hour. I hadn't had any guests—not even Ephialo—and my nerves cracked with sadness and boredom. I spent the hot afternoon asleep on a mat just inside the open door; the only sounds I heard were the chickens pecking in my yard. I dreamed stretched versions of actual happenings—babies crying behind their mothers' skirts when they saw me in the streets, small children wanting to play with the loose curls of my hair. I dreamed that I let Oignie's son and wife move into my house: in my dream I did all their cooking and cleaning, and I slept outside on a mat. When I finally woke, the sun was gone, and people were ending the long walk home from the fields. I sat on my porch but no one said hello. No one said go to hell. They just looked at me as they tromped by in the high grass, and in the crunch of their footsteps I heard their thoughts. *Go home, toubabi—don't you know we sent your Black ass away 400 years ago? We didn't want you then and we don't want you now. You were never meant to be here.* From my porch I could see the foundation of the wall, Oignie's last creation on this earth. The concrete gleamed in the light of the gibbous mid-month moon.

Elyse, the most enterprising of the villagers (besides the pornos, she had three radios, a mobylette, and a gas stove), brought out her black and white television set, which was hooked up to a car battery, and we watched *Family Matters*, which was dubbed over in French for TV Afrique. I hadn't gone home once since I had arrived in Africa, choosing instead to bank the money Peace Corps gave for my one trip to the States and avoid altogether the question of seeing Sam. Now, I had not only not done anyone any good, but I had killed someone. If Sam knew, he would laugh before he cried. The American characters on Elyse's television seemed foreign to me, the United States a far-off, happy place to which I could never really return. The laugh track sounded maudlin instead of merry, as though the characters were drugged circus clowns. I took out a chair and joined the circle of villagers watching television, but no one spoke to me. Even when the evening sitcoms ended, when Elyse was hitching up her television and car battery, no one said anything. *Bon nuit*, I said. *Good night*. No one replied.

I went inside, stripped down to nothing, and put a towel around my body. I took my lantern and a pail of fresh water I had raised from the well that morning, and I went out to bathe. I wet myself, tracing circles around my nipples like Sam had a couple of years before, running my hands down the sides of my body in memory of him. I had soaped up and was just about to rinse off when I heard a deep, mournful singing outside my latrine. The soap fell from my hand and slid away from me across the concrete floor as I stepped into the furthest corner of the little room. Three more voices joined the singing. The voices sounded neither male nor female, human nor animal: unrecognizable as part of this world.

The soap on my body dried and itched, but I didn't scratch it. Hours later, the voices stopped, but I never heard footsteps leaving. I turned down my lantern and sat there all night in my latrine, naked, soapy, and scared. I didn't move. When I saw through the hole in the wall that the sky was turning the same royal blue as when I left Oignie's funeral, I walked over and rapped against the inside of the latrine door. No one answered and nothing moved outside, so I rinsed myself off and put on my towel. I ran to my villa, dressed, and stuffed all the valuables I'd brought to the village—alarm clock, flashlight, a picture of my mother—in my backpack. I balled up as many clothes as I could. I took the spirit husband from the bookcase and jammed him down the side of the backpack.

I walked the short distance from my house to the main road, looking back over my shoulder the entire time, wishing I had grabbed one of the sweet purple mangoes that grew from the drooping tree beside my house. I half-ran, half-walked the six miles to Guedi, and caught the first morning bus making the trip south. That bus went to Daloa, where another bus waited for the remaining five hours to Abidjan. I didn't stop looking over my shoulder until I got there.

Ann Pancake

Dog Song

Him. Helling up a hillside in a thin snow won't melt, rock-broke, brush-broke, crust-cracking snow throat felt, the winter a cold one, but a dry one, kind of winter makes them tell about the old ones, and him helling up that hill towards her. To where he stweilerees her tree-tied, black trunk piercing snow hide, and the dog, roped, leashed, chained, he can't tell which, but something not right about the dog he can, tell, but he can't see, can't see quite full, and him helling. Him helling. His eyes knocking in his head, breath punching out of him in a hole, hah. Hah. Hah. Hah, and the dog, her haunch-sat ear-cocked waiting for him, and him helling. And him helling. And him helling. But he does not ever reach her.

This is his dream.

His dogs started disappearing around the fifteenth of July, near as he could pinpoint it looking back, because it wasn't until a week after that and he recognized it as a pattern that he started marking when they went. Parchy vanished first. The ugliest dog he ever owned, coated in this close-napped pink brown hair, his outsides colored like the insides of his mouth, and at first, Matley just figured he'd run off. Matley always had a few who'd run off because he couldn't bear to keep them tied, but then Buck followed Parchy a week later. But he'd only had Buck a few months, so he figured maybe he'd headed back to where he'd come from, at times they did that, too. Until Missy went because

Matley knew Missy would never stray. She was one of the six dogs he camper-kept, lovely mutt Missy, beautiful patches of twenty different dogs, no, Missy'd been with him seven years and was not one to travel. So on July 22nd, when Missy didn't show up for supper, Matley saw a pattern and started keeping track on his funeral home calendar. Randolph went on August one. Yeah, Matley'd always lost a few dogs. But this was different.

He'd heard what they said down in town, how he had seventy-five dogs back in there, but they did not know. Dog Man, they called him. Beagle Boy. Muttie. Mr. Hound. A few called him Cat. Stayed in a Winnebago camper beside a househole that had been his family homeplace before it was carried off in the '85 flood, an identical Winnebago behind the lived-in one so he could take from the second one parts and pieces as they broke in the first, him economical, savvy, keen, no, Matley was not dumb. He lived off a check he got for something nobody knew what, the youngest of four boys fathered by an old landowner back in farm times, and the other three left out and sold off their inheritance in nibbles and crumbs, acre, lot, gate, and tree, leaving only Matley anchored in there with the dogs and the househole along the tracks. Where a tourist train passed four times a day on summer weekends and even more days a week during leaf colors in fall, the cars bellied full of outsiders come to see the mountain sights—"farm children playing in the fields," the brochure said, "A land that time forgot"—and there sits Matley on a lawnchair between Winnebagos and househole. He knew what they said in town, the only person they talked about near as often as Muttie was ole Johnby, and Johnby they discussed only half as much. They said Mr. Hound had seventy-five dogs back in there, nobody had ever seen anything like it, half of them living outside in barrels, the other half right there in the camper with him. It was surely a health hazard, but what could you do about it? that's what they said.

But Matley never had seventy-five dogs. Before they started disappearing, he had twenty-two, and only six he kept in the camper, and one of those six was Guinea who fit in his sweatshirt pocket, so didn't hardly count. And he looked after them well, wasn't like that one woman kept six Pomeranians in a Jayco Pop-up while she stayed in her house and they all got burned up in a camper fire. Space heater. The outside dogs he built shelters for, terraced the houses up the side of the hill, and, yes, some of them were barrels on their sides braced with two-by-four struts, but others he fashioned out of scrap lumber, plenty of that on the place, and depending on what mood took him, sometimes he'd build them square and sometimes he'd build them like those lean-to teepees where people keep fighting cocks. Some dogs, like Parchy, slept in cable spools, a cable spool was the only structure in which Parchy would sleep, Matley could find cable spools and other almost doghouses along the river after the spring floods. And he never had seventy-five dogs.

Parchy, Buck, Missy, Randolph, Ghostdog, Blackie, Ed. Those went first. That left Tick, Hickory, Cese, Muddy Gut, Carmel, Big Girl, Leesburg, Honey, Smartie, Ray Junior, Junior Junior, Louise, Fella, Meredith, and Guinea. Junior Junior was only a pup at the time, Smartie was just a parttime dog, stayed two or three nights a week across the river with his Rottweiler girlfriend, and Meredith was pregnant. Guinea goes at the end of the list because Guinea was barely dog at all.

They could tell you in town that Matley was born old, born with the past squeezing on him, and he was supposed to grow up in that? How? There was no place to go but backwards. His parents were old by the time he came, his brothers gone by the time he could remember, his father dead by the time he was eight. Then the flood, on his twenty-third birthday. In town they might spot Matley in his '86 Chevette loaded from floorboards to domelight with twenty-five pound bags of Joy dog food, and one ole boy would say, "Well, there he goes. That ruint runt of Revie's four boys. End piece didn't come right."

Another: "I heard he was kinda retarded."

"No, not retarded exactly . . . . but he wasn't born until Revie was close to fifty. And that explains a few things. Far as I'm concerned. Old egg, old sperm, old baby."

"Hell, weren't none of them right," observes a third.

"There's something about those hills back in there. You know Johnby's from up there, too."

"Well." Says the last. "People are different."

Matley. His ageless, colorless, changeless self. Dressed always in baggy river-colored pants and a selection of pocketed sweatshirts he collected at yardsales. His bill-busted sweat-mapped river-colored cap, and the face between sweatshirt and cap as common and unmemorable as the pattern on a sofa. Matley had to have such a face, given what went on under and behind it. The bland face, the constant clothes, they had to balance out what rode behind them or Matley might be so loose as to fall. Because Matley had inherited from his parents not just the oldness, and not just the past (that gaping loss), and not just the irrational stick to the land, even land that you hated, and not just scraps of the land itself, and the collapsed buildings, and the househole, but also the loose part, he knew. Worst of all, he'd inherited the loose part inside (you got to hold on tight).

Now it was a couple years before the dogs started disappearing that things had gotten interesting from the point of view of them in town. They told. Matley's brother Charles sold off yet another plat on the ridge above the househole, there on what had always been called High Boy until the developers got to it, renamed it Oaken Acre Estates, and the out-of-staters who moved in there started complaining about the barking and the odor, and then the story got even better. One of Dog Man's Beagle Boy's Cat's mixed breed who-know-what's got up in there and impregnated some purebred something-or-other one of the imports owned, "and I heard they had ever last one of them pups put to sleep. That's the kind of people they are, now," taking Matley's side for once. Insider vs. outsider, even Muttie didn't look too bad that way.

Matley knew. At first those pureblood dog old people on High Boy appeared only on an occasional weekend, but then they returned to live there all the time, which was when the trouble started. They sent down a delegation of two women one summer, and when that didn't work, they sent two men. Matley could tell they were away from here from a distance, could tell from how they carried themselves before they even got close and confirmed it with their clothes. "This county has no leash ordinance," he told that second bunch because by that time he had checked, learned the lingo, but they went on to tell him how they'd paid money to mate this pureblood dog of some type Matley'd never heard of to another of its kind, but a mongrel got to her before the stud, and they were blaming it on one of his. Said it wasn't the first time either. "How many unneutered dogs do you have down here?" they asked, and, well, Matley never could stand to have them cut. So. But it wasn't until a whole year after the encounter that his dogs started disappearing, and Matley, of course, had been raised to respect the old.

The calendar was a free one from Berger's Funeral Home, kind of calendar has just one picture to cover all the months, usually a picture of a blonde child in a nightgown praying beside a bed, and this calendar had that picture, too. Blonde curls praying over lost dog marks, Matley almost made them crosses, but he changed them to question marks, and he kept every calendar page he tore off. He kept track, and for each one, he carried a half eulogy/half epitaph in his head:

Ed. Kind of dog you looked at and knew he was a boy, didn't have to glimpse his privates. You knew from the jog-prance of those stumpy legs, cock-of-the-walk strut, all the time swinging his head from side to side so not to miss anything, tongue flopping out and a big grin in his eyes. Essence of little boy, he was, core, heart, whatever you want to call it. There it sat in a dog. Ed would try anything once and had to get hurt pretty bad before he'd give up, and he'd eat anything twice. That one time, cold night, Matley let him in the camper, and Ed gagged and puked up a deer liver on Matley's carpet remnant, the liver intact, though a little rotty. There it came. Out. Ed's equipment was hung too close to the ground, that's how Mr. Mitchell explained it, "his dick's hung too close to the ground, way it almost scrapes stuff, would make you crazy or stupid, and he's stupid," Mr. Mitchell'd say. Ed went on August tenth.

Ghostdog. The most mysterious of the lot, even more so than Guinea, Ghostdog never made a sound; not a whimper, not a grunt, not a snore. A whitish ripple, Ghostdog was steam moving in skin, the way she'd ghost-coast around the place, a glow-in-the-dark angel cast to her, so that to sit by the househole of a summer night and watch that dog move across the field, a luminous padding, it was to learn how a nocturnal animal sees. Ghostdog'd give Matley that vision, she would make him understand, raccoon eyes, cat eyes, deer. And not only did Ghostdog show Matley night sight, through Ghostdog he could see also smells. He learned to see the shape of a smell, watching her with her head tilted, an odor entering nostrils on breeze, he could see the smell shape, "shape" being the only word he had for how the odors were, but "shape" not it at all. Still. She showed him. Ghostdog went on August nineteen.

Blackie was the only one who ever came home. He returned a strange and horrid sick, raspy purr to his breath like a locust. Kept crawling places to die, but Matley, for a while, just couldn't let him go, even though he knew it was terribly selfish. Blackie'd crawl in a place, and Matley'd pull him back out, gentle, until Matley finally fell asleep despite himself, which gave Blackie time to get under the bed and pass on. September second. But Blackie was the only one who came home like that. The others just went away.

Before Mom Revie died, he could only keep one dog at a time. She was too cheap to feed more, and she wouldn't let a dog inside the house until the late 1970's; she was country people and that was how they did their dogs, left them outside like pigs or sheep. For many years, Matley made do with his collection, dogs of ceramic and pewter, plastic and fake fur, and when he was little, Revie's rules didn't matter so much, because if he shone on the little dogs his heart and mind, Matley made them live. Then he grew up and couldn't do that anymore.

When he first started collecting live dogs after Mom Revie

was gone, he got them out of the paper, and if pickings there were slim, he drove around and scooped up strays. Pretty soon, people caught on, and he didn't have to go anywhere for them, folks just started dumping unwanteds along the road above his place. Not usually pups, no, they were mostly dogs who'd hit that ornery stage between cooey-cute puppyhood and mellow you-don't-have-to-pay-them-much-mind adult. That in-between stage was the dumping stage. The only humans Matley talked to much were the Mitchells, and more than once, before the dogs started disappearing, Mrs. Mitchell to Matley would gentle say, "Now, you know, Matley, I like dogs myself. But I never did want to have more than two or three at a time." And Matley, maybe him sitting across the table from her with a cup of instant coffee, maybe them in the yard down at his place with a couple of dogs nosing her legs, a couple peeing on her tires, Matley'd nod, he'd hear the question in what she said, but he does not, could not, never out loud say . . . .

How he was always a little loose inside, but looser always in the nights. The daylight makes it scurry down, but come darkness, nothing tamps it, you never know (hold on tight). So even before Matley lost a single dog, many nights he'd wake, not out of nightmare, but worse. Out of nothing. Matley would wake, a hard sock in his chest, his lungs a flutter, his body not knowing where it was, it not knowing, and Matley's eyes'd ball open in the dark, and behind the eyes: a galaxy of empty. Matley would gasp. *Why be alive*. This was what it told him. *Why be alive*.

There Matley would lie in peril. The loose part in him. Matley opened to emptiness, that bottomless gasp. Matley falling, Matley down-swirling (you got to hold), Matley understanding how the loose part had give, and if he wasn't to drop all the way out, he'd have to find something to hold on tight (yeah boy. Tight. Tight. Tighty tight tight). Matley on the all-out plummet, Matley tumbling head over butt down, Matley going almost gone, his arms outspread, him reaching, flailing, whopping . . . . Until, finally. Matley hits dog. Matley's arms drop over the bunk side and hit dog. And right there Matley stops, he grabs holt, and Matley . . . stroke. Stroke, stroke. There, Matley. There.

Yeah, the loose part Matley held with dog. He packed the

emptiness with pup. Took comfort in their scents, nose-buried in their coats, he inhaled their different smells, corn chips, chicken stock, meekish skunk. He'd listen to their breathing, march his breath in step with theirs, he'd hear them live, alive, their sleeping songs, them lapping themselves and recurling themselves, snoring and dreaming, settle and sigh. The dogs a soft putty, the loose part, sticking. There, Matley. There. He'd stroke their stomachs, fingercomb their flanks, knead their chests, Matley would hold on, and finally he'd get to the only true pleasure he'd ever known that wasn't also a sin. Rubbing the deep velvet of a dog's underthroat.

By late August, Matley had broke down and paid for ads in the paper, and he got calls, most of the calls people trying to give him dogs they wanted to get rid of, but some people thinking they'd found dogs he'd lost. Matley'd get in his car and run out to wherever the caller said the dog was, but it was never his dog. And, yeah, he had his local suspicions, but soft old people like the ones on the ridge, it was hard to believe they'd do such a thing. So first he just ran the road. Matley beetling his rain-colored Chevette up and down the twelve-mile-long road that connected the highway and his once-was farm. Holding the wheels to the road entirely through habit, wasn't no sight to it, sight he couldn't spare, Matley squinting into trees, fields, brush, until he'd enter the realm of dog mirage. Every rock, dirt mound, deer, piece of trash, he'd see it at first and think "Dog!" his heart bulging big with the hope. Crushed like an egg when he recognized the mistake. And all the while, the little dog haunts scampered the corners of his eyes, dissolving as soon as he turned to see. Every now and then he'd slam out and yell, try Revie's different calling songs, call, "Here, Ghostdog, here! Come, girl, come!" Call "Yah, Ed, yah! Yah! Yah! Yah!" Whistle and clap, cluck and whoop. But the only live thing he'd see besides groundhogs and deer, was that ole boy Johnby, hulking along.

Matley didn't usually pay Johnby much mind, he was used to him, had gone to school with him even though Johnby was a good bit older. Johnby was one of those kids who comes every year but don't graduate until they're so old the board gives them a certificate and throws them out. But today he watched ole Johnby lurching along, pretend-hunting, the gun, everyone had to assume, unloaded, and why the family let him out with guns, knives, Matley wasn't sure, but figured it was just nobody wanted to watch him. Throughout late summer, Mrs. Mitchell'd bring Matley deer parts from the ones they'd shot with crop damage permits, oh how the dogs loved those deer legs, and the ribcages, and the hearts. One day she'd brought Johnby along, Johnby'd catch a ride anywhere you'd take him, and Matley'd looked at Johnby, how his face'd gone old while the mind behind it never would, Johnby flipping through his wallet scraps, what he did when he got nervous. He flipped through the wallet while he stared gape-jawed at the dogs, gnawing those deer legs from hipbone to hoof. "I'm just as sorry as I can be," Mrs. Mitchell was saying, talking about the loss of the dogs. "Just as sorry as I can be." "If there's *any*thing," Mrs. Mitchell would say, "*Any*thing we can do. And you know I always keep an eye out."

Matley fondled Guinea in his pocket, felt her quiver and live. You got to keep everything else in you soldered tight to make stay in place the loose part that wasn't. You got to grip. Matley looked at Johnby, shuffling through his wallet scraps, and Matley said to him, "You got a dog, Johnby?" and Johnby said, "I got a dog," he said. "I got a dog with a white eye turns red when you shine a flashlight in it," Johnby said. "You ever hearda that kinda dog?"

What made it so awful, if awfuller it could be, was Matley never got a chance to heal. Dogs just kept going, so right about the time the wound scabbed a little, he'd get another slash. He'd scab a little, then it would get knocked off, the deep gash deeper, while the eulogies piled higher in his head:

Cese. Something got hold his head when he was wee little, Matley never knew if it was a big dog or a bear or a panther or what it was, but it happened. Didn't kill him, but left him forever after wobbling around like a stroke victim with a stiff right front leg and the eye on the same side wouldn't open all the way, matter always crusted in that eye, although he didn't drool. Cese'd only eat soft food, canned, favored Luck's pinto beans when he could get them, yeah, Matley gave him the deluxe treatment, fed him on top an old chest of drawers against the propane tank so nobody could steal his supper. Cese went on September ninth.

Leesburg. Called so because Matley found him dumped on a Virginia map that must have fallen out of the car by accident. Two pups on a map of Virginia and a crushed McDonald's bag, one pup dead, the other live, still teeny enough to suck Matley's little finger, and he decided on the name Leesburg over Big Mac, more dignity there. When that train first started running, Leesburg would storm the wheels, never fooled with the chickenfeed freight train, he knew where the trouble was. Fire himself at the wheels, snarling and barking, chasing and snap, and he scared some of the sightseers, who slammed their windows shut. Although a few threw food at him from the dining coach. Then one afternoon Matley was coming down the tracks after scavenging spikes, and he spotted a big wad of fur between two ties and thought, "That Missy's really shedding," because Missy was the longest-haired dog he had at the time, and this was a sizeable hair hunk. But when he got home, here came Leesburg wagging a piece of bloody bone sheathed in a shredded tail. Train'd took it, bone sticking out that bloody hair like a half-shucked ear of corn, and Matley had to haul him off to Dr. Simmons, who'd docked it down like a Doberman. Leesburg went on the thirtieth of September.

That sweet, sweet Carmel. Bless her heart. Sure, most of them, you tender them and they'll tender you back, but Carmel, she'd not just reciprocate, she'd soak up the littlest love piece you gave her and return it tenfold power. She would. Swan her neck back and around, reach to Matley's ear with her tiny front teeth and air-nibble as for fleas. Love solidified in a dog suit. Sometimes Matley'd break down and buy her a little bacon, feed it to her with one hand while he rump-scratched with his other, oh, Carmel curling into U-shaped bliss. That was what happiness looked like, purity, good. Matley knew. Carmel disappeared five days after Cese.

Guinea he held even closer, that Guinea a solder, a plug, a glue. Guinea he could not lose. Now Guinea wasn't one he found, she came from up at Mitchell's, he got her as a pup. Her mother was a slick-skinned beaglish creature, real nervous little dog, Matley saw the whole litter. Two pups came out normal, two did not, seemed the genes leaked around in the mother's belly and swapped birthbags, ended up making one enormous lumbery retarded pup, twice the size the normal ones, and then, like an afterbirth with fur and feet, came Guinea. A scrap of leftover animal material, looked more like a possum than a dog, and more like a guinea pig than either one, the scrap as bright as the big pup was dumb, yes, she was a genius if you factored in her being a dog, but Matley was the only one who'd take her. "Nobody else even believes what she *is*!" Mrs. Mitchell said. From the start, Guinea craved pockets, and that was when Matley started going about in sweatshirts with big muff-like pockets in front, cut-off sleeves for the heat, and little Guinea with him always, in the pocket sling, like a baby possum or a baby roo or, hell, like a baby baby. Guinea luxuring in those pockets. Pretending it was back before she was born and came out to realize wasn't another creature like her on earth. Matley understood. Guinea he kept close.

Columbus Day weekend. Nine dogs down. Matley collapsed in his lawnchair by the household. Matley spent quite a bit of time in his lawnchair by the household, didn't own a TV and didn't read much besides *Coonhound Bloodlines* and *Better Beagling* magazines, Matley would sit there and knuckle little Guinea's head. Fifteen years it had been since the house swam off, the household now slow-filling with the hardy plants, locust and cockaburrs and briar, the old coal furnace acrawl with poison ivy. Fifteen years, and across the tracks, what had been the most fertile piece of bottom in the valley, now smothered with the every-year-denser ragweed and stickweed and mock orange and puny too-many sycamore saplings. Matley could feel the loose part slipping, the emptiness pitting, he held Guinea close in his pocket. Way up the tracks, the tourist train, mumbling. Matley shifted a little and gritted his teeth.

The Mitchells had ridden the train once when they had a special price for locals, they said the train people told a story for every sight. Seemed if there wasn't something real to tell, they made something up, and if there was something to tell, but it wasn't good enough, they stretched it. Said they told that the goats that had run off from Revie decades ago and gone feral up in the Trough were wild mountain goats, like you'd see out West. Said they told how George Washington's brother had stayed at the Puffinburger place and choked to death on a country ham sandwich. Said they pointed to this tree in Malcolm's yard and told how a Confederate spy had been hanged from it, and Mr. Mitchell said, "That oak tree's old, but even if it was around a hundred and forty years ago, wasn't big enough to hang a spy. Not to mention around here they'd be more likely to hang a Yankee." Matley couldn't help wondering what they told on him, but he didn't ask. He'd never thought much about how his place looked until he had all the time these train people looking at him. He was afraid to ask. And he considered those mutt puppies, sleeping forever.

By that time, he'd made more than a few trips to Oaken Acre Estates despite himself (how old soft people could do such a thing). He'd sneak up in there and spy around, never following the new road on top the ridge, but by another way he knew. A path you picked up behind where the sheep barn used to be, the barn now collapsed into a quarter-acre sprawl of buckled rusty tin, but if you skirted it careful, leery of the snakes, there was a game path above the kudzu patch. He usually took four or five dogs, Hickory and Tick, they liked to travel, and Guinea in his pocket, of course Guinea went. They'd scramble up into the stand of woods between household and subdivision, Matley scuttling the path on the edges of his feet, steep in there, his one leg higher than the other, steadying Guinea with one hand. Matley tended towards clumsy and worried about falling and squashing Guinea dead. This little piece of woods was still Matley's piece of woods, had been deeded to him, and Matley, when he moved on that little land, could feel beyond him, on his bare shoulders and arms, how far the land went before. Matley angled along, keen for any dog sign, dog sound, dog sight, yeah, even dead dog odor. But there was nothing to see, hear, stink.

Then they'd come out of the woods to the bottoms of the slopey backyards, shaley and dry with the struggling grass where the outsiders played at recreating those Washington suburbs they'd so desperately fled. Gated-off, security-systemed, empty yard after empty yard after empty, everything stripped down past stump, no sign of a living thing up in there, nor even a once live thing dead. Hickory and Tick and whoever else had come would sniff, then piss, the lawns, been here, yeah, me, while Matley kept to the woods edge, kept to shelter, kept to shade. Guinea breathing under his chest. He had no idea where the pureblood dog people lived, and they left no sign, no dogs, no pens, no fences, and although the ridge was full, of lookalike houses garages gazebos utility sheds a swimming pool, it was the emptiest place he'd ever felt. How you could kill a piece of ground without moving it anywhere. And Matley'd watch, he'd listen, he'd sniff best he could. But no dog sights, no dog sounds, no smells, and nothing to feel but his own sticky sweat. Matley'd never discover a thing.

Matley tensed in his lawnchair, nine dogs gone, Guinea in his pocket, Junior Junior cranky in his lap. He listened to that train creak and come, the train was coming and coming it was always coming and you would never get away. The train slunk around the turn and into sight, its bad music an earbeat, a gutbeat, ta TA ta TA ta TA, locomotive slow-pulling for the sightseers to better see the sights, and how did they explain Matley? Plopped between Winnebagos and household with some eighteen doghouses up his yard. How did he fit into this land that time forgot? ta TA ta TA ta TA, the beat when it passed the joints in the rails, and the screee sound over the rail beat, and even over top that, a squealing, that ear-twisting song, a sorry mean ear-paining song. Starers shouldered up in open cars with cameras bouncing off golf-shirted bellies, and from the enclosed cars, some would wave. They would only wave if they were behind glass. And Matley would never wave back.

He comes to know. In the dream, he is a younger man than young he ever was, younger than he was born, and the hillside he hell-heaves, it's hill without end. The leaves loud under snow crust, his boots busting, ground cracking, the whole earth moanering, and him, him helling. Snow lying in dapples, mottles, over hillside, ridgeside, dog-marked like that, saddles, white snow saddles, see, his side seizing, breath in a blade, and the dog. Who he dream-knows is a girl dog, he knows that, the dog haunch-sat waiting pant, pant, pant. His hill pant, her dog pant, the blade in his ribs, who pants? say good dog "good dog" good, him helling and the dog roped leashed tethered to a cat-faced red oak black against the snow blank, dog a darker white than the snow white and. He cannot ever reach her.

Eventually it trinkled down to them in town. A few had seen. The fuel oil man. The UPS. Gilbert who drove the schoolbus to the turnaround where the road went from gravel to dirt. Dog Man blundering in bushes, whistling and yodeling some chint-chant dog-call, when few people besides the Mitchells had ever heard Muttie speak beyond shopping grunts. Of course, there were the lost ads, too, and although Matley wouldn't spend the extra dollar to print his name, just put a phone number there, well, the swifter ones put it together for those who were slow. Then somebody cornered Mr. Mitchell in the Super Fresh, and he confirmed it, yeah, they were vanishing off, and right away the story went around that Muttie was down twenty-seven dogs to a lean forty-eight. The UPS driver said he didn't think those old people out in Oaken Acre Estates were hard enough for such a slaughter, but then somebody pointed out the possibilities of poison, "people like that, scared of guns, they'll just use poison," a quiet violence you didn't have to see or touch. Yeah. A few speculated that the dogs just wised up, figured out Cat was crazy and left, and others blamed it on out-of-work chicken catchers from Hardy County. One (it was Mr. Puffinburger, he didn't appreciate the ham sandwich story) suspected the train people. Who knew to what lengths they'd go, Mr. Puffinburger said, the househole, the campers, the doghouses and Mr. Hound, that scenery so out of line with the presentation, so far from the scheme of decoration. Who knew how they might fix ole Beagle Boy and his colony of dog. He'd heard they tried to organize the 4-H'ers for a big trash clean-up. Then a sizeable and committed contingent swore Matley had done it himself and ate em, and afterwards either forgot about it or was trying to trick people into pity, "I wouldn't put anything past that boy."

"I wouldn't, either, now. He's right, buddy. Buddy, he. is. right."

"Hell, they were all of them crazy, you could see it in their eyes."

"And I heard Charles lives out in Washington State now, but he won't work. Say he sits around all day in a toolshed reading up on the Indians."

"Well," the last one said. "People are different."

Matley standing at his little sink washing up supper dishes, skilletsized pancakes and gravy from a can. His dogs have took up a dusktime song. An I'm gonna bark because I just want to song, a song different from an I'm barking at something I wanna catch song or I'm barking at somebody trying to sneak up song or I'm howling because I catch a contagion of the volunteer fire department siren-wailing different from I'm barking at a trainfull of gawkers song. A sad sad song. The loose parts in him. Daylight puts a little hold down on it, but with the dark, nothing tamps it, you never know. You got to hold tight. He'd seen Johnby again that morning, humping along through the ditch by the road, and now, behind his eyes, crept Johnby, hulking and hunching to the time of the song. Dogs sought Johnby because Johnby wasn't one to bathe much and dogs liked to pull in his scents, Johnby could no doubt bait dogs to him, Matley is thinking. The way Johnby's lip would lift and twitch. Muscles in a dead snake moving. Tic.

Matley stepped out, pulled Guinea from his pocket, and took a look. As sometimes happened, for a second he was surprised to see her tail. The dog song made a fog around them, from sad to eerie, Matley heard the music go, while Matley counted those dog voices, one two three to twelve. Matley hollowing under his heart (the part slipping), the fear pimpling his skin, and then he called, moany, a whisper in his head: *come out come out come out come out.*

He breathed the odor the place made of an evening, a brew of dropping temperature, darkness, and househole seep. A familiar odor. The odor of how things fail. Odor of ruin in progress, of must and stale hay, spoiling silage, familiar, and mildew and rotting wood and flaked paint; twenty-year-old manure, stagnant water, decaying animal hides, odor of the househole and what falls in it, the loss smell, familiar, the odor of the inside of his head. And Matley stroked little Guinea, in full dark now, the dog song dimming, and he heard Mrs. Mitchell again ("but I never did want to have more than two or three"), the not-question she used to ask, him not thinking directly on it, but thinking under thinking's place, and he knows if you get a good one, you can feel their spirits in them from several feet away, right under their fur, glassy and clear and dew-grass smelling. If you get a good one. You can feel it. No blurriness to the spirit of a dog, no haze, they're unpolluted by the thinking, by memories, by motives, you can feel that spirit raw, naked bare against your own. And dogs are themselves and aren't nothing else, just there they are, full in their skins and moving on the world. Like they came right out of it, which they did, which people did, too, but then people forget, while dogs never do. And when Matley was very young he used to think, if you love them hard enough, they might turn into people, but then he grew up a little and knew, what good would that be? So then he started wishing, if you loved one hard enough, it might speak to you. But then he grew up even more and knew that wasn't good either, unless they spoke dog, and not just dog language, but dog ideas, things people'd never thought before in sounds people'd never heard, Matley knew. And Matley had studied the way a dog loved, the ones that had it in them to love right, it was true, not every one did, but the ones that loved right, Matley stroking, cup, cradle, and hold, gaze in dog eyes, the gentle passing. Back and forth, enter and return, the gentle passing, passing between them, and Matley saw that love surpass what they preached at church, surpass any romance he'd heard of or seen, surpass motherlove loverlove babylove, he saw that doglove simple. Solid. And absolutely clear. Good dog. Good dog, now. Good. Good.

Meredith. Was just a couple weeks shy of dropping her pups, no mystery there, she was puffed out like a nail keg, and who in their right mind would steal a pregnant lab/Dalmatian mix? it could only be because they were killing them, if Matley'd ever doubted that, which he had. Which he'd had to. Meredith'd been a little on the unbrightish side, it was true, had fallen into the househole more than once in broad day, the spots on her head had soaked through and affected her brain, but still. And it was her first litter, might have made some nice pups, further you got from the purebloods, Matley had learned, better off you'll be. Meredith went on October seventeenth.

Muddy Gut. A black boy with a soft gold belly, and gold hair sprouting around his ears like broom sedge, soft grasses like that, he had the heaviest and most beautiful coat on the place, but the coat's beauty the world constantly marred, in envy or spite. Muddy Gut drew burrs, beggar's lice, devil's pitchforks, ticks, and Matley'd work tirelessly at the clobbed up fur, using an old currycomb, his own hairbrush, a fork. Muddy Gut patient and sad, aware of his glory he could not keep, while Matley held a match to a tick's behind until it pulled out its head to see what was wrong. A constant grooming Matley lavished over Muddy Gut, Matley forever untangling that lovely spoiled fur, oh sad sullied Muddy, dog tears bright in his deep gold eyes. Muddy Gut went on October twenty-first.

Junior Junior. Matley'd known it was bound to happen, Ray Junior or Junior Junior one. Although they were both a bit ill-tempered, they were different from the rest, they were Raymond descendants several generations down. Junior Junior was Ray Junior's son, and Ray Junior was mothered by a dog across the river called Ray Ray, and Ray Ray, Mr. Mitchell swore, was fathered by the original Raymond. In Junior Junior there was Raymond resemblance, well, a little anyway, in temperament for sure, and Matley didn't stop to think too hard about how a dog as inert as Raymond might swim the river to sow his oats. Raymond was the dog who came when Matley could no longer make the toy dogs live and who stayed until after the flood, and for a long time, he was the only dog Matley had to love. They'd found Raymond during a Sunday dinner at Mrs. Fox's Homestead Restaurant when Matley had stretched out his leg and hit something soft under the table, which surprised him. Was a big black dog, bloodied around his head, and come to find out it was a stray Mrs. Fox had been keeping for a few weeks, he'd been hit out on 50 that very morning and had holed up under the table to heal himself. Later, Revie liked to tell, "Well, you started begging and carrying on about this hit dog, and Mrs. Fox gave him up fast—I don't believe she much wanted to fool with him anyway—and here he's laid ever since, hateful and stubborn and foul-smelling. Then after we got done eating, Mrs. Fox came out of the kitchen, and she looked at our plates, and she said, 'You would of thought finding that hit dog under your table would of put a damper on your appetites. But I see it didn't!' It was a compliment to her cooking, you see." Junior Junior was Raymond's great-great grandson, and he disappeared on Halloween.

Matley in the bunk at night. He'd wake without the knowledge. He'd lose the loss in his sleep, and the moments right after waking were the worst he'd ever have: finding the loss again and freshly knowing. The black surge over his head, hot wash of saw-sided pain, then the bottom'd drop out. Raw socket. Through the weeks, the loss rolling, compounding, just when he'd think it couldn't get worse, think a body couldn't hold more hurt, another dog would go, the loss an infinity inside him. Like how many times you can bisect a line. They call it heartbreak, but not Matley, Matley learned it was not that clean, nowhere near that quick, he learned it was a heartgrating, this forever loss in slow-motion, forever loss without diminishment of loss, without recession, without ease, the grating. And Matley having had in him always the love, it pulsing, his whole life, reaching, for a big enough object to hold this love, back long before this crippling mess, he reached, and, now, the only end for that love he'd ever found being taken from him, too, and what to do with this love? Pummelling at air. Reaching, where to put this throat-stobbing surge, where, what? the beloved grating away. His spirit in his chest a single wing that opens and folds, opens and folds. Closing on nothing. Nothing there. And no, he says, no, he says, no, he says, no.

Come November, Matley was still running his ads, and he got a call from a woman out at Shanks, and though he doubted a dog of his would travel that far, he went anyway. The month was overly warm, seasons misplaced like they'd got in recent years, and coming home right around dusk, he crested High Boy with his windows half-down. At first, he wasn't paying much mind to anything except rattling the Chevette over that rutty road, only certain ways you could take the road without tearing off the muffler. But suddenly it came to him he didn't see no dogs. No dogs lounging around their houses, and no dogs prancing out to meet him. No dogs squirting out the far corners of the clearings at the sound of the car, even though it was dog-feeding time. No Guinea under the camper, no Hickory and Tick fighting over stripped-down deer legs, no welcome-home dog bustle. Not a dog on the place. None.

A panic began in the back of Matley's belly. Fizzing. He pushed it down by holding his breath. He parked the car, swung out slow, and when he stood up (hold on tight) there between the car seat and door, he felt his parts loosen. A rush of opening inside. He panic-scanned Winnebago and househole, sunken barns and swaying sheds, his head cocked to listen. Doghouses, tracks, bottom, and trees, his eyes spinning, a vacuum coring his chest, and then he heard himself holler. He hollered "Here!" and he hollered "Come!" and he hollered "Yah! Yah! Yah!" still swivelling his head to take in every place. Him hollering "Here Fella! Tick, C'mon now! Yah, Big Girl, Yah," his voice squawling higher while the loose part slipped. Matley hollered, and then he screamed, he clapped and hooed, he whistled until his mouth dried up. And then, from the direction of the sheep barn, way up the hill, he spied the shape of Guinea.

Little Guinea, gusting over the ground like a blown plastic bag. Matley ran to meet her. Guinea, talking and crying in her little Guinea voice, shuttling hysterical around his shins and trying to jump, and Matley scooped her up and in his pocket, stroking and trembling, and there, Guinea. There. And once she stilled, and he stilled, Matley heard the other.

Dog cries at a distance. Not steady, not belling or chopping, not like something trailed or treed. No, this song was a dissonant song. Off beat and out of tune. A snarling brutal song.

Matley wheeled. He charged up the pasture to the sheep barn there, grass tearing under his boots. He leaned into the path towards the subdivision, despite dark was fast dropping and he hadn't any light. He pounded that game path crazy, land tilted under his feet, his sight swinging in the unfocus of darkened trees, and the one hand held Guinea while the dead leaves roared. He was slipping and catching his balance, he was leaping logs when he had to, his legs bendy and the pinwheel of his head, and the parts inside him, unsoldering fast, he could feel his insides spilling out of him, Matley could no longer grip, he was falling. This land, this land under him, you got to grip, tight, Guinea crying, and now, over top the dry leaves' shout, he heard not only yelping, but nipping and growling and brush cracking, and Matley was close.

It was then that it came to him. He dreamed the dream end awake. Him helling up that endless hillslope, but the slope finally ends, and he sees the white dog tree-tied ear-cocked patient waiting, but still, Matley knows, something not right he can't tell. Black trees unplummetting out of white snow skiff, and Matley helling. Him helling. Him. Helling. He reaches, at last he reaches her, a nightmare rainbow's end, and he's known all along what he has to do, he thrusts his hand behind her to unleash her, free her, and then he understands, sees: behind the live dog front, she is bone. Her front part, her skin and face, a dog mask, body mask, and behind that, the not right he's always sensed but could not see, bone, and not even skeleton bone, but chunky bone, crumbled and granular and fragrant, the blood globbed up in chunks and clots, dry like snow cold day skiff and Matley moaning, he'd

broke free of the woods and into a little clearing below the subdivision, ground rampant with sumac and dormant honeysuckle and grape and

briar. It truly darkening now, and the way it's harder to see in near dark than it is in full dark, how your eyes don't know what to do with it, and Matley was stopped, trembling, loose, but he could hear. A house-sized mass of brush, a huge tangle of it making like a hill itself, dense looped and layered, crowned with the burgundy sumac spears. That whole clump asound with dog, and Matley felt himself tore raw inside, the flesh strips in him, and Matley started to yell.

He stood at a short distance and yelled at them to come out, come out of there, he knew inside himself not to dare go in, he knew before seeing what he couldn't bear to see. But nary a dog so much as poked its head out and looked at Matley, he could hear them snarling, hear bones cracking, see the brush rattle and sway, but to the dogs Matley wasn't there, and then he smelled it. Now the smell of it curled to him on that weird warm wind, as it had no doubt curled down to the househole and lured the dogs up, and he was screaming now, his voice scraping skin off his throat, ripping, and Matley, with the single ounce of gentle still left in his hand, pulled out Guinea and set her down. Then he stooped and plunged in.

Now he was with them, blundering through this confusion of plant, and he could see his dogs, saw them down through vine branch and briar. Louise, the biggest, hunkered over and tearing at it, growling if another dog got close, she held her ground, and Ray Junior writhing in it on her back, and Honey lavering his neck in dried guts. Big Girl drawn off to the side crunching spine, while Hickory and Tick battled over a big chunk, rared up on their hind legs and wrestling with their fronts, and Matley pitched deeper, thorns tearing his hands. Matley tangled in vine and slim trunk, the sumac tips, that odor gusting all over his head, and he reached for Tick's tail to break up the fight. But when he touched Tick, Tick turned on him. Tick spun around gone in his eyes, and he drew back his lips on Matley and he bared his teeth to bite, and Matley, his heart cleaved in half, dropped the tail and sprung back. And the moment he did, he saw what he'd been terrified he'd see all along. Or did he see? A sodden collar still buckled around a rotting neck, did he? The live dogs eating the dead dogs there, what he'd suspected horrified all along, did he? And then Matley was whacking, flailing, windmilling looney, beating with his hands and arms and feet and legs the live dogs off the dead things because he had nothing else to beat with, he was not even screaming any longer, he was beyond sound, Matley beyond himself, Matley reeling, dropping dropped down

Until Guinea was there. Against him. Hurtling up to be held. And Matley took her, did hold her. He stroked her long guinea hair, whispering, good girl, Guinea. Good.

Matley stood in the midst of the slaughter, shaking and panting, palming little Guinea's head. Most of the beat dogs had slunk off a ways to wait, but the bolder ones were already sneaking back. And finally Matley slowed enough, he was spent enough, to squint again through the dim and gradual understand.

There were no collars there.

Slowly.

These colors of fur, these shapes and sizes of bones. Were not dogs. No.

Groundhogs, squirrels, possums, deer.

Then he felt something and turned and saw: Johnby crouched in the dead grass, rifle stock stabbed in the ground and the barrel grooving his cheek. Johnby was watching.

Somehow it got going around in town that it had been a pile of dead dogs, and some said it served Muttie right, that many dogs should be illegal anyway. But others felt sad. Still other people had heard it was just a bunch of dead animals that ole Johnby had collected, lord knows if he'd even shot them, was the gun loaded? his family said not; could have been roadkill. Then there were the poison believers, claimed it was wild animals and dogs both, poisoned by the retirees in Oaken Acre Estates, and Bill Bates swore his brother-in-law'd been hired by the imports to gather a mess of carcasses and burn em up in a brush pile, he just hadn't got to the fire yet. Mr. Puffinburger held his ground, he felt vindicated, at least to himself, because this here was the lengths to which those train people would go, this here was how far they'd alter the landscape to suit themselves. What no one was ever certain about was just how many'd been lost. Were they all gone? had any come back? was he finding new ones? how many were out there now? Fred at the feedstore reported that Muttie wasn't buying any dog food, but the UPS truck had spied him along a creekbed with a dog galloping to him in some hillbilly Lassie-come-home.

Despite all the rumors, it must be said that after that, they didn't talk about Dog Man much anymore. Even for the skeptics and the critics, the subject of Matley lost its fun. And they still saw Muttie, although he came into town less often now, and when they did see him, they looked more closely, and a few even sidled up to him in the store in case he would speak. But the dogless Matley, to all appearances, was exactly like the dogful one.

These days, some mornings, in the lost dog aftermath, Matley wakes in his camper having forgot the place, the year, his age. He's always had such spells occasionally, losses of space and time, but now it's more than ever. Even though when he was a kid, Mom Revie'd only allow one live dog at a time and never inside, they did have for some years a real dog named Blanchey, some kind of wiener-beagle mix. And now, these mornings, when Matley wakes, believing himself eight in the flood-gone house, he hears Mom Revie's dog-calling song.

Oh, the way that woman could call a dog, it was bluegrass operatic. "Heeeeeere, Blanchey! Heeeeeeere, Blanchey, Blanchey, Blanchey," she'd yodel off the back porch, the "here" pulled taut to eight solid seconds, the "Blanchey" a squeaky two-beat yip. Then "You, Blanchey! C'mere, girl! 'mon!" fall from high-octave "here's" to a businesslike burr, and when Blanchey'd still not come, Revie'd switch from cajole to command. "Yah, Blanchey, Yah! Yah! Yah! Yah!" a bellydeep bass; while the "Here's" seduced, the "Yah's" insist, oh, it plunged down your ear and shivered your blood, ole Mom Revie's dog-calling song. And for some minutes, Matley lets himself hover in that time, he just lies abed and pleasures in the tones. Until she cuts loose in frustration with a two string riff— "comeoutcomeoutcomeoutcomeout"—rapid banjo plinkplunk wild, and Matley wakes enough to know ain't no dogs coming. To remember all the dogs are gone but one.

He crawls out of the bunk and hobbles outside. Guinea pokes

her head from his pocket, doesn't like what she sniffs, pulls back in. It is March, the train season is long over, but Matley hears it anyway. Hears it coming closer, moaning and sagging like it's about to split. Hears the haunty music that train plays, haunty like a tawdry carnival ride. Train moving slow and overfull, passing the joints in the rails, beat beat, and the screee sound over the railbeat, he hears it shriek-squeal over steel. And Matley stands there between household and Winnebago, the morning without fog and the air like glass, and he understands he is blighted landscape now. He is disruption of scenery. Understands he is the last one left, and nothing but a sight. A sight. Sight, wheel on rail click it on home, Sight. Sight. Sight. Then Matley does not hear a thing.

Lee K. Abbott

The Era of Great Numbers

Head coach Woody Knapp stood in the center of his office, a manorial layout that put him in mantic frame of mind. He had parquet floors, Coromandel screens, a cream brocade sectional sofa, a mile of Marie Antoinette moldings. Through a window which opened onto the players' locker room, he saw backfield coach Nate Creer methodically beating a sophomore second-string scatback named Krebs. Coach Knapp had one thought, possibly warmhearted, about the relationship of discipline to pedagogy; and another, this about what it meant to play football in the twenty-first century.

Near his desk his publicist, Lefty Mantillo, was on the phone, answering questions from a reporter for a special issue of Jane's Fighting Ships.

"They wonder if you'll use the Umayyad," Lefty said, "and how gravitons might complement the game plan."

Coach Knapp watched Nate Creer pummeling the benchwarmer. Groans were heard, as were thumps and bone-noise. He was reminded of the Turner painting of Piazza San Marco, *Juliet and Her Nurse*.

"Tell them I agree with Einstein," Coach Knapp said. "Football, like nature, is simple and beautiful."

Lefty had come to the team from the night world of rock n' roll. He had made famous The Unfinished Business of Childhood, a band that took turmoil as a theme to speak for the beleaguered.

"They're interested in the pregame meal," Lefty said. Coach adjusted his tie. It was silk, crafted by the adjunct faculty in the Division of Careless Movements.

"Mango sorbet," Coach began. "A milk concoction."

"They like that," Lefty told him.

Coach read the rest: West Beach Cafe taquito, beignets, grillades, Mardi Gras King cake, hearts-of-palm salad, Cat Château Pétrus, lobster medallions and rosettes of chestnut purée.

"One more question," Lefty said.

Lefty had the bald, thickly veined egghead of a B-movie Martian. He was said to have had in the old days an affiliation with the Montonero guerrillas of Argentina, a single-minded group with an explicit interest in hemispheric chaos.

"They want to know the pregame talk," Lefty was saying. "Chapter and verse, your perspective."

The pregame talk, Coach announced, would be the usual—about grief, how it is total and deep. "As I see it," he concluded, "we have three choices: move, ascend or vanish."

Nate Creer was finished with his player. Coach Knapp saw a puddle on the floor—necessary private fluids, perhaps—and he heard the sound of something pulpy, but in cleats, scraping toward the showers.

"Remember," Coach said, "truth is indifferent and men with guns are everywhere."

When Creer entered the room, Lefty exited in a flourish. Creer had been with Coach Knapp from the beginning, the intramural squads in the Louisiana playing fields of the Organization of American States. His virtues were a scientist's attention to detail, plus the wry imagination of a sneak-thief. He was thought to have a wife somewhere—in the First Republic of Albuquerque?—whose face had the texture of igneous rock.

"What was that beating all about?" Coach asked.

"Sloth," Creer said. "I spoke about digging deep within the self. I used the words 'ontology' and 'entelechy.' I appealed to the old conventions of manhood, of self-worth. I respected our differences within the mutuality of shared purpose. I aimed to address the issues of sacrifice, which leads to the loftimost, and puerilism, which does not. Then I pounded the stuffings out of him."

Coach Knapp picked up his briefcase, his silver whistle. "You mentioned Aquinas, I trust. And Vasco da Gama."

Nate Creer nodded. "Lordy," he said, "I love it when they smartmouth."

Woody Knapp walked through the locker room slowly. The air was stale, yellow, heavy. Several odors reached him: unguents, ointments, salves. His people, his players, were monodonists, ligubriates, inspired by Saracens. They spoke Igorot, Kimbundu, fluent New Orleans. Missing eyes, ears, toes, one or two limbs, they believed in firmaments, unified fields, what infants yearn for. In one locker, he noticed a two-page discussion of spasm-dose ratios, nuclear throw-weights; in another, a beaded reticule. He could see skull caps, djellabas, a garter belt, a life-size china snow leopard. They wore shawls, prophylacteries, vinyl jumpsuits. Coach Knapp heard a tape player somewhere, a tune called "More Facts About Life." It mentioned the pineal gland, what to do with the floccose. Like snowfall in July, its effect was eerie. One wall—this of Pentelic marble—was covered with graffiti unique to the intimate acts of man: birth, death, sport. The gods here were Cytrons and Maronites, metal constructions from the firms of Mattel and Fisher-Price in the old ages; and the atmosphere seemed basinesque, Caribbean, having to do with body-whomping and sly ways of using sweat. It brought to mind flickering torches, low but constant fevers, what can be accomplished by heedlessness.

At the entrance to the tunnel that led under the stands to the stadium, Coach Knapp met Eppley Franks, the editor of the alumni quarterly, *The Vulgate*. He was the ghostwriter for Coach's autobiography, *The Era of Great Numbers*.

"I got the galleys back yesterday," Franks was saying. His eyes were full of flecks and various luminous colors. In addition to talk linking him to specific jungle-spawned narcotics, he was said to like all things thalloid and most spore-bearing creatures.

"They want to delete the chain mail," he was saying. "They're in conference now about the anga coats and Mrs. K's silk turban. Textiles upset them."

"What do they want to substitute?"

Eppley Franks pawed through a folder of documents at his feet.

His was the handwriting of an Ostrogoth, but he had the virtue of a prose style direct enough to cause excruciating pain.

"There's talk of Huns, Hittites. I heard the name Ramses Two once. There's concern with subtext. 'Despotic' is a word that gets mentioned a lot."

"Where do we stand on this?" Coach wondered.

Eppley Franks glanced at his notes. At one time he'd apparently written on ox hide.

"Statute supports us on this one. We have Bishop De Quadra, Lord Robert. Prothalamion's our big gun. They, of course, control the paper and ink."

Coach Knapp was watching the cheerleaders practicing in the near end-zone. They seemed to have come from the only cities in the world: Islamabad and Trenton, New Jersey. Lithe and sufficiently buxom, they had a cheer artful and acrobatic enough to serve increase and weal.

"Touch my hand," Coach said. "What do you hear?"

"I hear compromise," Franks said. "Expediency."

Coach was watching the smokes in the southern distances—pink and yellow and green. Fires were said to be still smoldering in El Paso. There were rumors of fierce, eccentric hot winds and the habits of displaced housewives. One heard stories—set in other regions of the baked, white deserts—of hungry dogs and the howling food fleeing them.

"One more thing, Coach."

The cheerleaders were chanting about gore.

"Speak to me, Eppley. I'm in a hurry."

"No more philosophizing, okay? I'm getting grief from just about everybody. Stick to the basics, they say. Carnage, things you've won, why everybody loves you."

In his observation tower near the fifty-yard line, Coach Knapp was approached by his defensive line coordinator, Teak Warden. His was the face of a monast—bony, hollow-eyed, mean. At his belt flopped a walkie-talkie.

"I am lonely," Teak said. In his manner was the suggestion of loud voices, hanging meat. "I like to toy with my food. I'm starting to hear songs. I'm beginning to assign gender to inanimate objects, concepts. A phrase keeps popping up: 'the curves of time.' I can't sleep, I fear my bedclothes."

On a scrimmage field beyond the open end of the stadium stood the marching band, practicing a brassy, optimistic composition, basic oom-pah-pah with a fair amount of human shrieking in it. They had instruments of hair, vinework, dried fibers—flutes, bouzoukis, shells, bells. They liked to prance on the field at halftime, all five hundred of them, to form words or symbols. At the TCU game in Fort Worth, they'd spelled out a single declarative sentence: Being is not different from nothingness. They had names for man's slangy parts and knew where angst came from.

"I'm working on a purer vision," Teak was saying. "I keep seeing a place like this—vast, silent, full of rubble."

The walkie-talkie came to life: "Victor-Zulu-King, this is Almighty, do you copy?"

In the distance, the clouds were beasts, serpents, civil ruin. "I had a dream the other night," Teak said.

"Why are you telling me this?"

"It was profound. Religious. There was horror involved."

Down below, Coach's players were yammering in Pali, Tamil, Oriya. Moving in slow motion, the linebackers raised their fists, grunting. In helmets and pads, they brought to mind vaulted cisterns, limestone caves, the lamps the holy worship by.

"We're a serious people," Coach Knapp said.

Teak Warden nodded. "Ain't that the truth?"

"It's a lyric mode we seek, something to satisfy the animal in us. Wistfulness extends, diminishes our purpose. There is danger of ambiguity, of winding down."

The walkie-talkie crackled again: "Almighty, Almighty, this is Victor-Zulu-King, we have contact. Repeat: we have contact, do you copy?"

"These are sad times, Teak Warden," Coach said. "The saddest."

A hot wind had come up, like jet exhaust.

"We're in a strange business."

"Affirmative," Teak Warden said.

"There is the laying on of hands," Coach said, "and the hurling of bodies. Information is exchanged. We objectify, polarize. Screams are heard. There is hooting and other meaningful tumult."

"There are chains of being," Teak Warden said. "We are pre-science. I'm thinking matrix. I'm thinking the moral life, a negotiation of same."

Coach was watching the grandstands opposite him, tier upon tier of seats and gleaming metal benches. Plastered to the upper walls were banners from the pep club: "Refute Belief," "Visual Messages Are Not Discursive," "Self-Expression Requires No Artistic Form." There were impressive drawings from Tractatus Logico-Philosophicus and The Ape and the Child. Conference flags were whipping back and forth: Griffons, Knave-life, The Hidden Iman.

"Teak," Coach said, "who is that?"

He indicated a figure squatting beside a meager fire high up in the stands. It was a man, certainly, who seemed wrapped in a half-century of north-country outerwear.

The walkie-talkie hissed to life again. Someone was calling for help. "Accept no higher being," a voice said. "Let's go out there and thwart somebody."

"Don't know," Teak Warden said. "Student, possibly."
"Whose?"

Teak Warden waved, and yonder, out of the clothes, shot an arm. It snapped up and down several times, then disappeared. Something about it suggested delirium.

"Ours," Teak said, "definitely ours."

On the field, defensive line coach Archie Weeks, carrying a brushed-aluminum briefcase, had assembled his players in a semicircle. A dozen pens stuck out of his breast pocket. His view of sport was admirably cerebral. He was now referring to a chalkboard dense with numbers and letters, arrows and stars. He was very nimble for someone who sweated and twitched.

"I want penetration," he was saying. "Give me an emotion, lower organs. I want a rising up and a putting asunder."

His players—Cud, Onan, Redman, Univac, the Prince of Darkness—were serious, attentive. They had majors from every page in the catalogue: disquiet, vigor, happenstance. They were beef with heads that swiveled a little.

"I take failure personally," Archie Weeks was saying. "I want luridness out there tomorrow. Verve approaching madness.

Coach Knapp remained to one side. There would be several more lectures by his assistants, then he would have to say something. He was watching the mountains in the east. They were called the Organs and seemed associated with conditions best explained in poetry: rue, torment, befuddlement. Between them and him—indeed, all around, from horizon to horizon—lay the desert full of stunted trees, scrub, spines, thorns, savage hooks. People were believed to be out there—tribes of very unpleasant, dark-minded citizens. They had sores and mangy pelts, and every now and then they roared out of the spectacular wastes to watch football.

"I'm talking about conspiracies," Archie Weeks was saying. "Insinuations, betrayals. I'm talking about piling on, about getting one's licks in."

Next was Gene Jenks, offensive line coach. He looked like circus property. He had the need to lean into people's faces and yowl.

Gene Jenks spoke of the ideal sportsman. A half-winged creature, it could be any of the human colors, but it knew everything: how wish works, what to say when the glands call. It was a machine. Something with many fine parts. A quiet, high-speed operation with uncommonly expressive shoulder-work. It had a chemical description and delightful physical properties. It had girth and heft, and slammed about in the current hubbub being heroic.

"Things could be worse," Gene Jenks said. "Things could be much worse."

Vigorous applause greeted Coach Knapp when he stepped to the center of his players. He had visited each of their homes—their tents, cabins, lean-tos, caves. He had seen what they'd eaten, how they'd prepared themselves, and they had confessed to him their joys, their nightmares. Mesomorphs, hairy, porcine, thick as tree stumps—they were all the ilks folks come in. They read Erasmus, Cato, referred to themselves as loin or chop. Many of them slept upright and appeared better for it. They had thick parts and amusing ways of getting from hither to yon. They did not mumble. Nor did they lose direction, wander off. One would address them and, at the signal, they would go. Footwear was vital to them, as were rigor and single-mindedness. What did one say to such beings? He had met their parents, their distant relations. He'd met their mates—names came to him: Lulu, Jo Ann, Dottie. These women were life principles and part of winning itself. Coach's players believed in ritual and magic. They carried lucky thread, well-thumbed coins, medals that promised protection against smite itself. They had special words: miasma, columbine, Um-gang. They were held together—apart from the claim of the larger world—by tape and plastic, by miracle fabrics and bolts. One did not speak to them directly. One used an elaborate rhetoric of colors and numbers, a code of doing and being done to. "Blue, forty-six, slant left," one would say, and an instant later there would be a pile of very satisfied sportsmen. All over the fallen world such exchanges were being made: language became action and the human measure of it. Unusually large men were speaking to almost round things and beating each other for the sake of them. This was not war. It was earth and wind, fire and water. It was biology and the shedding of unnecessary parts. One said, "Red, dish-right, on eight," and immediately there was a collision and the crawling away from it.

"Sleep, eat, wash," Coach Knapp said, at last. "This is what we do. When we work, life is easy. We get to go places and hear ourselves talked about. This is what I like. Don't disappoint me."

In the locker room Coach Knapp came upon one of his people reading a book. The player was a free safety—a former woodchopper named Herkie Walls, Coach believed—and he wore a T-shirt with a picture of the new universe. There were curlicues, as well as runes, objects made important by desire. The kind of collapsed, special ruin hope had once lived in.

"I have questions," the kid said. "I have doubts, grow depressed. My vocabulary's shrinking."

A wind had risen, steady and full of faraway dirts.

Coach Knapp gestured to the book: "What're you reading?" Herkie Walls held the thing aloft, his playbook. It was open to the pages relevant to humbug and derring-do.

"I could have been a thousand things," the kid said. His eyes suggested fear. "For one birthday I received a field jacket. It was khaki, its hem bordered with formal Kufic lettering. I preferred to wear it with polychrome sateen. I had the need to stand out and be incorrigible."

Tension was involved here, a wariness. Worry was one parameter of Coach's profession; faith, the other. Eleven, sometimes twelve times a year he ushered his people onto one turf or another. He gave instructions, rules, rubrics. He urged them toward the manifest in themselves, put before them images of fleece and flax. He reminded his people what their opponents were: creatures without spawn, vermiculate matter that ambled on two legs. Coach Knapp created stories, narratives featuring a random collection of humans who find themselves in a remote, austere venue. In every version, the endings were identical: this collection—this cadre of gristle and girth—discovers unfamiliar and surprising things and returns to the world changed in some way.

"Where are you from, free safety?"

Almost black with blood, a hand appeared, pointed. "The Province of Florida, I think. You recruited me."

A light went on in Coach Knapp's memory. He saw—anew and in a way quite compelling—a thatched hut, a puny fire, a mewling thing. The common elements.

"I said you were a state of mind, I believe. I said if you ran very swiftly and were acceptably violent, you would be admired."

A smile came to the free safety, Herkie Walls. He had been bamboozled, the floor of his self given way, and now he was not.

"Thinking is a performing art, Coach. That's what you said."

Like father and son, they consulted the playbook. Its pages, light and precious as human skin, were garish with hexagons, exotic birds, palmette stars. Its language ran from border to border and defined the seat the self sits in. The product of a dozen minds, it avoided terms like "capitulation" and "surrender." Unlike the playbooks of the olden, icier ages—the times of Sooners and Razorbacks and Nittany Lions—this volume trafficked in parables, allegories, fables. It was to be read in a wild, silent place; it made the muscles tight and strong, set the organs tingling. Among other things, it spoke of love, which was the things that happened and what we said about them. Though it mentioned sulphur and brimstone, what speeds the stupid travel at, its effect was hortatory; its purpose, to heal and to promote fellowship.

"So what do we know now?" Coach asked.

In the kid's open locker was fabric that recalled mirth and what swine are for.

"We know one meaning of life," the kid said. "We've learned to discriminate, not to be deflected or deferred."

"We have learned not to read between the lines," Coach said. "To speak clearly and to hoist heavy things."

"Fucking A," the kid said.

Coach Knapp made his way across campus in his customary manner, in a straight line, his step springy as modernity itself. The sky had turned greenish-yellow, what blasphemy was said to look like once upon a time. Everywhere was evidence of scholarship: scrolls, cudgels, sacks to tote. In front of the music building, a dozen students dressed in shimmer stood in a precise file. They had fierce, determined faces, what kamikazes were thought to look like, and muttered into their fists. Admissions reported that there were thousands of students now—the craven and the mighty, fans of one science or another. They resembled hounds or crawling quadrupeds. Some had affiliated themselves with social clubs, drawn near one another by a shared interest in bombast or rowdiness. They were cowboys, memphitites, Janissaries. To class, they brought Jackstays, epodes, sporules. They dedicated themselves to epigraphy, to sponsion, to what inflammation means. In keeping with tradition, Coach Knapp had attended their parties. They celebrated complexity, nuance. They were the gummata, the kinematic. At the School of Applied Practice, they traveled in groups. One heard them in the early morning, theirs a singsong that had to do with kindredness. In other hours, one heard screech and riot given syntax. They painted their residences to resemble objects of desire and people they'd once loved.

"What is it we subscribe to?" one group was saying now. Their leader was a senior named Don, and around him in a ragged circle sat the females he hunkered with. They believed in tigers burning bright and gnarled trees of mystery.

"Where are we going?" Don hollered.

"Up," was the answer.

Don had a worried-man's face, a creased thing suffused with darkness. Soon he would graduate and toil in the outlands.

"When are we going?"

"Now," they said.

On the steps nearby, uncommonly rigid and sharp-eyed, had gathered the matriculants of the Department of Poesy. Each affected the face of his favorite versifier: Rah, the Sylphides, Lex Luthor. These were to be the next generation of litterateurs, Coach knew. They would produce books, tracts, documents that refuted the accepted wisdom. In the end, another generation would come along. Tricks would be played, points of view offered, positions debated. Scholars would hear of afflatus, disquisitions, stuff in dreadful tongues.

In its way, writing was like football itself: there was contact and joy at the end of it.

Outside the President's door sat a secretary using the phone. Several things about her—her whichaway hair, her upcast eye-balls, one hand sawing in the air—said motherhood, a concern for others.

"Are you listening?" she was saying as Coach Knapp stepped

by her. "First, it appears with green eyes, copper skin, a mouth tender as a child's. It has horns, fangs, forked appendages. It sprouts, blossoms, shrivels, has tendrils, converts easily to liquid. It serenades, wheedles, cajoles, barks. Its body is indescribable—features of goat, canine, scale of fish. It's made of dross, it's made of sputum. It causes a bloody flux."

The President was waiting. He was part Arab, part something else. Oklahoman maybe. Nobody knew. One of seven cousins who owned the college, he had discovered something in the Wadi, in the Heights, in the Gulf. It was a process, a refinement, a radical personal philosophy. Soon there was capital, assets, plunder, booty. Things were organized and produced. Titles were conferred. The cousins owned goods, services, personalities. Their logo—and the team's own name—was an arrangement of tiny but essential bones that had to do with longevity.

"I've been thinking about reality," the President said. "Particularly its specifications, the hardware vital to it. It's a big subject."

The President had a seal's slick hair, as well as the hands and precious feet of a jazz dancer. He liked to host parties that involved glee and out-of-body travel.

"Let us stand by the window," the man said. "We can watch."

Coach Knapp could still hear the secretary in the other room. "It's under the Ns," she was saying. " 'Nosology,' 'nos-tic,' 'nostril'—In there somewhere. It ravishes, torments, has gall. What a marvel it is."

In the distance, half in the shadows of the stadium itself, Coach Knapp saw his players moving like an army. They carried torches, penlights, smoky kerosene lamps, and they were headed for their dormitory, an exclusive facility that towered over its neighbors. Once inside, they'd prepare themselves. They would review, recapitulate, speculate. Out would go furniture, accoutrements, luxuries; in would come victuals and liquids, what the creature in them cried for. They were men who yearned for that agreement which could be found only in another man's bulky arms.

"I adore these moments," the President remarked.

"As do I," Coach Knapp said.

"Pads, headgear, scurrying in one direction—I am enamored of the whole thing."

"It is a spirit," Coach said. "Relationships, various coordinations. I'm humbled by the purity of it."

The men stood shoulder to shoulder. Below, on a stubbled, litter-strewn acre known as The Square of Past Mistakes, a pep rally was beginning.

"Still," the President said, "there are issues to guard against."

"One hopes to have a positive effect," Coach Knapp said. "Yet it is seldom the kids say anything to you. There's a barrier, I create it. My people don't call me Woody. My father's people used to call him Moe, and often I think it would be nice to be called Woody, to be friends. But that's not my job. My job is to treat them brutally; theirs, to love it."

From the other room came that voice again, the secretary. "Geniculation,'" she was saying, "the state of being geniculate."

Down below, the coach for the other team was being burned in effigy. His people were the Dukes, their mascot the dainty porringer of Count Ugo Malatesta. They were big, it was rumored. Like storybook farm life. And strong. They had one play, Wild Pinch Ollie, which did not involve the ball but which called upon an underclassman named Ham to lift his arms and pray in an annoying voice.

"I have the need to reveal myself to you," the President said. "I can trust you, I feel. I have confessions. At times, I am quite bad. I am headstrong, for example. I don't know any Greek. I give money away. Other times, I am surprised by my own goodness. I am generous to my wives. I like to breed. Ideas come to me, I scribble them down, attempt to bring them to fruition. I can make a scarf joint."

"You would have been an excellent weakside linebacker."

"Yes," the President said, "when one dashes off the field, there shouldn't be anything left."

"It's unfortunate you're not a coach," Woody Knapp said. "We could study film together, confide in each other. At halftime, you could stand up and make one hundred youngsters feel very inadequate."

"I could have been responsible for recruiting, say. Or the defensive backfield."

"You could show them what the world looks like and why there is so much screaming."

The fire below was beautiful. In the past, fans had charred the likenesses of Gator and Bruin. This season they would incinerate the Schismata, the Tartars. This year the Gentoo, the hymenopterous insects, the Galbanum—all the disgreeable, seductive notions they stood for—would go up in flames. The same songs would be heard, "Tell Me What You Know" and "All Hail the Power." Insights would be advanced, meanings detailed. Months from now one would have numbers to measure achievement.

"One more thing, Coach."

"Yes."

"Explain, please, the Strong G Wham."

Woody Knapp's hands fluttered like birds. He described movements, a frame of reference, what work the heart did. He discussed action in terms of phylum, genre, a specific ligament. He offered metaphor. Deep structure. Deconstruction. Tool and man.

"Check Magoo," he said. "Stem to cover Three. Willie Sam Flop One. The Cat's gotta get into the middle. Up blasts the Monster. Think turnover. Rover has deep responsibility, Red Ryder the underbody. We defoliate and make a Sweep. Then there's the Nether Parts."

"And Little Piggy?"

"Little Piggy stays home."

Outside, in the twilight, Coach Knapp moved quickly but deliberately. It was one of his precepts. "Pick a place and go to it," he would say. "Conceive and act." All around him, by contrast, wandered the distracted and the aimless. Sport—especially sport that required pain and constant doctoring—would have made everyone more saintly. There were things that could be understood only at the bottom of a mound of flesh. Coming toward him, accelerating like a steam train, charged Lefty Mantillo, the publicist. He was wearing a new outfit now, one of bangles and chrome hasps, his evening dress.

"I'm glad I found you," he said. "I got an inspiration."

Coach Knapp could see a line of lights on the mesa above the valley. Fans, he thought. Like players, they moved in bunches now. They wore red, or black, and had the look of humans who scrambled dawn to dusk. They could not gambol. Neither could they cavort.

"We do a movie," Lefty was saying, "a feature. Super eight, three-quarter tape, noise reduction—the works. We change your mother's name. Serena, Philomel—something with lilt. We allude to catamites. You moralize, hector. I have ideas for vistas, soft focus, stop-action, you in the misty twilight, leaves on the ground, billowy cloudwork. A narrator. Flow and irony. We loop in the bullshit in post-production."

Coach Knapp was saddened by the image of himself. There was so much to learn nowadays—where beautiful women came from, what to make of metaphysics, the subtleties of the shuddery arts.

"The first reel's all special effects," Lefty continued. "Birth, youth, rites of passage. The second, I don't know yet. Hoopla, maybe. Hurly-burly. Bad things happen. You emerge. Football enters the current times."

"I like it," Coach said.

"I hums, sahib. It says tie-in, promotion, scratch 'n' sniff. It's killer material, that's what it is. Contemplative but with the rough stuff left in."

"I have to go, Lefty."

Mantillo's eyes went out of focus, came back. He hugged himself as if something—a crucial tissue, a fluid—were about to spill out.

"Ten-four, Coach. I gotta get back to work. I'm excited, I tell you. It's like getting aroused. I love this art business."

Coach Knapp ducked around one corner. And another. Direction signs stood up all over, from the folks in Orientation:

ESCHEW GLUTTONY; THE TIMES ARE NEVER SO BAD; GO BACK, THIS IS NOT FOR YOU. A few people in that department were former players who held convocations to propose answers to impossible questions. They quoted Karl Barth, the Wallendas, seers from the dark atomic years. "Suck it in," they ordered. "Stand up tall. Don't be a drag-ass."

Now Coach Knapp was aware of someone following him. There was shambling, a trepidation. Nerve was being summoned. Soon there would be a clearing of the throat. Then speech.

"Who are you?" Coach asked.

Out of the gloom shuffled a figure, something wrought. It was the person in the stands earlier in the afternoon, the one who'd waved.

"I know you," Coach said. "Your name is Griggs. Emile, possibly. You were called the Snake, I believe. This was ages ago. The Lizard. A member of the reptile family."

The man came closer, smiling.

"Height, six-two. Weight, one ninety-six. I never forget these statistics. Your favorite dinner, what you dreamed. You attended school in Cupertino, I remember. Had trouble with world geography."

"Culver," the man said. "It's not there anymore."

Griggs looked like the poorly fitted parts of many other men. His posture said "Assemble with care." It said "Close cover before striking."

"What do you want, Mr. Griggs?"

"Football," he answered. "I want to wear what everyone else does. I want to take directions from somebody named Lance or Butch. I want knowledge alien to the outside world."

A fiber had let go in Coach Knapp, a link to memory. Here was ash, here was dust.

"Are you still fast?"

Griggs raced away, darted back. "I'm fast."

"Are you strong, mean?"

"I could apply myself," Griggs said. "Things could be applied to me."

"What about age?" Coach said. "You must be middle, late thirties."

"I have wisdom," Griggs insisted. "I know things. The fornix, for example. How to foregather, where to look for ground water. I have enthusiasm."

"I could've used you ten years ago."

Griggs edged forward, his posture an underling's.

"You could use me now," he said. "I could be a conduit, a transitor, your voice in the muddle. I could be a moral value. Truth, say. Something vaunted, an idealization. I'd be a whirlwind."

A noise composed of yowling and shouting had risen in the west. Coach Knapp believed it the cries those in history were famous for. Ideas, in the form of people, were colliding. Bad, or weak, ideas would be seen in the morning like trash on a beach.

"You are staying nearby?" Coach asked.

Griggs nodded. He had a residence. Four stakes in the dirt, a rag to crawl under in the dark.

"Go there," Coach said.

"You'll call for me?"

Coach thought he might.

"I could offer myself elsewhere," Griggs said. "I have a list—opponents, those without scruple. I can't take much more wandering. I thirst, I hunger."

Griggs was moving off, bent and sly, the animal half of him alert and watchful. In the distance, the shrieking had become speech, then prattle again. A concord was being reached, disunion overlooked.

"Griggs?" Coach called. "What's your greatest thrill?" The man had a smile like daylight.

"To break the plane of the goal line," he yelled back. "I want to vault forward and dance by myself in front of eighty thousand people."

Outside his office, Coach Knapp found Nate Creer interrogating a player. The kid was strapped to a chair, a gooseneck lamp over his head, its light a noontime glare. Around them, on the floor, were scattered groundnuts, alkaloids, an overnight bag. "We've been here a while," Creer explained. The kid was in shock, eyes bulging, sweating.

Nate was name-calling. "Hydroid dipstick, muck-faced fart-breath," he was screaming. "Colewort motherhumper. Salmon slime!"

"What's the problem here?" Coach asked.

"He says he's hurt."

The kid's face went three or four directions.

"I'm hurt," the kid said. "I'm hurt."

"He denies he's a dickweed."

"I deny," the kid blubbered. "I deny."

"He swears on his mother, his father."

The kid's jaw dropped. He swore, he swore.

"What's his story?"

"The usual," Nate began. "Parturition, a time of running about unsupervised, body hair. Hormones, friendship—the years all run together. A succession of pets, an allowance. A world view develops, life becomes complicated. An attitude is adopted. Vocabulary expands, paperwork accumulates. Courtship, a tearful reunion, admissions of guilt. There is commingling, disappointment."

"Then what?"

Nate Creer pounded his fist in exasperation.

"Then this squirrel-faced, rat-eyed squamoid yellow-belly fractures his wrist."

Up went the kid's arm. Knobby and blue, it looked like a peculiarly cunning but soft club.

"I figure an hour more, then I let him go," Nate Creer said. "I got things to say here, a position to defend."

"This is a bad sign, Nate."

The man shrugged. "Bad signs are everywhere, Coach. I tend to ignore them."

In his office, Coach Woody Knapp kept the lights off. The dark had its comforts. It encouraged reflection, maximum self-awareness. It allowed for a summing up, a casting forward. He would be home in an hour. There would be food, badinage. Mrs. Knapp, Helen, would tend to him. All had been done that could be. There would be sleep, morning. Time would shrink, disappear. Then he would be back here again, his people ready, his advice delivered. There would be football then.

And nothing else.

Chris Offutt

Decirculating the Monkey

Housing developments in Lexington are as interchangeable as sectional sofas covered in vinyl. I live in a two-story wood house with a stoop. I'd rather live in a brick house with an ivy-clad porch, but five years ago my wife died and I gave up on the idea of home. My furniture is lawn chairs and card tables. Most of the walls are covered by bookshelves and I have read most of the books.

Most people do not choose where they live. They stay near family or go somewhere for a job. And the sad part is that most people hate their job and don't get along with family. But not me. I just hated the jobs that Max offered. In the early years, Max and I worked as equals, but after his bloody clinching of street power, my role was subordinated to one of counsel and crucial operations. I cleaned up after Max. He sent me into the night with satchels of money for transactions. I made surprise visits to people whose influence he sought, or whose ambitions he desired to halt. I threatened with fist, feet, club and gun. I shook down pimps, blackmailed crooked politicians, and made extremely meaningful small talk with corrupt men of the cloth. I picked up payoffs from chop-shops, bookie joints, and hot sheet hotels. Twice I'd disencumbered Max of business rivals intent on compelling him to eschew his habit of breathing. I was bagman, strong-arm man, gunman, madman. Amphetamines cut with whisky put me on the kill. Combat calmed me. Sex was a buffer to sleep. Then my wife got sick and I quit working for Max.

I spent the next five years raising my son. You'd think we'd be close, but without my wife as mediating go-between, we drifted apart, became strangers and finally enemies. Our family home transformed to a barracks. He moved out for college. Now I sat in my living room and inspected the contents of the envelope Max had handed me. Errors occur in the details, and a professional occupies the minutae while fully engaging the grander picture. With cash up front, I needed to treat the job as any other. Usually this required a few weeks of clandestine surveillance, an enormously boring activity that primarily consisted of sitting in a car with binoculars, eating caffeine pills and pissing in a bottle. But Max lived in an upscale neighborhood, where a strange car would stick out within a couple of hours. And since the monkey never left the house it would be like watching a hermit.

Max had included a detailed diagram of the house with points of entry marked and positioning of motion-sensitive lights. He'd listed the schedule for a cleaning woman, garbage pickup, local school bus. He'd included security codes to bypass the alarm system and housekeys.

His wife was in and out of the house with a community social life that included library volunteer, board of the Children's Museum, a begonia club, Wildcats Booster Club, Kentucky Horse Park Foundation board, and a ladies book club. She was also involved with a highway beautification organization, which had apparently contributed nothing yet since our auxiliary roads are still ugly as homemade sin. Louise was as solid a citizen as I'd ever known. I'd met her a few times over the years and liked her, although she remained aloof since I was one of Max's business associates and not part of Lexington Society. She was deeply feminine—makeup, heels, nylons, jewelry—and used southern politesse as armor. Still, she was married to Max, which meant she possessed more backbone than a dinosaur.

One daughter was "away" at college, which meant the semi-controlled environments of co-ed dorms at U.K. The oldest daughter was doing graduate work in Indiana. The youngest daughter was Mindy the monkey owner, a senior at Loveland-Moore, the most elite private high school in town. Though wealthy, the students dressed in ragged clothes. Their primary means of rebellion was their hair, which came colored, shaved, mohawked, faux-hawked, dreadlocked and dirty. The publicity material front-loaded photographs of light-skinned Black, Hispanic, and Asian kids to prove that Loveland-Moore was diverse while simultaneously reassuring skittish parents that the minority students were fittingly appropriate—conservative and well-to-do. Student activities included demonstrating against sweatshops, NAFTA, out-sourcing, and corporate tax breaks—the very entitites that provided the kids with their safe enclave. Due to their outrageously poor performance at sporting events, the boys were called the Loveland Smores. The girls were known locally as the Loveland Whores.

Mindy was home from school by 4:00 in the afternoon. Louise completed her errands by the same time in order to meet her daughter. The house was only confirmed vacant on Tuesday and Thursday afternoons from one to four. A night mission was out of the question since the family slept in the house. A daylight operation meant a hot prowl of the house, a vehicle visible on the street, and my face in the neighborhood. I didn't like it. But then, nobody truly likes this kind of work except sociopaths, and they're not to be trusted. For years I wondered if I fit that category, until I did considerable reading. I have sociopathic tendencies but I'm non-delusional, follow orders, and obey most laws. My thinking is organized. My operational mode boiled down to three steadfast rules—I do not underestimate, I do not overlook, and I never screw around.

The objective consisted of achieving clandestine entry, decirculating the target, and exfiltration without incident. A one-man mission with no recon required a direct but flexible plan. With more time I could conceal a sedative in the monkey's food supply, or acquire a gun that would fire a needle loaded with a tranquilizer. But Max desired quick completion. Photographic verification of the target wasn't really necessary.

In my bedroom, I pushed aside the dresser and rolled a section of a ratty carpet to expose the painted planks. Years ago I'd used a drill and a hole saw to carefully carve out a section of flooring and built a storage compartment for ordnance between the joists. I pried the lid up with a knife. The weapons lay in orderly rows, tipped at a slight angle so the oil in the bore wouldn't drain into the stock. A few small pouches of silica absorbed moisture. The SIG-Sauer P229 is the official handgun of choice for the FBI, the DEA, the Secret Service, the Coast Guard, the U.S. Postal Service, Immigrations and Customs. Recently the SIGARMS company received a 24 million dollar contract to supply the Department of Homeland Security with sidearms. All those splendid machines are made in Exeter, New Hamphsire, just down the road from America's most elite boarding school.

I went with the smaller P225, a double-action automatic. The magazine capacity was only eight rounds. It wouldn't bulge beneath my clothes, but was powerful enough to nullify most mammals. My backup was a .38 revolver made by Smith & Wesson, a snub-nose five shot known as a Chief's Special. I took two magazines, a speed-loader for the .38, an ankle-holster and a belt-clip holster.

I slid the lid in place, blew dust into the cracks, unfurled the rug and shifted the dresser in place. As I wiped my hands, it occurred to me that household dust was always pink or gray and I couldn't for the life of me figure out why. I owned nothing in either color. Downstairs I sat at the card table and cleaned the guns. The SIG-Sauer is a Swiss/German gun—quite the combination—and I don't like either bunch. The Swiss are nothing but a gang of hypocrites hiding behind a public camouflage of watches, chocolate bars, and cheese. Switzerland likes to play neutral politics but for seventy years their government's corrupt banking system concealed international criminals. Their whole stance of no-standing-army chaps my ass since nobody really wants their fucking country anyhow. They can trot out the Red Cross till the cows come home but the fact is, the Swiss designed the most effective killing pistol ever made. To circumvent their pansy-ass gun laws that banned weapons production, the Swiss collaborated with a German company for manufacture. Germans are a disciplined and orderly people, which makes them splendid Americans, but left to their own devices, Germans make the worst Germans. They're always starting trouble with their neighbors, which in Kentucky is a dangerous habit. It hasn't worked out well for the Germans either.

After loading the weapons, I laid them out on my card table and retrieved my ready-bag from two hooks inside my bedroom closet above the door. People rarely look there, making it the most quickly available hiding place in the house. The bag is made of waterproof nylon, reinforced at the seams, with a zipper that's supposedly unjammable. I inspected its contents, arranging everything in careful order. Five thousand in C-notes, credit card and passport under a false name, unregistered .22 pistol with extra ammo, Ka-Bar knife, hoodie and hat, twenty MREs, water-purifying kit, first-aid kit, sewing kit, mini-tool kit, fifty feet of cord, a never-used cell phone, an atlas, caffeine pills, waterproof poncho, heat-reflective blanket, and a pair of binoculars. If the mission fell apart and I needed to disappear in plain sight, I was confident of going black for a good long while. The only thing the ready-bag lacked was a rifle and a large caliber pistol. But as my training officer always said, the best gun in a gunfight is the one you have with you.

I slid the web harness over my body and holstered the SIG under my left arm. The little .38 snuggled against my right hip. I wore dark clothes, a faded jacket, a ball cap, sunglasses and pair of 5.11 H.R.T. Assault Boots. I preferred a side-zip paratrooper style, but these had Kevlar side panels. Into my jacket pocket, I slid a fully charged taser and the keys to Max's house.

My garage held an old pickup truck. It was registered to a dead man and the plates were obscured by mud. I placed a shovel and a rake in the bed, carefully positioned so the business ends were visible. I opened a cabinet and removed two large magnetic signs and affixed them to the truck doors. They said "Jackson Landscaper" and listed a phone number. I threw my ready-bag on the passenger side floorboard, fired up the engine, and drove to Max's slicked-up neighborhood. The streets were clean and empty, the sidewalks sparkled from embedded quartz, and every tree appeared to be carefully groomed for a contest. Driveways appeared from behind hedges flanked by iron posts. The foliage was already budded out as if summer had been mandated to arrive early for the high tax bracket of the residents. I parked a block from Max's fortress of brick and fake-weathered siding. Two kids on bicycles rode past staring at me, each with a handlebar basket containing a skateboard. They were white boys, one with a shaved head, the other wearing dreadlocks. I ignored them. I didn't belong here. I would never belong here. Any attempt to blend in would fail, which meant I had to capitalize on not belonging.

I left the truck and walked purposefully, holding a clipboard sheaved with papers. I approached Max's house from the ivy-covered side, halted at the lawn's edge and glanced from the clipboard to the house twice, then stepped back as if double-checking the address stenciled on the gently sloping curb. I nodded once to myself and walked across the cropped grass. The yard was like a shag carpet with thick foam padding beneath the sod. A privacy fence shrouded by vines protected the side yard. I crouched by the basement window and peered inside.

The large room contained a pool table, a foosball table, and a refrigerator. Books and magazines lay on a couch. Scattered along the floor were open tubes of Pringles, plastic-wrapped MoonPies, and empty pop bottles. There was a portable CD player fashioned after the style of a 1940s automobile, garish and silver and large. The next window held the fogged glass of a bathroom. I moved through a maple's dappled shade to the rear of the house where a deck jutted into the vast backyard like a pier. Beside it was an enclosed hot tub, infinity pool, and barbeque pit. The back fence rose high above a pool house the size of a gas station. Deep in the corner beneath an ancient oak leaned a series of rocks marking the rounded humps of pet graves dug by Max's daughter. There were no sightlines from the neighbors.

I slid along the rear wall until I could see through a glass door. Recessed fixtures illuminated the room with funnels of overlapping light. The area resembled the aftermath of a tornado in a trailer park, strewn with debris, garbage, books and magazines, scattered articles of clothing, a torn-apart laundry basket, a shattered guitar, ripped pillows, dismantled furniture, and an amazing array of disassembled electronic parts. An electric-blue reclining chair stood in the corner with a halogen lamp beside it. Leaning back with the footrest fully raised was a monkey holding a book.

In a languid motion, the monkey stretched a long arm, extended its fingers, and turned the page of its book, and I wondered how often it had watched Max's daughter sit in the same chair and read. Monkey see, monkey do. The monkey turned another page and drank from a green bottle of Ale-8. His erection quivered in the air like the bowsprit of a model ship. It occurred to me that maybe Max was playing an elaborate joke and had hired a midget in a costume, a notion I quickly discounted because he wouldn't risk homicide in his house even if it was just a midget. This was definitely a monkey—it smelled bad, there were no seams, and its genitalia was legit.

I leaned the clipboard against the wall and walked around the house. My plan was simple—divert the monkey into the guest bedroom, assault through the entrance, subdue the monkey with a Taser, fill the tub with water, throw the boombox and monkey into the tub, and pull back. A houseful of roaming teenagers would make it easy for the police to conclude that someone had left the boombox in the bathroom. I didn't like those damn things anyhow. People carried them like a shroud of music to irritate the world. Maybe Max could sue the manufacturer.

I pecked on the window of the bedroom, then ran around the house to the walk-out entrance. The blue chair was empty. The monkey was investigating my diversion. I inserted the key in the door, swung it open and stepped inside, leading with the taser held before me. Something hard struck my knee. My instinct was to retreat but my training propelled me toward the attack. The monkey hit my forearm hard with a broken chair leg. It was a quick blow of the sort cops use with a baton and I dropped the Taser. The monkey grabbed it with his foot and pulled it to him. I took two steps back and withdrew the SIG.

We stared at each other in a situation I'd experienced before—two adversaries assessing the other's abilities before attack. I'd never sized up a monkey before. It crouched without motion, back to the wall, nostrils flared wide, dark eyes never leaving mine. He was a fierce-looking little spud. I had the advantage of height, weight, reach, brain, and pistol. There was little option save killing it on the spot. I lowered the gun barrel to aim at the monkey's center of mass. One shot, none of that double-tap movie crap that gives away a professional. Then I'd break a window and ransack the house like a meth freak looking for a score.

The monkey flicked its wrist and the chair leg flew through the air at an alarming speed, striking me in the face. I blinked and twitched my head. The monkey grabbed my gun hand and twisted to the precise point where one centimeter more would render a distal radius fracture. I recognized the maneuver from close-quarters hand-to-hand combat training, but the monkey's speed and strength surpassed anyone I'd faced. It stared as if waiting for me to recognize my own vulnerability. Glinting in its eyes was the same adrenalized calm I'd seen in men taking fire. The monkey would break my wrist as readily as turning a switch. I released the pistol. The monkey caught it with his other hand and withdrew. I flexed my hand, the pain sizzling up my arm. I'd been disarmed only once before, by my training officer, who promptly taught me how to defend against the attack.

The monkey aimed the SIG at me, holding it with an awkward delicacy like a child cradling an egg. I was about to be killed. Nothing flashed through my mind but a spreading sense of shame and despair. I'd bungled the job, let down my only friend, and betrayed my training. It was an embarassing death, neither combat nor murder. I thought of my son. I loved him and I hadn't told him so in years.

The monkey pressed the heel magazine release and the clip dropped into his other hand. I exhaled a fierce rush of air, instinctively preparing a counter-attack. The monkey pulled the slide to check the chamber, slammed the magazine back into the pistol, and set the safety. He repeated this process three times, his hands moving by rote—unload, load, check the barrel, set the safety. Then he reversed the weapon in his hand and offered it to me. I took it. The monkey stretched its spine and stood upright, suddenly resembling a man in an animal suit standing at attention. I gathered breath to shoot on the exhale, and the monkey held its position. I underwent the strange and fleeting knowledge that the monkey was seeking my approval, as both an eager apprentice of weaponry and an animal expecting a reward for having performed correctly. For the second time in my life I hesitated at a crucial moment, confused by circumstances that made no sense, and a sudden fear zipped through my body as I remembered the outcome of the last instance in which I had faltered. My military career had ended shortly thereafter.

A door slammed upstairs and I heard the rapid tapping of a woman's heels crossing the hardwood floor of the entry hall. Carpet dulled the sound briefly, then changed pitch as she strode along the tiled kitchen floor directly overhead. A chair scraped. The irritatingly modulated voice on the telephone answering machine informed the world of three messages. Max's wife had come home early.

I lowered the SIG. It was time to abort this cluster-fuck. The monkey extended its paw as if expecting me to return the weapon. Instead, I gestured at the ceiling and held a finger to my lips, then pointed the gun at the Taser. The monkey retrieved the weapon and passed it to me. I slipped the Taser into my pocket. The monkey maintained its upright stance as if waiting further instruction. I aimed at its chest, and moved the SIG quickly to indicate my desire to stop blocking my passage. He did so, and I opened the door slowly, hearing a female voice chatter from the machine overhead. As I stepped from the house, the monkey followed. I shook my head and jerked the gun barrel toward the interior of the house. The monkey shook its own little head. Then it gestured to a window overhead, aimed two fingers at its eyes, and pointed at me. I heeded the warning and back-stepped against the house. The monkey pointed at me, tapped its chest, and stretched its arm toward the side of the house. I understood the meaning, having been trained in silent communication with the same signals, using an economy of motion. When nothing made sense, it's time to say fuck it. In this case, fuck the monkey, too. And fuck Max most of all.

I eased the door shut and locked it, holstered the SIG, grabbed the clipboard, and moved to the sheltered shadows of the tree. I used the shade until reaching the empty street. I strolled along the sidewalk with the clipboard, crossed the street without hurry, got into my pickup and turned the key. I put the truck in gear. Peripheral movement snared my attention and I turned my head as the monkey vaulted with the ease of an athlete into the back of the truck. He lay prone below the sides of the bed. I depressed the accelerator carefully. As I turned the corner, I passed the same two kids on bicycles I'd seen before—baldy and dreadlocks. They were staring at me. Periodically I checked the rearview mirror. Wind rippled the monkey's fur like bluegrass in a field.

I parked in my garage and left the truck carrying my pistol and ready-bag. The monkey sat on the wheel-well, patient as a Marine facing deployment. I remembered Max telling me that this was not a normal monkey, and now despite the failure of my primary objective, I was deeply curious about the animal. Its hair was long and parted in the middle of its forehead like an old-time pharmacist. Its hands were much bigger than its head. I looked into his eyes, surprised by the depth of intelligence, the mind's apparent awareness of itself, and a ruthless quality possessed by combat survivors. Behind that, like a scrim through which light shone, I saw an overriding despair—not so much the hopeless variety, but a tragic optimism as if he perceived existence on its own terms—boring, short, and full of pain. I abruptly realized that the monkey was observing me as well. We were momentarily as interchangeable as an earthen well and a cloud in the sky regarding each other, foreign and familiar, empty and vast.

Ron Rash

Corpse Bird

Perhaps if work had been less stressful, Boyd Candler would not have heard the owl, but he hadn't slept well for a month. Too often he found himself awake at three or four in the morning, his mind troubled by engineering projects weeks behind schedule, possible layoffs at year's end. So now, for the second night in a row, Boyd listened to the bird's low, plaintive moan. In a few minutes he got out of bed. Boyd left the house where his wife and daughter slept to stand in the side yard that bordered the Coleman's property. He was barefoot and the cold late-October dew dampened his feet. The neighborhood was utterly still. No dog barked or car passed. No air-conditioner or heater murmured. Boyd waited like a man in a doctor's office expecting a dreaded diagnosis. In a few minutes it came. The owl called from the scarlet oak behind the Coleman's house, and Boyd knew with utter certainty that if the bird stayed in the tree another night someone would die.

Boyd Candler had grown up among people who believed the world would tell you all sorts of things if you would only pay attention. As a child he'd watched his grandfather, the man he and his parents lived with, find a new well for a neighbor with nothing more than a limb from an ash tree. He'd been in the neighbor's pasture as his grandfather walked slowly from one fence to the other, the branch's two forks gripped like reins, not stopping until the tip wavered, then dipped toward the ground as if yanked by an invisible hand. He'd watched the old man plant crops and cut trees by "the signs."

Boyd had learned to read the signs as well, learned it as another person in a different culture might learn a particular dialect.

Years later as a teenager Boyd had heard the corpse bird in the woods behind the barn. His grandfather had been sick for months but had recently rallied, eating more and getting out of the bed some. The old man had heard the owl as well, and it was a sound of reckoning as final as the thump of dirt clods on a coffin.

"It's come to fetch me," the old man had said of the owl, and Boyd had not the slightest doubt it was true. His grandfather had lived his life by the signs and now he would die by them. Three nights the bird called from the woods behind the barn. Boyd had been in the room those nights, had been there the night his grandfather had passed as the corpse bird called the old man out into the darkness. Boyd had borne witness to this event and it had been as real and tangible as a tree or a rock.

The next morning at breakfast Boyd did not mention the owl to his wife or daughter. He wanted to believe the owl might have been a dream brought on by the stress he'd been under at work, the kind of thing he'd learned about in his college psychology class. After he'd finished his second cup of coffee, Boyd looked at his watch.

"Where's Jennifer," he asked his wife. "It's our week to carpool."

"No pickup today," Laura said. "Janice called while you were in the shower. Jennifer's been sick. She ran a temperature over a hundred all weekend. It still hasn't broken so Janice is staying home with her."

Boyd felt not a shadow, but something like that, pass over his face. It was as though he were outside on a blue-sky day and a cloud had suddenly blotted out the sun.

"Have they been to the doctor?"

"Of course," Laura said. "He told them it was just a virus, something going around."

Allison looked up from her bowl of cereal.

"I bet I get it next, Momma. If I do I want lots of ice cream to cool me off."

"But nothing to worry about?" Boyd asked his wife.

"No," Laura said, her back turned to him as she finished packing Allison's lunch.

"Did the doctor tell Janice anything else?"

Laura turned to face him. The expression on her face wavered between puzzlement and irritation.

"It's a virus, Boyd. That's all it is."

"I'll be outside when you're ready," Boyd told his daughter, then walked out into the yard. The neighborhood seemed less familiar, as though many months had passed since he'd seen it. The subdivision had been built over a cotton field. A few young dogwoods and maples grew in some yards, but the only big tree was a scarlet oak that grew in the undeveloped lot behind the Coleman's house. Boyd imagined it had once been a shade tree, a place for the people who'd worked that cotton field to escape the sun a few minutes when they took water breaks.

The owl was still in the oak. He knew this because as a child in Madison County he'd heard the older folks say a corpse bird always had to perch in a big tree. It was one way you could tell it from a barn or screech owl. Another way was that the bird returned to the same tree, the same branch, each of the three nights. No one had ever said why this was so. Like most of what he'd learned back then it was not something to be debated or explained but acknowledged and, if possible, acted upon.

His family had moved to Asheville soon after his grandfather's death. Boyd had been an indifferent student in Madison County, assuming he'd become a farmer, but the farm had been sold, the money divided among Boyd's father and aunts. He mastered a new kind of knowledge of theorems and formulas, a knowledge where everything could be explained down to the last decimal point. His teachers told him he should be an engineer and helped Boyd get loans and scholarships so he could be the first in his family to attend college.

They offered him a world where the sky did not matter, where land did not blacken your nails or cling to your boots but was seen, if seen at all, through the glass windows of buildings and cars and planes. A world irrelevant and mute. They had believed he could leave the world he had grown up in, and perhaps he had believed it as well.

He remembered the morning his college sociology class watched a film about the folklore of the Hmung tribesmen of Cambodia. After the film there had been a discussion. When the professor had asked if similar beliefs could be found in other cultures, Boyd had raised his hand.

When Boyd had finished speaking, the professor and the other students had looked at Boyd as though he had a bone piercing his nostrils, a necklace of human teeth around his neck.

"So you've actually witnessed such things," the professor had asked.

"Yes, sir," he had replied, knowing his face had turned a deep crimson.

A student behind him, like Boyd an engineering major, snickered.

"And this folklore, you believe in it?" the professor asked.

"I'm just saying I once knew people who did," Boyd said. "I wasn't talking about myself."

"Superstition is nothing more than an ignorance of cause and effect," the student who had snickered said.

This was exactly the same rational, educated response Boyd knew his neighbors would have. Most were transplants from the Northeast or Midwest, all white-collar professionals like himself. They would assume that since it was October the owl was migrating. It would be nothing more than a bit of nature that had managed to find its way into the city, like the occasional possum found on the carport eating the cat food.

"We're making cardboard black cats and jack-o-lantern's today," Allison said as they rode to the elementary school. "Mr. Watson said we can decorate our front doors with them. Is that ok?"

"Sure," Boyd said. "As long as you use tape."

"If I have time I'm going to make Jennifer some, too," Allison said.

"That's a very thoughtful thing to do," Boyd said. "I'm sure Jennifer would appreciate that."

They did not speak again until Allison was getting out of the car.

"Don't worry about Jennifer, Daddy," Allison said. "Mom's right. It's just a virus."

"I won't, Baby, " Boyd said.

But he did worry, off and on all morning and afternoon. Concern for the sick girl, a girl his own daughter's age, became entangled with concerns about timetables and supplies. There had been times he or Laura had taken the thermometer out of Allison's mouth and found the red line risen over three digits, but he could never remember such a fever lasting three days.

He thought about calling the Colemans' house to check on Jennifer, but he knew how strange that would seem. He and Laura had known Janice and her husband ever since they had moved to Raleigh from Chicago. They carpooled their children together and Jennifer and Allison were bosom buddies, but the adults were more acquaintances than friends. In the six years they had lived next door to one another, the two families had never shared a meal together.

Because Boyd was tired and kept thinking about Jennifer, he found he had to stay nine hours to get done what should have been finished in eight. Halloween was five nights away, and as he drove home he saw gap-toothed pumpkins already placed on porches and steps. A skeleton shuddered above a carport, its eyes two black o's.

It was almost full dark when he pulled into the driveway behind Laura's Camry. He saw her through the kitchen window fixing supper. Laura had built a fire and Allison sprawled in front of it doing her homework. The first frost of the year had been predicted for tonight and from the chill in the air Boyd knew it would be so.

He stepped into the side yard and studied the Colemans' house. Lights were on in two rooms upstairs as well as in the kitchen and dining room. The Colemans' two vehicles were both in the carport. He was about to go inside when he heard the owl.

Boyd walked into the backyard to where his land bordered the Colemans'. The scarlet oak's leaves caught the day's last light. Lambent, that was the word for it, Boyd thought, like red wine raised to candlelight, but more viscous than wine. He slowly raised his gaze but did not see the bird. He clapped his hands together, so hard his palms burned. Something dark lifted out of the tallest limbs of the oak, hung above the tree a moment, then resettled.

"How is Jennifer?" he asked when he came into the kitchen.

Laura took off her apron.

"No better. Janice called and said she was going to keep her home again tomorrow."

"Did she take her back to the doctor?"

"Yes. The doctor gave her some antibiotics and took a strep culture."

Allison came in from the living room, her face flushed from sitting near the fire.

"Momma says you need to go out to Mr. Hampton's farm and cut us some more firewood," she told Boyd. Allison placed her books in a backpack draped on a chair.

"Do you hear me, Daddy?" she said.

"Yes," he said.

Boyd turned back to Laura.

"But she's still running a high temperature?"

"Yes."

"I think she needs to see somebody else, somebody besides a family doctor."

Allison came into the kitchen.

"Why do you think that, Daddy?"

"Because I think she's real sick."

"But she can't miss Halloween," Allison said. "We're going to be ghosts together."

"How do you know that?" Laura asked. "You haven't even seen her."

"I just know."

Laura stared at him as if he were suddenly someone she did not seem to know well.

"What's going on with you, Boyd?"

She looked at Allison and said nothing more.

"What's wrong, Daddy? Allison asked. "Don't you want me and Jennifer to be ghosts?"

He waited until after supper to knock on the Colemans' door. Laura had told him not to go, but he went anyway. As he walked across the lawn he wondered how to say this improbable thing and make the Colemans believe it. He knew he couldn't, not in a straightforward way at least. Jim Coleman opened the door. Boyd stood before a man he suddenly realized he knew hardly anything about. He did not know how many siblings Jim Coleman had or what kind of neighborhood he'd grown up in or if he had ever held a shotgun or fishing rod in his hand. He did not know if Jim Coleman had once been a churchgoer or had always spent his Sunday mornings working in his garage or yard.

"I've come to check on Jennifer," he said.

"She's sleeping," Jim said but did not invite him in.

"I'd still like to see her, if you don't mind." Boyd raised the cardboard cat and jack-o-lantern in his left hand. "Allison made these for Jennifer. She'd be real disappointed if I didn't deliver them."

For a moment Boyd thought he would say no, but Jim Coleman stepped aside.

"Come in then."

He followed Jim down the hallway and up the stairs to Jennifer's bedroom. The girl lay in her bed, the bedsheets pulled up to her neck. Jennifer's hair was matted by sweat and her face glistened a pale sheen like the face of a porcelain doll. In a few moments Janice joined them in the room. She pressed her palm against Jennifer's forehead and let it linger as though bestowing a blessing on the child.

"What was her temperature the last time you checked?" Boyd asked.

"One hundred and two. It goes up in the evening."

"And it's been four days now?"

"Yes," Janice said. "Four days and four nights. I let her go to school Friday. I probably shouldn't have."

Boyd looked at Jennifer. He tried to put himself in her parents' situation. He tried to imagine what words could connect what he had witnessed in Madison County to some part of their experience in Chicago or Raleigh. But he knew there were no such words. What he had learned in the North Carolina mountains was untranslatable to the Colemans.

"I think you need to get her to the hospital," Boyd said.

"But the doctor says soon as the antibiotics kick in she'll be fine," Janice said.

"You need to get her to the hospital," Boyd said again.

"How can you know that?" Janice said. "You're not a doctor."

"I know," Boyd said. "When I was a boy, I saw someone sick like this. That person died."

"Doctor Underwood said she'd be fine," Jim said, "that plenty of kids have had this. He's seen her twice."

"You're scaring me," Janice said. She looked at her husband.

"I'm not trying to scare you," Boyd said. "Please take Jennifer to the hospital. Will you do that?"

Janice turned to her husband.

"Why is he saying these things?"

"You need to leave," Jim Coleman said.

"Please," Boyd said. "I know what I'm talking about."

"Leave. Leave now," Jim Coleman said.

Boyd walked back into his own yard. For a few minutes he stood there. The owl did not call but he knew it was there in the scarlet oak, waiting. He sensed its presence like a huge, black pall draped over the Colemans' house. When he came inside Laura had sent Allison to bed.

"We need to talk," she said. "Janice just called and she's royally pissed off."

They sat at the dining room table for half an hour. As Boyd

spoke he heard his words as he knew she heard them, and it sounded like the ravings of a lunatic. It did not help matters that she had not heard the owl either night. That made it all seem even more ludicrous.

"I know where you grew up people, people who had no education, could believe such a thing," Laura said when he'd finished. "But you don't live in Madison County now. You know better. It's your job, the stress of it, that's doing this to you. Can't you see that, Boyd?"

She paused.

"You need to talk to Doctor Harmon. He can give you some AMBIAN to help you sleep, maybe something else to ease the stress. Doctor Harmon can take care of this."

Later that night he waited in bed for the owl to call. An hour passed on the red digits of the alarm clock and he tried to muster hope that the bird had left. He slept, only a few minutes according to the clock but long enough to dream about his grandfather. They were in Madison County, in the farmhouse. Boyd was in the front room by himself, waiting though he didn't know what for. Finally, the old man came out of his bedroom, dressed in brogans and overalls, a sweat rag in his back pocket. *We got work that needs doing*, his grandfather said.

The sound of his grandfather's voice was replaced by the corpse bird's call and Boyd was instantly awake. He looked at the clock and saw it was nearly midnight. Boyd got out of bed and put on pants and shoes and a sweatshirt. He did not know if what he was going to do would save Jennifer, for the landscape the corpse bird inhabited transcended the corporal in some if not all ways. What Boyd did know was that he had to try.

He went into the basement to get the chainsaw. The machine was almost forty years old, a relic, heavy and cumbersome, its teeth dulled by decades of use. But it still ran well enough to cut scrub oak into firewood.

He filled the gas tank and checked the spark plug and chain lube. The chainsaw had belonged to his grandfather, had been used by the old man to cull trees from his thirty-acre farm for firewood. Boyd had often gone into the woods with him, helped load the logs and kindling into his grandfather's battered pick-up. After the old man's health had not allowed him to use it anymore, he'd given it to Boyd.

"You can make you some money with it," the old man had said, "once you get stout enough to heft it." But Boyd had left Madison County before that had happened. Two decades had passed before he found a use for it. A co-worker owned some farm land near Cary and offered Boyd all the free firewood he wanted as long as he cut it himself. Boyd had put in a new spark plug, cleaned out the carburetor and filter, and sharpened the chain as best he could. Even then he was surprised the thing still ran.

He pulled the cord eight times before the machine sputtered to life. As soon as it idled he shut it off. He carried it upstairs, pausing to take the flashlight from a kitchen drawer before he went outside.

It was colder now, the air sharp and clean feeling. The stars seemed more defined, closer, as though picked-up and polished, then reset closer to the earth. A bright-orange harvest moon rose in the west. He clicked on the flashlight and let its beam trace the upper limbs until he saw it. Despite being bathed in light, the corpse bird did not stir. Rigid as a gravestone, Boyd thought. The unblinking yellow eyes stared toward the Colemans' house, and Boyd knew these were the same eyes that had fixed themselves on his grandfather.

Boyd laid the flashlight on the grass, its beam aimed at the oak's trunk. He pulled the cord and the machine trembled to life in his hands. The vibration shook his whole upper body. Boyd stepped close to the tree, extending his arms, the weight tensing the biceps and forearm muscles.

The scrub oaks on Billy Hampton's land had come down quickly and easily. But he'd never cut a tree the size of the scarlet oak. The bark was thick and the teeth on the blade so worn it looked as though a file had been used on them. A few bark shards flew out as the blade hit the tree, then the blade skittered down the trunk until Boyd pulled it away and tried again.

It took eight attempts before he made the beginnings of a wedge in the tree. He was already breathing hard, the weight of the saw straining his arms, back, and even his legs as he steadied not only himself but the machine. He angled the blade as best he could to widen the wedge. By the time he finished the first side, sawdust and sweat stung his eyes. His heart banged against his ribs like something trying to break out of a cage.

Boyd thought about resting a minute but when he looked back at his house and the Colemans, he saw his bedroom light was on, as was the Colemans' back deck light. He carried the saw to the other side of the trunk. Three times the blade hit the bark and skittered away. It seemed to Boyd to be something wild and alive that was trying to get away from him. He looked toward the houses. Jim Coleman was crossing his back yard, coming towards Boyd, his mouth open and arms gesturing.

Boyd eased the throttle and let the chainsaw idle.

"What in God's name are you doing?" Jim shouted.

"What's got to be done," Boyd said.

"I've got a sick daughter and you woke her up."

"I know that," Boyd said.

Jim Coleman reached his hand out as though to wrest the chainsaw from Boyd's hand. Boyd shoved the throttle and waved the blade between him and Jim Coleman.

"I'm calling the police," Jim Coleman shouted at him, then hurried back toward his house. Laura was outside now as well, her hand clutching her bathrobe as she and Jim Coleman spoke to one another a few moments before he went into his house. When Laura approached Boyd screamed at her to stay away and she did and that was a good thing because the oak was ready to fall. He made a final thrust deep into the tree's heart. He dropped the saw and stepped back. The oak wavered a moment, then came crashing down. As it fell, something beaked and wings rushed past inches in front of Boyd's face. He picked up the flashlight and shone it on the bird as it flew off in the opposite direction of the Colemans' house. The corpse bird crossed over the vacant lot and disappeared into the darkness it had been summoned from. Boyd knew the girl was safe now. He clicked off the flashlight and sat down on the trunk of the oak.

His wife and neighbor stood beside each other in the Colemans' back yard, their eyes on him. They spoke softly to one another, as though Boyd were a wild animal they did not want to reveal their presence to.

Soon blue lights splashed against the sides of the two houses. Other neighbors came and joined Jim Coleman and Laura in the back yard. The policeman talked to Jim and Laura a few moments. Boyd watched them but to him they were like a crowd of people glimpsed from a train or car. They were all, even Laura, strangers.

One of the policemen spoke into a walkie-talkie. Then he and his partner started walking toward Boyd. Boyd sat up, arms held out before him, the palms turned upward, like a man who had just set something free.

Andrew Hudgins

Mother

Down the long, wide, and closely trimmed acres of Mammon,
plate toppling with saffron potato salad, I followed my shadow
to an appealing dilapidated pond. Ghostly koi coasted under ripples
undulating to the tempo of hidden pumps. Fish mouths
mouthed my shadow, and among them moved a golden
adumbration. Voluptuous fins feathered the water, blossoming
like massive chrysanthemums that opened and opened
—bud to blowsy, blowsy to blown—and gently closed.
Gold propelled itself on delicate explosions, dissolving
and resolving in aureate metamorphoses, golden fish to golden flower,
flower to fish. But fins I thought petals were actually,
I could not believe this, wings. It was a trained bird, a pullet,
slipping under silk lilies. Before I could even be astonished,
the shadow of wealth stood beside my shadow, a large man,
sly look worn always openly. "I call that one Mother," he said,
and laughed. "Then I'll call her Mother too," I answered, laughing with him
because on Fridays I'd gathered balls while he snapped chip shots,
one after one, over the hood of his Benz, yellow balls
arcing black lacquer I'd polished and onto a green I'd swept.
He never thwacked a door panel, dimpled the hood, or, dear god,
as I prayed from behind a rigid grin, slapped a frosted star
through safety glass. "Risk," he explained. "Risk makes you concentrate."
Orange carp gulped hopefully at our reflections. A sandblasted dolphin,
nearly amorphous with calculated age, shot filtered water into filtered water.
This is America, he told me. Though I was the help, of course I was invited.
At our feet, Mother, never surfacing, lapped the pool like an Olympian.

Kathy Conner

The Widow Sunday

Milla hears the news from Thomas, that the Widow Sunday has gone up to Jackson to have her horn removed, a surgical procedure rarely attempted in Mississippi. Milla listens, perched on the wooden railing of her back porch. Her legs hang, white in sunlight, one heel drumming against lattice below. She tilts her chin up toward a broken ceiling fan, toward wisps of cobwebs gathered between the blades, and she plans how she will steal the horn once the Widow has brought it back, unattached.

"It took a whole team of doctors," Thomas says. "You should of seen it, all over the news up there." He showed up on the porch this morning, the first time he has come here in the weeks since her father left, since the whole house became only Milla's, nothing to ramble through rooms but her own skinny legs, her own fingers to sweep across bookshelves, to trail paths in layers of dust.

"I'll bet," Milla says, "she'll keep the horn." She points across the yard at the hill that blocks the Widow's house from her own. To see the house, Milla must climb the hill, and then its big gray back emerges more and more—the edge of a roof, a window snaked with ivy so thick that Milla, when she tries, can never make out much inside.

"The doctors will take it from her," Thomas says. "They'll ship it off somewhere like Birmingham."

"It's hers," Milla says. "She's got a right to bring it here." She tells herself that she too has a right—the right to steal it because she has always understood these things, horns, disfigurements and the like. The wood is hot beneath her thighs and she arcs her back, throws her shoulders open to Thomas, who stands above. She imagines the horn, swaddled in cloth at the bottom of Widow's suitcase, or boxed up in tissue like a present, propped in Widow's lap for the drive home. It was a thick five inches before the Widow left for surgery, a yellowish stalk in the center of her forehead that curved down toward her nose. It started as something nubbish, like a cyst or a small bone. She was not a widow back then; when it started she was not yet middle-aged. Even now, Widow is only sixty, but thirty years older than Milla herself and as a child, Milla bought with her father's money the fat bread rolls, home-made, that Widow sold with the other Catholic ladies, a wide straw hat jammed on her head to hide what everyone knew was there. She has lived next to Milla for as long as Milla can remember, before Milla's mother left town, before her father went off to Whitfield, the mental institution up in Jackson. Voluntary commitment that, for all Milla can tell, will continue for years.

Thomas leans with his back against the wooden railing, beside her. He presses a hand on her thigh just beneath the hem of her shorts, and his palm is damp against her skin. "What do you want with a horn?" he says.

She stares straight ahead and not at all down at the hand on her thigh. She is conscious of her knee twitching involuntarily, conscious too of her course skin and how it must feel to him, all angle and bone. She has the sudden fear that her knee will pop up against her will, smash him right in the face.

He takes his hand away—and how to answer? How to explain to someone who, like her, has lived here all his life and should already understand? It was with him that, years ago as a child, she snuck into the Widow's house, with him that she crept all over the bottom floor. Together they searched the Widow's rooms; they ran their palms over the slick wood tables, behind them, narrow hallways that stretched on and on and disappeared into black. And the walls there, everywhere papered in brown flowers—crisp and real, dried upside down and pasted on by Widow's quick hands, her smooth pink fingers.

She curves her throat up to him. "A horn is a rare thing, Thomas," she says. "Really something." A good way of putting it, she thinks, because it is something—a thing that for so many years was always there, always topic of conversation, an extension of the whole place and everyone in it. "What makes us different," her father always said. "And we live right next to that woman, right behind her house." It was her father's obsession, and then hers too, the horn and all deformities. Books and books of deformities piled on her father's desk, books that he left behind, and she has poured over them again and again—the glossy photos of men and women born limbless, two-headed babies, soldiers exposed to nerve gas, their noses twisted to one side, muscles drawn severely down as if stretched by wire.

If only she can get the horn—she thinks how she will hold it in her fist, the smooth curve of bone, hollow like blown glass, its point pricking her palm. It will be hers only and she will not share it with her father because her father is gone, and not with her mother because her mother is gone too, gone even before her father. Both gone and now there is only Thomas and sometimes there is not even him.

Propped against the wooden railing, arms folded over his chest, he says, "If it's rare, Widow will want it herself. And she'll take care not to leave it where anyone can get it." His hair clumps over his forehead, oily black, sticky, Milla thinks, if she touched it, if she pulled the tacky curls through her fingers.

"Know what I think?" she says. "That you're going to help me steal it."

"Why should I?" His face hangs just above, and she finds the flaws there, the pock marks on the forehead, the splotch of red on the line of his jaw that is there, always, every time she looks.

"You have nothing else," Milla says. "Not one thing else, nothing to do. So you'll help."

"I have other things," Thomas says.

"What things?" she says. "What do you have, Thomas?" But she knows that he does have things, things he will not share. He has his job as manager of a hardware store. He has his hopes too, pinned on running the new branch in Jackson. He travels at least three times every month up there on business. What he does there, how he occupies his time, Milla does not know. In her mind, a flash of rooms clouded in smoke and the deep slur of men's voices, the slap of palms against tables. Sometimes, her father there as well, the circle of his face bathed in the green light of a bar lamp, and Thomas just beside—a flush of cheek and lip egging him on.

"Think of it," Milla says to Thomas. "You can take the horn up to Jackson, show it off. You can take me too and we'll go all over with it. We'll charge people to see it and we could make a fortune, I'll bet."

"If I take you," he says, "where would I put you?"

"Stash me where you want," she says. "I won't annoy you." Because he wouldn't want to show her off too. She is not worth showing, she knows.

Thomas only looks at her, a corner of his mouth curled up, a half-smile. She has not seen him in weeks, but he is always the same—the flap of black hair over one pale eye, white cheeks, collar bone so sharp it seems about to pierce through his skin. She ran from him as a child, came out nights to hide behind tree trunks, her arms clapped at her sides. They spent whole summers this way, an ongoing hide-and-seek in the night. She roamed over every neighbor's yard in that part of town, and she learned them all, their angles and the dark spots, the places that sucked her in, swallowed her whole body in shadow. Thomas knew these places too, and back and forth they searched the lawns and all of the ditches and the bald dirt trails that glowed, bare in moonlight, and that led eventually to nowhere, to the wooden back of a neighboring fence, to a black tower of vines and trees. They might have kept going, could have broken through but to them this was it, everything, and there was nothing beyond.

In her parents' room there are double French doors that open onto a small balcony. From here, Milla watches the street below. The Widow came back from Jackson this morning, Thomas had said.

"She's hornless," he said. "They saw her on the way to mass."

"Who? Who saw her?" This was on the phone, late morning and Milla still in bed, a thin sheet pulled to her neck. "You?"

"Not me. But I heard enough about it," Thomas said, "to see it clear in my mind." But Milla had hung up before he could describe it to her, had flung the sheets away, skidded in her bare feet across the wood floor, down the hall to her parents' bedroom and the balcony where she can see the street. Widow will pass this way when she comes back from mass. She always passes this way—in the past, Milla's father calling for her to come see, to have another look at Widow's car, the sticker on the bumper *Caution! Never drive faster than your angels can fly!* and Widow behind the wheel, sometimes alone, or sometimes with one of the Catholic ladies, both of them white-gloved and flower-hatted. Milla waits this morning to see it again, the car and the woman and this time, all of it different without the horn flopping out of Widow's hat like a part of the hat itself, some elaborate ornament done up over her forehead.

At eleven o'clock there are still thirty minutes before mass will end. Milla returns to the inside of the room, leaving the balcony doors open behind her. The room is crammed with the furniture, the clothes and shoes, stacks of records, photos and all the other items that her parents have left behind, and as Milla waits, she finds reasons for touching these things, more and more. The perfume bottles and silver combs of her mother's must be polished, and she finds a rag in the bathroom, wipes down the tall oval mirror of the vanity, the framed picture of her father as a seven-year-old, his face freckled and burnt and fat with childhood. One of his books lies on the vanity as well—perhaps the one he had been reading when he snapped, suddenly, after he heard from friends in Memphis that her mother—fifty years old by now, but a beauty still—had taken up with a college boy up there. A boy younger than Milla herself and handsome like Apollo, if the rumors are true. A boy that wouldn't look at Milla—she knows the type, beautiful boys with sneering mouths and half-closed eyes that never see her at all.

Milla runs her finger along the book's shiny jacket—*A World of Genetic Mutations*. She flips through the pages, finds the one with the edge folded back—her father never bothered with book marks. This is where he stopped, on a polydactyl woman, her hand held high and the six fingers spread wide, each fingernail polished a bright pink. Milla turns the page, then again, page after page. She could take it to her father at Whitfield, an empty book. She could tell him how she ripped each page from the spine while sprawled on his bed, how she tore them all into bits, every book in the house. She could tell him this, though none of it would be true.

She takes the book out onto the balcony and is flipping through it still when Widow's long gray Buick rumbles up the street. Milla pauses, book still in hand. There is a stop sign just past Milla's house, and Widow's car slows as it approaches. The sun throws a glare across the windshield. Milla can see nothing of the Widow inside. The car will soon be gone and she must stop the car and before she knows it, she is leaning far out over the railing, waving her arms. "Hello!" she shouts. "Good to see you! Hello!"

The car moves on and so Milla flings the book over the balcony. It lands on the grass, far short of the street, but the movement has caught the Widow's attention. The car stops; the window rolls down and for a moment Milla finds Widow, her profile, naked now, nothing save for the mild slope of her nose, the jut of her bottom lip that Milla notices for the first time, horn gone. Widow tips her chin up to the balcony, her face a bright circle floating below. They look right at one another, Milla saying, "Christ, Christ, Christ" and waving her hands in greeting. Widow raises her own gloved hand, waves back.

Suddenly, Milla is glad that her father is gone, glad that he has missed this—Widow's forehead wrapped in gauze, the one square in the center, glaringly white. A clean empty square and a damn shame, her father would say, to take from the woman what nature had given her. As a child, Milla spent hours with her father, sprawled on the rug in the den, books passing from his hands into hers. "Look here," he would say, tapping a page, "a fetus with pointed ears, like the devil." And Milla would peer over his shoulder at these images, would remember them later, most of them in black and white, unnaturally shiny, and she would sketch crude copies of them during school, never as horrific as the originals themselves.

She could never get the horn right especially, could never capture the curve of it, not really a curve so much as a drop, like gravity had pulled it down, down. And she wonders now if someday it would have grown all the way down to Widow's feet, if it would have curled between her legs to drag behind her in the grass. She will never know and Widow will never know and Milla waits there, on the balcony, long after her car has disappeared. She waits there and she props her arms on the railing, stares down at her father's book where it lies in the grass. The sun beats against her arms and face and, sweating and exhausted, she stumbles inside; she falls on her back onto her parents' bed and balls her hand into a fist that she presses against her damp forehead.

Thomas is a fool to argue with her, a fool to say that it could ruin him. What is there to ruin? Milla asks him this as they crouch outside a window in front of Widow's house.

"I won't go in," Thomas says. "I'm here to watch only."

"You can't watch from outside," Milla says. "You can't see anything from outside. Widow's made sure of it." Milla paws at the ivy that covers the glass, thick masses of it, layers that have grown one on top of the other, year after year. The Widow is not home; Milla and Thomas have watched her drive off in her Sunday clothes—bright heels, a flowing blouse and long skirt, though today is only Tuesday.

"Where's she going?" Thomas says.

"It doesn't matter." There is a latch here, somewhere, if Milla can remember how to position her fingers so that they scrape against the lock, just so. And there it is, like it was years back. Her arms press against the glass before she snaps the lock and pushes the window up, beneath all that ivy. Then she turns to Thomas.

"We'll part it like a curtain." She sweeps her arms through the air, demonstrating.

"That's not how you part a curtain," Thomas says.

Milla plunges one leg deep into the ivy, leaves and stems scratching her thigh. She claws at it, breaks it apart with her whole body. For a moment, she is swallowed up in it—all that ivy crowded everywhere, and she cannot see, and she sucks air through her teeth when she smacks her elbow against the window sill, and then, she finds her footing. She is inside.

"Now you've made a mess," Thomas says, through the window.

She is in Widow's kitchen and when she looks around, she knows the kitchen, though this should not be possible. She has been here only the one time, but feels that it is all the same, everything placed just as it was before. A wooden owl with sharp, pointed beak sits in the middle of a long white table. The yellow curtains, frilled at the edges, are tied not back, but up, their ends looped over shiny yellow rope. The door to the living room is propped open with the same brass ornament, and Milla picks it up, lets the door swing shut behind her.

In the living room, she hears Thomas knocking on the front door, and the sound is louder, more hollow than in her own home, startling in the midst of all that solid furniture and the dark folds of drapery. A number of fancy sofas line the walls, a large one angled in the center of the room, each with legs and arms carved from dark wood. Milla sits on the center one, crosses her ankles, lady-like, taps one heel against a sofa leg. She tries to place the Widow here, feet propped on a stool, a novel in her hands, or on the phone with one of the Catholic ladies, receiver cradled to her ear. But this is wrong somehow, and Milla cannot help picturing her, always, with the horn drooping over her forehead like something wilted, dead.

She opens the door for Thomas and he rushes inside, shuts and then locks the door behind him. "Someone could see us," he says.

The brass doorstopper is still in Milla's hand, and she holds it out to him. "Remember this?" she says.

"Not a bit."

"Look around. It's all the same." Milla points to several spots in the room. "That lamp. And over there, the red Christmas candles."

"There wasn't that grandfather clock," Thomas says.

"Sure there was," Milla says, but she cannot be sure she remembers it there, tall over the mantle. She cannot be sure that she remembers any of it, and she pinches the ruffle of a pillow between her fingers, runs a palm over the rough nap of fabric. But none of it brings back any physical image, any tangible memory of interacting with these things. When she tries to conjure something up, what comes instead resembles her own home, her own cushions too plumped and clean save for the fine skim of dust that covers everywhere; so much dust that Milla can never get it all, no matter how often she scrubs, back bent over table after table and her nose raw with sneezing.

"No horn," Thomas says.

Milla moves toward the hallway, and Thomas follows. They search the bottom floor and find nothing, more furniture, a guest room with a hope chest filled only with linens, a bathroom with a cabinet stocked with common toiletries.

Thomas touches her arm. "This is ridiculous," he says.

"Upstairs," Milla says. She reaches the top of the stairs and turns to see Thomas still below. "Come on, Thomas," she says. "You've gone this far."

"I could lose my job," he says.

Milla takes off without him. There is a long hallway here with walls papered, like the ones below, with dry flowers that crinkle beneath Milla's fingers. She moves quickly down this hall, peeping into rooms. In an office with a big black desk, she finds a glass vase filled with pens and pencils, and she tucks it under her arm, carries it back to the top of the stairs.

"Here," Milla says, holding it high above her head. "Come on, or I'll do something drastic." Thomas only blinks up at her, so she turns the vase over, pens and pencils falling in a clatter to the floor, some of them rolling down the stairs.

"That's not all that convincing," Thomas says.

"I'll throw the vase too," Milla says. She waits only seconds before flinging it against the wall, shards of glass flying up and just missing her legs.

"Fucking could have killed yourself," Thomas says, and when she darts off down the hall again, she hears him, stomping up the stairs after her.

She finds Widow's bedroom at the end of the hall. She waits for Thomas to catch up with her, and then they both go into the room together. Here, everything is red, deep, vivid red—red satin on the bed, sheer red canopy, red and gold curtains.

"Jesus, it's like a whorehouse," Thomas says. "One of those fancy ones."

"How do you know, Thomas?" Milla says. But she walks full into the room, without waiting for his answer. In here, it smells strongly of cologne, something heavy that seems to hang in a cloud over the room.

"A room like this, a woman wants someone to see," Thomas says.

Milla runs her fingers over the slick top of a table set up as a vanity, a mirror hung above. There is a stool with a red velvet cushion, and Milla sits, props her elbows on the table, chin in her hands. Thomas is there, reflected in the mirror, a motionless figure, like a photo, a painting. Not real. She forces her eyes down, glances over the items scattered across the table, several brushes, combs, perfumes, and then a man's shaving kit in the corner. The case is old brown leather and inside, gleaming as if recently polished, are a straight razor, a pair of silver scissors and a small round mirror. Her husband's? Milla does not remember a husband or any man ever connected with the Widow. There must have been one—one that died. She reaches to grab the leather case, to study it, and she knocks a hair brush and a bottle of cologne off of the table. The bottle hits the carpet without breaking, but the glass stopper comes ajar, heavy odor spilling into the room, right up Milla's nose, and she backs away, backs into Thomas. He catches her by the shoulders, says, "What's wrong with you? That's expensive I bet." He takes the leather case from her hands, sets it back on the table. He grabs her by both wrists, bends his head close to her ear. "Let's get this over with," he says.

Milla does not answer and for a moment, they stand close together without speaking. She can feel the hot rush of his breath, the pulse of his thumb against her wrist. Once, long ago, he had kissed her. How old had they been, their skinny legs and arms, their voices like music, like the sing-song chants of schoolyards? She cannot remember the age, only how it felt, all that wet and heat, the click of his teeth accidentally against hers, and she had bitten him, his tongue, hard enough to draw blood that she tasted, metallic and salty and hotter than anything else. He had pushed away, shoved a finger in his mouth, pulled it out red and held it up to her, said, "You did that, Milla."

She is close enough to kiss him now, and for a moment she lets her chin rub against his shoulder. She breathes into his neck, her own hot breath coming back at her. The backs of her knees are slick with sweat. She should smell him, this close, but her nose is filled only with the heavy, flower-ish scent of Widow's cologne.

"What's it smell like in a whorehouse, Thomas?" Milla looks at him, at his fingers pushing at all that black hair over his forehead.

"I never can remember," he says.

A room a woman wants someone to see, Thomas had said, and Milla decides to take her time, see it all and touch it too. While Thomas dabs the carpet with a wet rag, she opens Widow's closet. It is a large walk-in and inside she finds only empty hangers, a mess of boxes and suitcases stacked on the floor. She falls to her knees and snaps open the lid of a suitcase. It is full to the brim, clothes neatly folded inside, each pocket of the lining stuffed with garments—delicate white handkerchiefs, tangles of hosiery, long satin slips. She opens another and pulls out a blouse with gold buttons at the cuffs.

"I'll drag you out of there," Thomas says, from the doorway.

"You see this?" Milla says. She points to the boxes. "Where's she going?"

"On a trip, it seems."

There are more suitcases, more traveling bags and thick cardboard boxes piled on the closet shelves. "Christ," Milla says. She jumps to her feet, spins around to Thomas. "I bet she's moving."

"Nothing else is packed."

"Because she'll leave the other things behind," she says. "She's taking just this stuff here and she's leaving town for good."

"Let her leave then."

Milla clasps her head with her hands. Her forehead has gone numb, has disappeared, nothing there now to hold her features in place. "Of course you don't care." She is screaming at him. "You're not here anyway." She shoves him back and slams the closet door, shutting him out. She stands there for a moment in the dark, then fumbles around for the light switch. Thomas is knocking on the door from the outside, calling to her. The door is not locked and he could simply turn the knob, but he doesn't.

"She could be home any time," he says.

"Get out of here, Thomas." Milla rummages through the boxes until she finds a floor-length formal skirt and a thick, cream-colored blouse. She kicks off her shoes and strips from her own clothes to try these on. The Widow is a small woman, almost bony, and her clothes would be too tight on Milla, if they weren't all flowing and loose, like scarves. Milla twirls to make the skirt fly out around her legs. She tucks the blouse into the waist, adjusts the buttons.

Something is missing. There are hat boxes in one corner, stacked almost to the ceiling and when she pulls one out, several of them fall around her, lids popping open and hats tumbling across the closet floor. She lifts them one by one—this one black felt and this one red with silk flowers clustered at the front. Some have fruit instead of flowers, and some have netting; some are plain. There are so many that Milla must take her time to go through them all. On the other side of the door, Thomas is quiet. She wonders if he has left her here alone, but will not ask.

She decides, finally, on a sun-bleached straw hat with ribbon, and she shakes her hair over her shoulders, places the hat on her head. It faces the right direction, bow at the back, but in the center of the brim, over her forehead, is a groove, an indention not meant for decoration. Milla realizes at once that Widow's horn has caused this, pressed too often, always, in the same spot. Milla takes another hat from the floor, finds the same groove. The horn has molded itself into most of these hats, and she fits her fingers into the grooves, measures their width, their length. She can squeeze three fingers in, side-by-side.

"Christ, she'll have to get all new ones," she says aloud.

When she steps from behind the closet door, Thomas sits on the edge of Widow's bed, his arms folded across his chest. Milla walks right up to him and grabs him by the shoulders. He jerks his head back to look at her. He pinches the sleeve of her blouse between a finger and thumb. "Not your style," he says.

Milla pulls the brim of the hat over her eyes. "I think so," she says.

"You're not even looking for the horn."

"She's got it on her I bet. I'm waiting for her."

"No, no." Thomas jumps to his feet. "You'll be alone then. I won't get caught here." He whirls around, walks quickly to the center of the room, stops. "When did you get so bold?" he says. His eyes are wide round circles beneath his brow.

"I've got nothing to lose," Milla says.

"I do."

Milla moves toward him, swinging her hips to make the skirt swish around her legs. Odd, that in these old-fashioned clothes she feels somehow naked, exposed in a way that makes her skin tingle pleasantly beneath the thick satin. She wraps her arms around Thomas's shoulders. The wide brim of the hat jabs his chin and she sweeps it from her head, drops it to the floor. She presses her mouth to his neck, tastes his skin all the way up to his earlobe that she takes between her lips. He is tense beneath her hands, his jaw strained tight and suddenly he bends his head and kisses her back. His palms press against her back and his mouth buries her own, and this time when she bites him, when she nips the edge of his lower lip, it is on purpose. His hands pull her closer, so that her body is flattened against his and it is right then that Widow's car sputters into the driveway.

Both pause, and then Milla draws back. She stoops to pick up the hat. She jams it far down on her head and from beneath the brim, she gazes up at Thomas. He flushes a bright red and sweat shimmers across his brow. He rubs his temples with his fingers, squeezes his eyes shut and before he can open them, Milla slips from the room. She runs down the hall in her bare feet, dodging the broken glass near the top of the stairs. In the driveway, the crunch of the car door closing, the click of Widow's heels against the pavement. Then the sharp hiss, a spat curse, and Milla knows that she has found the broken ivy and open window. There is a chance, a possibility that Widow will be too afraid to come in. But Milla makes a bet with herself: the Widow will be bold, and so Milla stands at the top of the stairs and waits for her.

"You ruined my kudzu," the Widow says right away. She gapes up at Milla on the staircase.

"Not on purpose," Milla says.

"Come on down from there."

Milla obeys, holding the hem of her skirt so not to trip on her way down the stairs. Up close, the Widow is a mess, the skin around her eyes dark and her face puffed with bruises still visible beneath a layer of powder. She is hatless, her hair swept away from her face in a bun, the bandages on her forehead whiter than her too-white skin. She tugs lightly at a corner of one. Her lips are lined in bright red, her mouth a brilliant splotch of color in the midst of all the white powder, the white gauze. In her hand is something small wrapped in paper, and with her other hand she reaches, taps Milla's shoulder. "You came for my clothes?" she says.

"No."

"The hat you can have," Widow says. "I have lots of hats."

"I know about your hats."

"Of course."

Beneath the brim of the hat, Milla's eyes flit again and again to the something wrapped in paper that Widow holds in her hand. It is too crinkled, too hidden under Widow's fingers to determine its shape, but it could be curved; it could be half-mooned. Milla can study it all she wants, without the Widow seeing, because only the lower half of Milla's face, her chin and lips, tip of her nose, is visible with this hat. Milla decides that she will keep the hat. "Listen," Milla says. "Something I was wanting to ask. When they cut the horn off," she says, "did they tell you where it came from?"

"You'll have to pay for my kudzu." The Widow flaps her hand at a sofa. "Go on and sit."

Milla makes sure to choose a chair that faces the staircase, so the Widow will sit with her back to it. The Widow places the parcel wrapped in paper in her lap, folds her hands over it. Then she leans toward Milla. "All those hats and it was sun damage," Widow says. "That's what they told me. But they don't know. I never did like the sun."

"Sun can't do that."

"A skin lesion," Widow says. "Not many people have that reaction, they said." Her hands flutter up to her forehead. The paper in her lap, brown and creased and exposed—maybe, after all, it is empty. Only shaped like what it carried just this morning, when Widow left in all her fancy clothes.

Milla says, "You've been gone for hours."

"It takes that long to drive up to Jackson and back."

"You're moving there."

"Not there." Widow's fingers, as she speaks, play at the paper in her lap, unfolding it, corner by corner. "Somewhere better. Charleston, Nashville. I could go overseas to London if I wanted." When she has finished unwrapping it, the horn lies on its back, point curved up to the Widow's face, smaller, less yellow than Milla remembers. One end, the end that grew from Widow's head, is ragged, cracked in several places, stained a dark brown. At the other end, the point is sharp and unblemished and the Widow taps it with her finger.

"You have no idea what they want for it," Widow says. "It's worth more than anything has a right to be." She scoops it up in her palm, holds it out to Milla.

Milla reaches for the horn, its smooth, round width suddenly hers. It is lighter than she expected, delicate, and Milla is careful not to touch the one end, the brown and ugly end from Widow's head. She runs her hands over the rest of it, all the way to the tip, the point that is not sharp enough to puncture holes, but sharp enough to tickle the flesh where she rubs it down the length of her arm.

"You're selling it," Milla says.

"Of course I'm selling it. It's a blessing, a gift from God. I'll make enough off it to do whatever I want the rest of my life." She smiles, lips stretched tight, red lipstick clumped in the corners of her mouth.

A movement on the staircase catches Milla's attention, and she glances over the Widow's shoulder at Thomas. He takes a step, pauses, takes another until he is half-way down and then he stops, his eyes on Milla and the horn in her hand. Milla wraps her fingers around it in a loose fist. She has the sudden urge to squeeze it tight, to break it by its middle and keep one end for herself, for Thomas. A half is all she needs and why shouldn't the Widow share her blessing? Even broken, the horn must be worth something.

"Saw your father up there," Widow says. "I showed him the horn."

Milla squints at her. "You went to the asylum?"

"No. I saw him at brunch at Julip's. He was with a crowd."

Thomas hears this, Milla sees, because he shakes his head rapidly back and forth, as if denying it. He has reached almost the foot of the stairs by now and the front door is only a few feet away. He could make a run for it, but he waits.

"That wasn't him," Milla says. "It couldn't have been him." She stands from her chair, still holding on to the horn.

"Sure it was. He was with a red-haired woman and three other couples," the Widow says. "He looked happier than I've seen him in years." She holds her hand up and wiggles her fingers. "Give that back now."

Thomas is all the way down the stairs and still, the Widow is unaware of his presence. He is posed ready to bolt for the door, but waiting for a signal from Milla. Milla holds the horn by its middle, both ends sticking out from her fist. "I think I'll keep it," she says.

The Widow jumps to her feet. "Oh," she says, "I knew you'd want it. You and your father both. Always watching me and looking and everyone looking." She grabs Milla by the arm, peers hard into her face. "You don't know what that's like," she says. "No one watches you."

Milla finds the Widow's eyes, dark pits sunken into the bruised and swollen face. Bandages all over. Beaten up with it, beaten and worn and ready to retire and Milla knows: Widow will not miss it, this thing that sprouted up out of nowhere, that ruined all her hats and hung in front of her eyes like a wayward hair that she could never swat away. She will not miss it but Milla will, its presence always in the back of her mind, a thing to be reckoned with, a thing that should not be and somehow is. Now, in her hand, an insignificant scrap, a shell of what it was and it will never be the same, unattached.

"Take it," Milla says. "Take it away. Get rid of it." With sudden violence, she pushes it at the Widow. It drops to the floor between them. "Go," Milla says. "Go on. Go!" Behind the Widow, Thomas runs for the door and in seconds is gone. Milla gathers her skirt in her arms and darts after him.

"Wait," the Widow yells. "I'll need those clothes back before you leave."

She pauses at the front door and turns to look over her shoulder. The Widow is crouched over the horn, clasping it tight in both hands. Stray hairs float around her face like tiny snakes and posed this way, bent almost to the floor, she is like some fallen Medusa.

"Said I want those back," Widow says.

Milla runs. She is out the front door, flying over the porch, across the yard and she hears the Widow behind, yelling how Milla is a grown woman now and too old for this kind of thing. But Milla does not stop, and the slope of the hill pushes her faster, down, down. Thomas is far ahead, and Milla focuses on him, on his long back, his swift legs carrying him forward until he rounds a corner and drops out of sight. Milla makes wind with her speed, air that rushes up and blows the hat off of her head as she flies down the hill, arms spread for balance, hem of the skirt still clutched in one fist. She will not stop for the hat, cannot stop now because the hill is too steep. Stopping would be falling, and when she is half-way down, she sees her own porch and Thomas there already, panting and slouched against the wooden railing. No one watches her; the Widow is right. But Thomas is watching now, and she runs to him.

The hill brings her closer and closer, and he comes into focus—his white face, eyes hidden beneath the mess of black hair, and from this distance, from up here, he is like a man waiting for what he loves, gazing up the hill as if he has nothing but this. But he has other things, and he will leave again any day for Jackson. He will go there, and eventually he will come back, but he will always go again. He will leave her here and she runs to him anyway, like she ran from him as a child. Hide-and-seek that lasted hours in the dark, when night after night, Milla found Thomas, or he found her and either way she would go home, legs sore with all that running, and she would lie beneath her bedroom window until her parents stopped crashing around, until the house grew quiet and still, and she would tap her blistered heels over and over against the glass. This time, when she gets down there, she will take something heavy, something denser than the horn, and she will smash right through.

Tom Franklin

Smonk Gets Out Alive

It was the eve of the eve of his death by murder and there was harmonica music on the air when E. O. Smonk rode the disputed mule over the railroad tracks and up the hill to the hotel where his trial would be. It was October the first of that year. It had been dry and dusty for six weeks and five days. The crops were dead. It was Saturday. Ten after three o'clock in the afternoon according to the shadows of the bottles on the bottle tree.

Amid the row of long nickering horsefaces at the rail Smonk slid off the mule into the sand and spat away his cigar stub and stood glaring among the animal shoulders at his full height of five and a quarter foot. He told a filthy blond boy holding a balloon to watch the mule, which had an English saddle on its back and an embroidered blanket from Bruges Belgium underneath. In a sheath stitched to the saddle stood the polished butt of the Winchester rifle with which, not half an hour earlier, Smonk had dispatched four of an Irishman's goats in their pen because the only thing he abhorred more than an Irish was an Irish goat. By way of brand the mule had a fresh .22 bullet hole through its left ear, same as Smonk's cows and pigs and hound dog did, even his cat.

That mule gits away, he told the boy, I'll brand ye balloon.

He struck a match with his thumbnail and lit another cigar. He noted there were no men on the porches, downstair or up, and slid the rifle from its sock and snicked the safety off. He backhanded dust from a mare's flank to get her the hell out of his way (they say he wouldn't walk behind a horse) and clumped up the steps into the balcony's shade and limped across the hotel porch, the planks groaning under his boots. The boy watched him: his immense dwarf shape, shoulders of a grizzly bear, that bushel basket of a head low and cocked, as if he were trying to determine the sex of something. His hands were wide as shovels and his fingers so long he could palm a man's skull, but his lower half was smaller, thin horseshoe legs and little feet in brand-new calf opera boots the color of chocolate, loose denim britches tucked in the tops. He wore a clean pressed white shirt and ruffled collar, suspenders, a black string tie with a pair of dice on the end and a tan duck coat. He was uncovered as usual—hats made his head sweat—and he wore the blue-lensed eyeglasses prescribed for sufferers of syphilis, which accounted him in its numbers. On a lanyard around his neck hung a whiskey gourd stoppered with a syrup cork.

He coughed.

Along with the Winchester he carried an ivory-handled walking cane with a sword concealed in the shaft and a derringer in the handle. He had four or five revolvers in various places within his clothing and cartridges clicking in his coat pockets and a knife in his boot. There were several bullet scars in his right shoulder and one in each forearm and another in his left foot. There were a dozen buckshot pocks peppered over the hairy knoll of his back and the trail of a knife scored across his belly. His left eye was gone a few years now, replaced by a white glass ball two sizes small. He had a goiter under his beard. He had gout, he had the clap, blood-sugar, neuralgia and ague. Malaria. The silk handkerchief balled in his pants pocket was blooded from the advanced consumption the doctor had just informed him he had.

You'll die from it, the doctor had said.

When? asked Smonk.

One of these days.

At the hotel door, he paused to collect his wind and glanced down behind him. Except for the boy slouching against a post with his balloon, an aired-up sheep's stomach lining, there were no children to be seen, a more childless place you'd never find. Throughout town the whorish old biddies were pulling in shutters and closing doors, others hurrying across the street shadowed beneath their parasols, but every one of them peeping back over their shoulders to catch a gander at Smonk.

He pretended to tip a hat.

Then he noticed them—the two slickers standing across the road beside a buckboard wagon covered in a tarp. They were setting up the tripod legs of their camera and wore dandy-looking suits and shiny derbies.

Smonk, who could read lips, saw one say, There he is.

Inside the hotel the bailiff, who'd been blowing the harmonica, put it away and straightened his posture when he saw who it was coming and cleared his throat and announced it was no guns allowed in a courtroom.

This ain't a courtroom, Smonk said.

It is today by God, said the bailiff.

Smonk glanced out behind him as if he might leave, the hell with the farce of justice once and for all. But instead he handed the rifle over, barrels first, and as he laid one heavy revolver and then another on the whiskey keg the bailiff had for a desk, he looked down at the gaunt barefaced Scot in his overalls and bicycle cap pulled low, sitting on a wooden crate, the sideboard behind him jumbled with firearms deposited by those already inside.

Smonk studied the bailiff. I seen ye before.

Maybe ye did, the man said. Maybe I used to work as ye agent till ye sacked me from service and my wife run off after ye and cast me in such doldrums me and my boy Willie come up losing ever thing we had—land, house, barn, corn crib, still, crick. Ever blessed thing. Open up ye coat and show me inside there.

Smonk did. You lucky I didn't kill ye.

The bailiff pointed the rifle. That 'n too.

The one-eye licked his long red tongue over his lips and put his cigar in his teeth and unworked from his waistband a forty-one caliber Colt Navy pistol and laid it on the wood between them.

Keep these instruments safe, fellow. Maybe I'll tip ye a penny for looking after em good.

I wouldn't accept no tip penny from you, Mister Smonk, if it was the last penny minted in this land.

Smonk had coughed. Do what.

I said if it was to happen a copper blight over this whole county and a penny was selling for a dollar and a half and I hadn't eat a bite of food in a month and my boy was starving, I wouldn't take no penny from you. Not even if ye paid me a whole nother penny to take it.

But Smonk had turned away.

Angry harmonica notes preceded him as he twisted his shoulders to fit the door and stepped into the hot, smoky diningroom, cigar ash dusted down his tie like beard dander. The eating tables had been shoved against the walls and stacked surface to surface, the legs of the ones on top in the air like dead livestock. Justice of the Peace Elmer Tate and the lawyer and the banker and two or three farmers and the liveryman and that doctor from before checking his watch and Hobbs the undertaker, all deacons, looked at him. The talking had hushed, the men quiet as chairs. The nine ball flashing its number across the billiard table in the corner didn't make its hole and ticked off the seven and stopped dead on the felt.

Smonk leaned against the wall; it gave a little. He coughed into his handkerchief and dabbed his lips and stuffed the cloth into his pocket, the conversation and game of billiards picking back up.

For a moment nothing happened except the quip of a mockingbird from outside and Smonk unstoppering his gourd. Then the door opened at the opposite end of the room and into the light walked the circuit judge, a Democrat, Mason and former army officer equally renowned for his drinking and his mutton chops. He acknowledged no other man as he excused his way through them and stepped onto the wooden dais erected for this occasion and seated himself behind the table set up for him, a glass of water there and a notepad, quill and ink bottle. He wore a black suit and hat like a preacher and for a gavel used the butt end of a new Smith & Wesson Schofield .45.

Order now, order, he called, removing his hat. Be seated, gentlemen. He screwed his monocle in.

Ever body set down, called the bailiff. And git ye got-dern cover off.

The men snatched off their hats and scuffed into chairs. In the rear of the room, Smonk kept standing. He ashed his cigar. For once he wished he wore a hat so he could leave it on. A sombrero, say.

Let's see. The judge cleared his throat. First on the docket here is the people of Old Texas Alabama versus Eugene Oregon Smonk.

Not first, the defendant growled. The whole docket. Today I'm yer whole fucking docket.

Anger charged the diningroom: the state flag in the corner seemed to quiver though the air between the men was as still as the inside of a rock. From somewhere out beyond the dusty desiccated sugarcane came the high parched yap of a mad-dog.

Afternoon Gentlemen. Smonk grinned. Judge.

He pulled his shoulders off the wall and hung his cane on his arm and puffed his cigar and stopped up his gourd. But he'd only made two steps toward his table when he paused and raised his head.

Something was different.

Somehow, the red-headed farmer glaring at him was not the same farmer Smonk had beaten with a coiled whip. The town clerk was not the same town clerk he had slapped down in the street, whose face he'd ground in the mud and money purse taken. Somehow that one there wasn't the banker he'd swindled out of seventy-five acres of bottomland including a creek. That one was not the liveryman whose daughter he'd won at rook and taken in the feed room in the back. Hobbs the undertaker was another undertaker entirely and Tate yonder wasn't the same spineless justice of the peace Smonk had been blackmailing near a year. They were all other faces, all other men.

He didn't know them. He didn't know them.

The bailiff wasn't a bailiff now but another man altogether. They were scuffling to their feet in a mob as the judge banged his pistol so hard the ink bottle jumped off.

Order! he called. God damn it, I said order!

But there was no order left.

Instead there were fire pokers and riding crops. An ash shovel. There were bricks and unlooped belts and letter openers and knots of kindling. An iron pump handle. A broken window's flashing knives. One soaked noose, cue sticks, table legs with nails crooked as fangs, the picks and pikes of splintered chairs.

The men advanced on Smonk with leery sidesteps. He ducked

the hurled eight-ball which smashed a window. He dropped his cigar to the floor and didn't bother to toe it out and it lay smoking between his boots. He took off his glasses and folded them away into his breast pocket, in no hurry despite the men closing in behind their weapons, so close the ones in front could see his red teeth.

Get him, said somebody in the corner.

But Smonk raised the prongs of his fingers and his assailants froze. He leaned back, haled a long tug of air and held it, as if he might say some truth they needed to hear.

They waited for him to speak.

Instead he coughed, blood smattering those faces closest. And in the same moment each fellow in the room tall enough to see witnessed Eugene Oregon Smonk's eye uncork from his head into the air.

For an instant it glinted in a ray of light through the window, then McKissick the bailiff caught it like a marble.

He opened his palm and grinned.

When he looked up Smonk had a derringer in one hand and sword in the other and he was backing toward the sideboard where all those lined-up rifles and pistols lay gleaming.

Well have at it, he yelled, you hongry bitches.

Meanwhile, the sun had shied behind a cloud. The horses along the rail outside were bland and peaceful, many with their eyes shut. Even the flies had landed. Across the street, the two photographers stood on either side of their wagon cracking their knuckles and glancing up the deserted street and down it.

The blond boy had tied his balloon in the raw hole in the mule's ear and was climbing into the saddle. He wiggled his behind. The stirrups, adjusted for Smonk, hung too far down so he didn't use them, even as the mule backed up on its own and faced east.

When the first shot came from inside, the photographers let fall their tripod and leaped into the wagon and flung away a green tarp to reveal a 1908 Model Hiram Maxim water-cooled machine gun bolted to its metal jackstand. One man checked the lock while the other twirled vises and tightened the petcock valve.

I heard he killed his own momma, he said.

For starters, said the other.

The blond boy slapped the mule across its withers and gigged it with his bare heels. Let's git to that orphanage, he said, saluting the machine gunners as they waited, one slowly returning the salute. The mule began to walk, and then trot, the bailiff's son not looking back despite the storm of gunfire, the balloon bobbing above them like a thought the mule was having, empty of history.

Laura Benedict

Witches, All

There's a knock on the dressing room door, and something inside, this voice in my head that speaks up now and again when I'm stone-fucking sober tells me to stay where I am and not to answer it. It's the same voice I heard the night my old man hanged himself in our garage, the same voice that warned me away from the dancer in Tallahassee who screwed me blind and nine months later gave me the kid, now ten years old and as ugly as his old man. The time it told me not to get on an airplane, I did listen, and the plane was delayed on LaGuardia's tarmac for six hours. As men go, I'm not completely stupid. But I'm not going to listen to it now because I never know when that voice might be just screwing with my head.

Once upon a time, I would've opened the door to a vibrating group of tight-ass teenage girls, all made up to look like their big sisters or slutty mothers, pretty white teeth straightened by just-popped braces, tits straining to burst from their itty-bitty tee shirts, the ones with my name emblazoned across their fronts as big as that Rolling Stones mouth with the tongue hanging out. Chances are tonight it's one of those girls all grown up and divorced with brats of her own, her tits shrunken and sagging, and her hair either dulled with age, or way too blond. Still, it's like opening up a Christmas present every time there's a knock on a dressing room door. Because I remember that other voice, the one that didn't shut up for six years until people started to forget "Unjust Love" and "Give Me You" and there was no more record contract, the voice that said *They want you! Can you fucking believe it, you lucky bastard?*

She's looking at me shyly, like she doesn't know why she's standing there.

"Can I come in?" she says.

And what am I going to tell her? "Sorry, but there's this voice inside my head—actually two voices, and one's telling me I should let you in and do you on the piece of shit yellow vinyl couch and the other's telling me that you're trouble, that you may be, in fact, the agent of my death."

She looks like someone's sister, the way she walks in with her shoulders pushed back and her purse dangling from her hand by a shiny satin ribbon. Her skirt is long in that old-fashioned hippie way of wives who've given up caring if anyone knows what's underneath. But the skirt isn't what I notice first. It's her tits, of course, which are bound up, lifted and pushed out by some kind of witchy corset peeking out of her see-through black top. They are creamy and pale and lovely and, I know—I know this like I know the shape of my own face when I shave it—I'm going to see them in their full, up-close, delicious, and possibly suffocating glory.

But years of practice have allowed me to cover well and I am looking at her face before she even knows that I was staring at her tits.

"So, young lady," I say. "Where's your backstage pass?"

She laughs and it is a knowing little laugh. I give her a smile. It hurts that the stage manager didn't even give enough of a shit to run interference. And really, what else did he have to do? We sold only about ten tickets over the number needed to keep the show on the schedule.

"You probably think I do this all the time," she says, following the script. Her hair is brown like her irises. She hasn't bothered to make up her eyes, but the remainder of her face—with the exception of her russet lips—is covered with a thick layer of powder. The effect is freakish and theatrical, like she's one of those Japanese Kabuki guys made up to look like a woman. I think about what the kid's doing back at my mother's house in Mobile—sleeping, probably, or parked under the sheets with a flashlight reading a book. I get a mental image of this woman coming at him through the dark. She's hungry, this woman, and I know that she would eat him.

"You want a drink?" I say. I push the mess on the dressing table around until I come up with a sleeve of plastic cups. "Got 'em."

She smiles as I hand her a couple fingers of Wild Turkey.

She downs the whiskey without a breath, like she's taking medicine that she doesn't like, and holds out the cup for more. "You didn't want ice with that, anyway," I say.

She laughs again and it's a pretty laugh, a laugh that's supposed to put me at ease.

She tells me her name is Chloe and that she lives with her brother in a house not far from the theater, if I want to go there with her for some dinner, or maybe another drink.

Of course the voice—the one that's getting some quieter now that I've swallowed my own few fingers of the bird—wants me to show her the door and then hang around in the dressing room long enough for her to give up and go away, or at least until the stage manager kicks me out. But I tell the voice to shut the hell up and ask it did it see those tits.

"Will your brother be there?" I say. Then I realize it's kind of an asshole thing to say, like I'm worried I won't get to fuck her if he's there, and, if not, why should I go. "I mean, will I get to meet him, too, Chloe?"

She gives a dismissive shake of her head. "Oh, him," she says. "He's never around."

She helps me load up my bag and I try to forget how long it's been since I've had someone to do that shit for me. I grab my guitar case. As the stage manager lets us out the door to the alley, I mutter, "Fuck you very much." He doesn't hear me, but Chloe laughs.

Chloe's house has marble columns across the front of it twenty feet tall. Shrubbery cut into animal shapes comes at us out of the darkness like some giant baby's toys left outside. The air smells like sulfur and rain. In the distance, I hear sounds from a beach, some body of water. I try to remember what city I'm in, but as I step across the threshold of the front door, I give up. Chloe tells me that her great-great-great grandfather kept slaves and I believe her.

"Over here," she says.

We're in a room filled with books and she's dropped the blouse and the skirt and they're nowhere that I can see and she's wearing only the corset and she doesn't look half bad. If she's twenty-five or forty, I don't know because there's only light from the fireplace and I don't care, anyway. The voice is piping up, of course, telling me to keep my shit together and get the hell out of there, but I know it's only because I didn't drink enough of the bird. Then, I see the decanter on a table over by the fireplace and there looks to me to be whiskey in it and glasses standing by. She sees me looking and tells me to go ahead.

But even as I drink it, the voice is telling me that it's poison, some kind of witch's potion to go with her witch's costume—that leather and lace corset thing she's wearing, the only thing she's wearing—but I don't listen because it's been a long time since something even vaguely worth screwing showed up at a dressing room door. It doesn't matter if she's Dracula's second wife and six hundred years old, because, for fuck's sake, she's got those tits, and I don't care at that moment if they're attached to a three-legged cow.

I drink and it's sweet fire going down my throat and spreading in my gut. She drinks, letting it spill a little over her chin and onto those tits, and I lean close to her to lick the droplets off and I am grateful that she smells of powder and perfume and not like an old witch just pretending to be a woman with great tits.

She pulls me over in front of the fireplace where, it seems like only seconds before, there was a spread of sparkling tiles on the floor, blues and greens and gold flashing in the firelight, but now there's a bear rug—I shit you not—an actual hide of a bear that must've gone half a ton and eight feet tall. Its mouth is open and the glass eye that I can see looks murderous and I wonder if it's glass at all. The voice is screaming that it can't be, that the bearskin wasn't there when we came in. I tell it that of course it can be because she's a witch and witches can do anything and why the hell isn't it shutting up now because whatever was in the decanter is settling in just fine. I strip down, warmed by the booze and the heat from the fire.

Chloe—if that is her name, and I wouldn't put it past a witch to choose a name she thinks might please me, and it does somewhat please me—is soft. And I don't mean that she has baby-soft skin like in the commercials. Her flesh is so malleable that I'm afraid that if I grip her too tightly, I will leave impressions like I would in a pile of dough.

It's unkind to express disappointment when a woman offers herself the way the Chloe/witch/person has. I'm not an asshole like a lot of guys. A smile plays on her lips—those lips that are like the entrance to a dark, deep well nested in the powdered-white curves of her face—as she helps me unlace the corset. Our fingers tangle. Mine are shaking. When the thing finally opens and each side falls to the floor, her breasts, what there is of them, fall as well, and I see that I have been fooled.

It's tough to keep going in the face of such a deception. I think that a witch should be able to concoct herself a decent body, one that will stay together on inspection, one that doesn't disappoint.

The Chloe/witch/person doesn't seem to get what I'm thinking and she closes her eyes and makes little moaning noises like I'm doing something good to her. But I can barely bring myself to touch those sorry tits.

I make a go of it, thinking that I'll just do her and get out, that at least I can do that, because even though she's a witch, she's still a woman-witch and I've screwed a lot worse. But despite all the moaning she's doing, I find that she's not even ready for me and I can't get into her with all that dry, folded flesh between her legs. And that's the icing on the fucking cake, because who the hell needs that kind of rejection? Not that she'd gone into what a big fan she was or that she'd always fantasized about having me right here on her living room floor. Wasn't that implied? Wasn't that what the whole see-through shirt thing was all about? She's messing with my head is what she is doing. That's what witches do, and all of a sudden it's clear to me that she isn't the first witch to fool me. My erection dies.

When her eyes open, the voice tells me to look away from her, to just get up and put on my jeans, pick up my guitar and get the hell out of there. It doesn't want me to look into the witch's eyes. I think the voice is afraid.

"What?" the witch says.

"You know what," I tell her.

"What happened to you?"

Her witch's mouth is serious, but her eyes are wide and glittering and I can hear the laughter that's hiding behind them and the voice is telling me not to listen to it, but it gets louder and louder and drowns out the voice. It's witchy, cartoon laughter, like a Halloween gag. The noise makes me cover my ears.

She reaches for me and now her mouth is open and I can see inside, deep, deep inside, all the way to her rotting core and I know that she is trying to devour me, to bite into my flesh. I think that if I let her, maybe she will not bother my boy—even though he's far away, I know that he's not safe, because she is a witch and she only has to think about being with him and she will be there. But I know I will die if those teeth touch me. I feel I'm dying already from the laughter, that it's eating the inside of my head.

I look away to the fire, hoping, praying that by looking away, the noise will stop. It doesn't.

When I reach for the iron poker leaning against the fireplace, there's a break in the laughter, a pause like a breath in which both the laughter and the voice are silent and I know in that one clear moment that I'm doing the only thing that can save the boy and myself.

I push the witch back onto the bearskin with my free hand and jam the poker into her open mouth, working, working it into the back of her throat until it rests in the rotting, shuddering flesh.

There is blood on my arms and I can feel it, wet on my face, but it doesn't matter because the only sound I hear is of the popping of the wood in the fireplace. Gargoyles leer down at me from their perches on the mantelpiece, and the shadows of the room are long and black. My eyes have been opened. I can finally see the world as it really is, and what I see makes me afraid. I want to get away from the witch, away from this evil place.

I look for my clothes, but the witch has hidden them. Away from the fire, I'm cold and I start to worry that I'll never find them. I'm about to go out to check the front hallway—could I have been in such a hurry to sleep with *that thing* that I had undressed there?—when I see the brother standing in the open doorway.

In silhouette, his head is enormous and shaggy, his shoulders sloping down, down into the heavy cloak he's wearing despite the temperature outdoors. We're frozen there together in time, the distance between us vast, the tiles on the floor shining like a silvery lake that neither one of us wants to cross. Then the quiet is broken by a small whimpering sound, a pitiful sound that reminds me of one the boy would make when he was small and was tired or had a tummy ache. And I can't believe it, but the sound is coming from the brother, which is fucking weird because he's so big—six-four or five—and I can see what they call evening clothes peeking out from the cloak and it's not a man's sound at all. He takes a step forward into the room and I think he's coming for me and I go into a half-crouch, set to run. But he's not even looking at me. Now that he's closer, the light from the fire hits his face, and I can see that it's scarred like he got the worst in some ancient fight: jagged stripes of raised flesh stretch across his cheek to his jaw, and one of his eyebrows has been torn away. The hand he raises to his face is more like a paw with the stubs of the fingers fused together and I know that he's not a man, but he's some kind of animal. His parents—his and the witch's—they must have been beasts from Hell, and I'm flooded with a sense of their vile rutting in the very room where I stand as though I'm in some kind of fucking sty or barn, and doesn't that make me an animal, too? I have lain with the witch/beast, or at least had her vile tongue in my mouth, my mouth on her breasts.

Still making that awful, mournful sound, the brother/beast moves silently to where the witch lies on the floor, and I see that he is as much lion as he is man.

I watch as he kneels beside his sister and touches her hair tenderly. His sad eyes (black, black eyes with only the barest hint of white at their corners) turn to me as he opens his mouth and twists his head to the side to clench the shaft of the poker in his teeth. He rests one hand/paw against the shaft to steady it as he struggles to wrest the thing free of her and I think that it should be easier given that the witch's flesh was so rotten. (Why, then, had she smelled so nice? Why hadn't I been able to tell that she was rotten as I tasted her? Because she was a fucking witch, that's why.) Two streams of saliva—a long one that makes contact with the witch's bloodied chest, and a shorter one that ends in mid-air—hang from the beast's lips. As he tugs, grunting deep in his throat, he watches me, and I know he wants me to see what he's doing, how tough it is for him. For the briefest of seconds I think I might go over and give him a hand, but I'm still not stupid.

Finally, he gets the thing free, jerking his head so that the poker flies against a giant copper firewood bucket and makes a clanging sound that echoes through the room, a sound that gets louder and louder like some bastard is ringing one of those big temple gongs right beside my ear. The entire house begins to ring—I can feel it around me—and the floor vibrates under my bare feet.

I am afraid again—but I'd be lying if I said I hadn't been afraid right along, ever since I walked into this hell house.

The beast/brother throws his head back and lets out a roar that makes my fucking blood shoot through my veins like a jolt of fine horse. And I know there's something magical, something demonic, something really fucking *wrong* about this ringing and roaring because the witch/beast sits straight up like something out of a Boris Karloff movie and turns her face to the brother and smiles at him even though she looks like an exploded stromboli sandwich from her upper lip to her tits. She looks at me, and the beast/brother who looks satisfied that he's done his job does, too, and I finally understand that the voice, which shows no sign of speaking up again, wasn't messing with me, that I should've just let this witch/beast/woman wait at the dressing room door until we were both rotting corpses.

They make no move toward me, but only stare, the witch/beast's eyes as black as her brother's.

I run for the front door.

If this isn't real life, but the kind of horror film I can't wait to take the kid to when he's older, the door will lock itself about two seconds before my hand reaches out to touch the knob, but I count *one, two* and the door pulls open so quickly that I nearly hit myself with it. As I run down the pile of steps, they crumble under my bare feet, and I try again to remember what the hell city I'm in, but I can't think. I can't think. There's laughter far behind me, that same witch's laughter and I know I haven't killed her. Maybe she was never alive.

I look back at the open door because I can't help myself and I expect to see her standing there. But there's only darkness, like the darkness in her witch's mouth.

All around me are massive houses like the witch's, probably portals to other hells, but I tell myself that's a crazy thought and for a moment I want the stupid voice to come back because now my head is just full of echoes of that laughter and a weird kind of fuzziness that I remember from when I was a kid and I had scarlet fever. I keep my head down, not wanting to look into the windows of the houses I pass because whatever's living there might come out and drag me inside. But how could I stop the people, the *things* in the houses if, when you jab a poker into one of their sorry-ass throats, they don't even die? Even the cops with those little Glocks they're so fond of couldn't stop one.

This bugs me. The witch can't die. But I can. And the boy is more vulnerable than I am.

Whoever is in the car coming toward me either doesn't see me on the sidewalk or is trying to fool me, because they don't slow down. The laughter follows me. I walk faster. I'm not safe.

I like being without my clothes. I like the way the air passes over my skin, between my legs. I can taste the air, which is no longer sulfury, but over-sweet, like rotting fruit. *This is how animals live. I will tell the boy.*

Here come two girls at me, their dark faces shining in the streetlamp light. Black girls never liked my music except for Deirdre, who used to tease me that I looked like that Nelson brother, the one who died, the one she said her mother, who had a thing for "lame-ass white-boy singers," got in trouble for having a picture of when she was a kid. They push at each other and laugh when they see me—they are not afraid. I wonder what they will do if I bare my teeth or growl at them, so I do it just to get their reaction. It feels good, growling, and makes the hairs on my chest feel like they're standing at attention, but the girls just keep laughing and I know what they are. They keep coming toward me, daring me. *Go on, Freak Man*, one of them, the girl with a thousand braids shouts at me. Daring me. Daring me. Daring me. Still they walk wide of me, drifting into a yard at the edge of the sidewalk, but I feint at them—growling again because it feels so fucking good—and let them think that I won't really bother them, that I'm just some crazy, stoned bastard who doesn't like to wear clothes. They jump back but don't look away from my eyes. They think they're challenging me. But when they're past, they start giggling again and I know I've fooled them.

Those assholes who made fun of me as a kid because of my long skinny legs should see me now because it takes me only a couple of strides to reach the witches, the young witches who thought they could get by me, and I leap like a fucking cheetah and land on the back of the one with a thousand braids and we drop to the ground. She makes a comic-book sound under me *—oof!—* and I feel some part of her break beneath the leg I've wrapped around her, and my head is filled with the other witch's screaming and I try to get the witch/girl's shirt off because I want to get to her skin, I want to peel back that skin and see what kind of witch she is beneath it, but the thing is so fucking tight on her body that I can't get to it through all that hair and it makes me fucking mad! The other witch, the screaming one is kicking me now, in the side, in the jaw—*shit, shit, shit*—and it hurts like hell and I reach out for her foot to pull her off balance and try to keep the other one beneath me at the same time, but that one is moving now, trying to crawl away and I realize I've got an erection as big as a hog's leg and I push her down with it because it feels strong and I know I can do it. But the kicking, screaming witch shakes her leg loose and gets me between two ribs with one of her fucking pig sticker heels and for a second all I can think is *pigsticker, hogleg* and I wonder if it's a pig I'm turning into, but the thought doesn't last because the heel catches in my ribs and she falls down on the ground, but her fucking shoe stays inside me and it's my turn to scream.

Everything shuts down, focusing into one tiny dot of banshee screaming in my head.

When I come to, I'm alone. The damp grass is soft against my face, but the rest of my body feels like it's been pushed through a fucking meat grinder and squeezed back together again. I dreamed of hunting in the woods with my old man and raising his .30-.30 to take a shot, but I couldn't see the target clearly. He screamed at me, "Take the shot! Take the shot!" When I tried to pull the trigger, it turned into the belt from a woman's dress and I grabbed it and pulled, but nothing happened and I knew my old man was going to think I was some kind of pussy. And then I was in the kitchen of the house next door to my parents' and Cleta, the old woman who lived there, was shaking her head and pulling things from a barrel and sticking them in her purse. At first, I thought they were rotten apples, but I looked more closely and saw they were the shrunken heads of children and my old man was poking me with a stick, telling me to get along and take the shot. He poked and poked and that was how I woke up to realize the girl-witch's shoe was still stuck in my ribs.

I reach down to rip the thing away before I can change my mind. It's slick with blood, my own blood, and not the witch's, I'm sure. Just touching it sends a shockwave through my body, but I pull it out anyway because I'm not going to be able to save anyone with a fucking shoe in my side. I clench my teeth, trying not to scream. I do scream some, but I can't help it. I throw the thing into the shadows of the yard where I lie and press my hand against my side to keep the blood in.

Rest. What I need is rest. Maybe a doctor. Definitely a doctor. But there's no time because I have to find the boy. I can't see them, but I know Chloe, the witch/beast, and her brother are looking for us. When I turn my head a certain way, I can hear the witch/beast laughing loud and clear again, like I'm some kind of psychic radio.

In the house behind me, there are lights on, but no one comes outside. I limp over to where one of the witch-girls has dropped her purse and a long gauzy scarf that sparkles with hundreds of tiny rhinestones like the ones David Bowie used to have on his weirder costumes and I think that this gauze stuff must be peculiar to witches, and that David Bowie may even have been one of them all along and we never knew it.

I wrap the scarf around my ribs, pulling it as tight as I can. Through it, I touch the hole in my side. Fucking witch. She wants me to bleed to death.

When I open the purse, its flowery stench makes my stomach roil. Inside, there's a busted bottle of perfume, its glass so fragile that it crumbles between my fingertips. I toss what I can onto the ground. There's a cell phone, a couple of condoms, a tube of lip gloss, and a lighter, but no cigarettes, which is a damned shame. I shut the purse and put the strap over my neck and work one of my arms through. I head toward the sound of the water.

The witch/wife tried to take the boy once before. He was a tiny thing then and she hid him in a bag she carried, telling my mother that he was sleeping in his bed, and, of course, my mother believed her because that's the sort of trusting person she is. But they weren't hard to find. The witch/wife always goes to water to try to hide herself, thinking that the water is big and noisy and blue and safe for witches like her. She was wrong that time, as she's wrong this time. I found them three days later in the pool house of some rich bastard who'd fallen for the softness of her silky witch hair and tricks of her hands. The boy had to stay in the hospital two days because she hadn't given him enough to drink.

Dark. The whole damned city is dark. Everyone's hiding behind their windows, watching me. I know they can't hear me—no shoes, no sound. A dog, a white-faced cur, trots out of an alley, looking straight ahead, but it notices me and stops, baring its yellowed teeth, one fang missing. I stare it down, and it rolls onto its back. When I see the rows of black teats, I think of all those young girls who did the same for me for all those years and I wonder if this bitch was once one of them.

I keep close to the walls of the ugly brick buildings lining the road above the beach. Across the asphalt and sand, I see a row of five bungalows, but only one has a light on inside, and I know I'm in the right place. I hear the screech of some night bird, some freakish thing fishing the angry black waves in the darkness.

The street is brightly lighted, and I don't want to cross it, even though I can hear the laughter behind me. My eyes crave the dark, now. When I look at the light it burns, and I want to curl into a ball in some warm place and close my eyes and let them rest. I think of the witch's house, the warmth of the witch's fire. If they find me, they will take me back there, I know, and they will force me to watch them feast on the boy.

"Garrett, look!"

A boy of about twelve stands over me, his black hair falling into his eyes. In his hands are a long metal rod and a plastic bag full of stones and shells. Why am I on the ground, looking up at him? I put my hand out to balance and I see that it's covered in blood. Fucking witch and her fucking shoe!

"Check out this bozo," the one who isn't Garrett says. A second boy comes around a corner to stare at me.

I recognize the shape of him silhouetted against the streetlamp. I try to say his name, but only a gurgling sound comes out. I think of the lion/brother/witch and the roar from deep in his furred chest.

"Where are your clothes, asshole?" the first boy says. He pokes at my knee with the rod. "Some kind of crazy drunk."

No man should have to bear being called a crazy drunk in front of his only son. I grab the rod with a speed that astonishes even me and jerk the boy toward me so that he falls. As he lands on me, I'm overcome by the boy-smell of him: sour chewing gum, sweat, peanut butter, salty earth.

Frantic, he pushes at me to get up, landing one of his filthy hands on the soaking scarf wrapped around my ribs and I finally find my voice.

"Wait!" I scream after the other boy, my boy. He is running, running, and I have to go after him.

I pick up the rod, ignoring the nasty little fuck who is crawling away like a scared, piss-ant dog.

My boy is fast. He gets that from me.

I'm not worried, because I know that he's headed for the bungalow on the beach, the one with the light. He is safe. Almost.

The metal rod is sturdy and tries to bury itself into the sandy soil as I walk. My progress is slow, which means I might be toast before I can even reach him, but I have to take the chance.

Coming up the steps of the bungalow's tiny front deck, I can see the place is in bad shape. The witch/slut/wife was never any kind of housekeeper. I take the steps carefully because I don't know what the witch/slut/wife might have lying in wait for me.

I trip on a pile of tarp lying on the peeling floorboards. When it moves, I lift the edge of it with the rod. A cat, a seal-point Siamese, raises its blue marble eyes to me. Its mouth is purple with the guts of the animal that lies ripped open, shredded, beneath it. As I crouch down to see what it is, the pain in my own gut forces me all the way to my knees. The Siamese watches. I tug on an undamaged paw of the dead thing to pull it into the light.

It's a second cat. Male or female, it's too late to tell. There's something about the jeweled red and purple and the bloody aroma of the feast in its cavity that makes me want to put my mouth to it to taste it. But I cannot. Not yet.

The door in front of me opens, and the cat shoots past me, into the scrub around the deck.

"I'll show you there ain't nobody out here," says a voice from the doorway. But the woman sees me and we regard each other for a moment—she with a mute look of surprise on her ugly, old face. So, this is what the witch/slut/wife has become? A shrew in baggy orange shorts and a soiled white hoodie, wrinkled mouth stretched into a slack "O" of surprise. Her hair is different, and where are the stunning breasts she once so proudly strutted across titty stages and slick-topped bars all over Georgia and Alabama?

But she's a witch, the voice says. *She can be anything!*

"Yes," I say, and throw myself at her before she can shut the door in my face.

It's right that the boy doesn't see me kill his mother. I push myself up off of the witch/slut/wife, bringing the stick with me.

I don't have much time. I am dying and they are coming.

The house is a mess of pizza boxes and soiled clothes. The vile, human smell of it assaults me. I make my way, hands and feet to the floor. The remnant carpet is slick beneath my fingers and toes.

I can bear the smell of the boy. He is my own.

I call his name.

"Come out," I tell him, but he doesn't answer. I smell his fear, and it makes me sad.

That first night, the night the witch/slut/wife gave birth to him, I carried him up to the roof of the hospital—stole him, really, but he was my son, and my business and mine to do with whatever the hell I chose. I held him to the sky so he could see the stars that fell one, two, four at a time, some scheduled shower that my manager had told me about, and I can't believe I remembered he'd even told me because I had been stoned out of my mind. What a stupid asshole of a man I was—a worthless human. The boy was in danger up there, wrapped in the hospital's thin blanket and held only by my shaking hands. I held him up like an offering to God, so that God himself could see what he'd sent through the fetid canal of the witch/slut/wife (though I didn't know what she was then, even though the voice had warned me—oh, yes, it had warned me).

But even as I offered him up, the stars stopped falling, and I knew there was something wrong. And now I know that I was not worthy to make the offering. I wonder if I have made myself worthy, now.

"Come out," I say, again.

The room is empty but for a bed and a bureau with a guitar

leaning against it. I recognize the guitar for what it is, but I know my hands cannot play it anymore, because animals know nothing of music. The boy has been playing, though, and I wonder why he hasn't told me.

I smell the urine from the closet.

Stay the fuck away from the kid, the voice in my head says.

But I want to see him, want to touch him, want to hold him against me, shelter him from that other death—the one that's coming.

"Shut up!" I scream at the voice.

When I hear the laughter from the living room, I know the witch has found me and it's almost too late.

Stay the fuck away from the kid, the voice says, again, not in my head this time.

It pains me to turn around, and the room seems to turn with me, its shabby, unpainted walls melting into waves.

Looking up, I see the witch, the lower half of her jaw completely gone, now, her eyes alive, but empty. The brother seems to support her, as though she is failing, but he's truly angry now, and his mouth is purple and I know that he has finished the cat's snack on the porch and I'm a little jealous because I am hungry. There is a third beast with them, a wretched, red-nosed dwarf with fur growing from his long ears and a suit so tight that it might have belonged to a small child. The dwarf has a gun, a small Glock, the kind the cops are so fond of.

The voice says, *Close your eyes,* just before the shot enters my chest, at the bud of the thorny rose tattooed over my right nipple. I'm thrown back against the bureau—just like in the movies—and I fall over the guitar, and the feel of the strings against my skin is familiar, almost a comfort.

I open my eyes to see the witch pushing the dwarf out of the way, so she can reach me first, and I think about that deceitful corset she wore, and how I was fooled. But as she lowers her shattered, hungry face to the wound in my chest, I am hopeful that my flesh will sate the beasts, that the boy will be safe.

William Gay

The Paperhanger

The vanishing of the doctor's wife's child in broad daylight was an event so cataclysmic that it forever divided time into the then and the now, the before and the after. In later years, fortified with a pitcher of silica-dry vodka martinis, she had cause to replay the events preceding the disappearance. They were tawdry and banal but in retrospect freighted with menace, a foreshadowing of what was to come, like a footman or a fool preceding a king into a room.

She had been quarreling with the paperhanger. Her four-year-old daughter, Zeineb, was standing directly behind the paperhanger where he knelt smoothing air bubbles out with a wide plastic trowel. Zeineb had her fingers in the paperhanger's hair. The paperhanger's hair was shoulder length and the color of flax and the child was delighted with it. The paperhanger was accustomed to her doing this and he did not even turn around. He just went on with his work. His arms were smooth and brown and corded with muscle and in the light that fell upon the paperhanger through stained-glass panels the doctor's wife could see that they were lightly downed with fine golden hair. She studied these arms bemusedly while she formulated her thoughts.

You tell me so much a roll, she said. The doctor's wife was from Pakistan and her speech was still heavily accented. I do not know single-bolt rolls and double-bolt rolls. You tell me double-bolt price but you are installing single-bolt rolls. My friend has told me. It is cost me perhaps twice as much.

The paperhanger, still on his knees, turned. He smiled up at her. He had pale blue eyes. I did tell you so much a roll, he said. You bought the rolls.

The child, not yet vanished, was watching the paperhanger's eyes. She was a scaled-down clone of the mother, the mother viewed through the wrong end of a telescope, and the paperhanger suspected that as she grew neither her features nor her expression would alter, she would just grow larger, like something being aired up with a hand pump.

And you are leave lumps, the doctor's wife said, gesturing at the wall.

I do not leave lumps, the paperhanger said. You've seen my work before. These are not lumps. The paper is wet. The paste is wet. Everything will shrink down and flatten out. He smiled again. He had clean even teeth. And besides, he said, I gave you my special cockteaser rate. I don't know what you're complaining about.

Her mouth worked convulsively. She looked for a moment as if he'd slapped her. When words did come they came in a fine spray of spit. You are trash, she said. You are scum.

Hands on knees, he was pushing erect, the girl's dark fingers trailing out of his hair. Don't call me trash, he said, as if it were perfectly all right to call him scum, but he was already talking to her back. She had whirled on her heels and went twisting her hips through an arched doorway into the cathedraled living room. The paperhanger looked down at the child. Her face glowed with a strange constrained glee, as if she and the paperhanger shared some secret the rest of the world hadn't caught on to yet.

In the living room the builder was supervising the installation of a chandelier that depended from the vaulted ceiling by a long golden chain. The builder was a short bearded man dancing about, showing her the features of the chandelier, smiling obsequiously. She gave him a flat angry look. She waved a dismissive hand toward the ceiling. Whatever, she said.

She went out the front door onto the porch and down a makeshift walkway of two-by-tens into the front yard where her car was parked. The car was a silver-gray Mercedes her husband had given her for their anniversary. When she cranked the engine its idle was scarcely perceptible.

She powered down the window. Zeineb, she called. Across the razed earth of the unlandscaped yard a man in a grease-stained T-shirt was booming down the chains securing a backhoe to a lowboy hooked to a gravel truck. The sun was low in the west and bloodred behind this tableau and man and tractor looked flat and dimensionless as something decorative stamped from tin. She blew the horn. The man turned, raised an arm as if she'd signaled him.

Zeineb, she called again.

She got out of the car and started impatiently up the walkway. Behind her the gravel truck started, and truck and backhoe pulled out of the drive and down toward the road.

The paperhanger was stowing away his T square and trowels in his wooden toolbox. Where is Zeineb? the doctor's wife asked. She followed you out, the paperhanger told her. He glanced about, as if the girl might be hiding somewhere. There was nowhere to hide.

Where is my child? she asked the builder. The electrician climbed down from the ladder. The paperhanger came out of the bathroom with his tools. The builder was looking all around. His elfin features were touched with chagrin, as if this missing child were just something else he was going to be held accountable for.

Likely she's hiding in a closet, the paperhanger said. Playing a trick on you.

Zeineb does not play tricks, the doctor's wife said. Her eyes kept darting about the huge room, the shadows that lurked in corners. There was already an undercurrent of panic in her voice and all her poise and self-confidence seemed to have vanished with the child.

The paperhanger set down his toolbox and went through the house, opening and closing doors. It was a huge house and there were a lot of closets. There was no child in any of them.

The electrician was searching upstairs. The builder had gone through the French doors that opened onto the unfinished veranda and was peering into the backyard. The backyard was a maze of convoluted ditch excavated for the septic tank field line and beyond that there was just woods. She's playing in that ditch, the builder said, going down the flagstone steps.

She wasn't, though. She wasn't anywhere. They searched the

house and grounds. They moved with jerky haste. They kept glancing toward the woods where the day was waning first. The builder kept shaking his head. She's got to be somewhere, he said.

Call someone, the doctor's wife said. Call the police.

It's a little early for the police, the builder said. She's got to be here.

You call them anyway. I have a phone in my car. I will call my husband.

While she called, the paperhanger and the electrician continued to search. They had looked everywhere and were forced to search places they'd already looked. If this ain't the goddamnedest thing I ever saw, the electrician said.

The doctor's wife got out of the Mercedes and slammed the door. Suddenly she stopped and clasped a hand to her forehead. She screamed. The man with the tractor, she cried. Somehow my child is gone with the tractor man.

Oh Jesus, the builder said. What have we got ourselves into here.

The high sheriff that year was a ruminative man named Bellwether. He stood beside the county cruiser talking to the paperhanger while deputies ranged the grounds. Other men were inside looking in places that had already been searched numberless times. Bellwether had been in the woods and he was picking cocklebus off his khakis and out of his socks. He was watching the woods, where dark was gathering and seeping across the field like a stain.

I've got to get men out here, Bellwether said. A lot of men and a lot of lights. We're going to have to search every inch of these woods.

You'll play hell doing it, the paperhanger said. These woods stretch all the way to Lawrence County. This is the edge of the Harrikin. Down in there's where all those old mines used to be. Aliens Creek.

I don't give a shit if they stretch all the way to Fairbanks,

Alaska, Bellwether said. They've got to be searched. It'll just take a lot of men.

The raw earth yard was full of cars. Dr. Jamahl had come in a sleek black Lexus. He berated his wife. Why weren't you watching her? he asked. Unlike his wife's, the doctor's speech was impeccable. She covered her face with her palms and wept. The doctor still wore his green surgeon's smock and it was flecked with bright dots of blood as a butcher's smock might be.

I need to feed a few cows, the paperhanger said. I'll feed my stock pretty quick and come back and help hunt.

You don't mind if I look in your truck, do you?

Do what?

I've got to cover my ass. If that little girl don't turn up damn quick this is going to be over my head. TBI, FBI, network news. I've got to eliminate everything.

Eliminate away, the paperhanger said.

The sheriff searched the floorboard of the paperhanger's pickup truck. He shined his huge flashlight under the seat and felt behind it with his hands.

I had to look, he said apologetically.

Of course you did, the paperhanger said.

Full dark had fallen before he returned. He had fed his cattle and stowed away his tools and picked up a six-pack of San Miguel beer and he sat in the back of the pickup truck drinking it. The paperhanger had been in the Navy and stationed in the Philippines and San Miguel was the only beer he could drink. He had to go out of town to buy it, but he figured it was worth it. He liked the exotic labels, the dark bitter taste on the back of his tongue, the way the chilled bottles felt held against his forehead.

A motley crowd of curiosity seekers and searchers thronged the yard. There was a vaguely festive air. He watched all this with a dispassionate eye, as if he were charged with grading the participants, comparing this with other spectacles he'd seen. Coffee urns had been brought in and set up on tables, sandwiches prepared and handed out to the weary searchers. A crane had been hauled in and the septic tank reclaimed from the ground. It swayed from a taut cable while men with lights searched the impacted earth beneath it for a child, for the very trace of a child. Through the far dark woods lights crossed and recrossed, darted to and fro like fireflies. The doctor and the doctor's wife sat in folding camp chairs looking drained, stunned, waiting for their child to be delivered into their arms.

The doctor was a short portly man with a benevolent expression. He had a moon-shaped face, with light and dark areas of skin that looked swirled, as if the pigment coloring him had not been properly mixed. He had been educated at Princeton. When he had established his practice he had returned to Pakistan to find a wife befitting his station. The woman he had selected had been chosen on the basis of her beauty. In retrospect, perhaps more consideration should have been given to other qualities. She was still beautiful but he was thinking that certain faults might outweigh this. She seemed to have trouble keeping up with her children. She could lose a four-year-old child in a room no larger than six hundred square feet and she could not find it again.

The paperhanger drained his bottle and set it by his foot in the bed of the truck. He studied the doctor's wife's ravaged face through the deep blue light. The first time he had seen her she had hired him to paint a bedroom in the house they were living in while the doctor's mansion was being built. There was an arrogance about her that cried out to be taken down a notch or two. She flirted with him, backed away, flirted again. She would treat him as if he were a stain on the bathroom rug and then stand close by him while he worked until he was dizzy with the smell of her, with the heat that seemed to radiate off her body. She stood by him while he knelt painting baseboards and after an infinite moment leaned carefully the weight of a thigh against his shoulder. You'd better move it, he thought. She didn't. He laughed and turned his face into her groin. She gave a strangled cry and slapped him hard. The paintbrush flew away and speckled the dark rose walls with antique white. You filthy beast, she said. You are some kind of monster. She stormed out of the room and he could hear her slamming doors behind her.

Well, I was looking for a job when I found this one. He smiled philosophically to himself.

But he had not been fired. In fact now he had been hired again. Perhaps there was something here to ponder.

At midnight he gave up his vigil. Some souls more hardy than his kept up the watch. The earth here was worn smooth by the useless traffic of the searchers. Driving out, he met a line of pickup trucks with civil defense tags. Grim-faced men sat aligned in their beds. Some clutched rifles loosely by their barrels, as if they would lay to waste whatever monster, man or beast, would snatch up a child in its slaverous jaws and vanish, prey and predator, in the space between two heartbeats.

Even more dubious reminders of civilization as these fell away. He drove into the Harrikin, where he lived. A world so dark and forlorn light itself seemed at a premium. Whippoorwills swept red-eyed up from the roadside. Old abandoned foundries and furnaces rolled past, grim and dark as forsaken prisons. Down a ridge here was an abandoned graveyard, if you knew where to look. The paperhanger did. He had dug up a few of the graves, examined with curiosity what remained, buttons, belt buckles, a cameo brooch. The bones he laid out like a child with a Tinkertoy, arranging them the way they went in jury-rigged resurrection.

He braked hard on a curve, the truck slewing in the gravel. A bobcat had crossed the road, graceful as a wraith, fierce and lantern-eyed in the headlights, gone so swiftly it might have been a stage prop swung across the road on wires.

Bellwether and a deputy drove to the backhoe operator's house. He lived up a gravel road that wound through a great stand of cedars. He lived in a board-and-batten house with a tin roof rusted to a warm umber. They parked before it and got out, adjusting their gun belts.

Bellwether had a search warrant with the ink scarcely dry. The operator was outraged.

Look at it this way, Bellwether explained patiently. I've got to cover my ass. Everything has got to be considered. You know how kids are. Never thinking. What if she run under the wheels of your truck when you was backing out? What if quicklike you put the body in your truck to get rid of somewhere?

What if quicklike you get the hell off my property, the operator said.

Everything has to be considered, the sheriff said again. Nobody's accusing anybody of anything just yet.

The operator's wife stood glowering at them. To have something to do with his hands, the operator began to construct a cigarette. He had huge red hands thickly sown with brown freckles. They trembled. I ain't got a thing in this round world to hide, he said.

Bellwether and his men searched everywhere they could think of to look. Finally they stood uncertainly in the operator's yard, out of place in their neat khakis, their polished leather.

Now get the hell off my land, the operator said. If all you think of me is that I could run over a little kid and then throw it off in the bushes like a dead cat or something then I don't even want to see your goddamn face. I want you gone and I want you by God gone now.

Everything had to be considered, the sheriff said.

Then maybe you need to consider that paperhanger. What about him?

That paperhanger is one sick puppy.

He was still there when I got there, the sheriff said. Three witnesses swore nobody ever left, not even for a minute, and one of them was the child's mother. I searched his truck myself.

Then he's a sick puppy with a damn good alibi, the operator said.

That was all. There was no ransom note, no child that turned up two counties over with amnesia. She was a page turned, a door closed, a lost ball in the high weeds. She was a child no larger than a doll, but the void she left behind her was unreckonable. Yet there was no end to it. No finality. There was no moment when someone could say, turning from a mounded grave, Well, this has been unbearable, but you've got to go on with your life. Life did not go on.

At the doctor's wife's insistence an intensive investigation was focused on the backhoe operator. Forensic experts from the FBI examined every millimeter of the gravel truck, paying special attention to its wheels. They were examined with every modern crime-fighting device the government possessed, and there was not a microscopic particle of tissue or blood, no telltale chip of fingernail, no hair ribbon.

Work ceased on the mansion. Some subcontractors were discharged outright, while others simply drifted away. There was no one to care if the work was done, no one to pay them. The half-finished veranda's raw wood grayed in the fall, then winter, rains. The ditches were left fallow and uncovered and half filled with water. Kudzu crept from the woods. The hollyhocks and oleanders the doctor's wife had planted grew entangled and rampant. The imported windows were stoned by double-dared boys who whirled and fled. Already this house where a child had vanished was acquiring an unhealthy, diseased reputation.

The doctor and his wife sat entombed in separate prisons replaying real and imagined grievances. The doctor felt that his wife's neglect had sent his child into the abstract. The doctor's wife drank vodka martinis and watched talk shows where passed an endless procession of vengeful people who had not had children vanish, and felt, perhaps rightly, that the fates had dealt her from the bottom of the deck, and she prayed with intensity for a miracle.

Then one day she was just gone. The Mercedes and part of her clothing and personal possessions were gone too. He idly wondered where she was, but he did not search for her.

Sitting in his armchair cradling a great marmalade cat and a bottle of J&B and observing with bemused detachment the gradations of light at the window, the doctor remembered studying literature at Princeton. He had particular cause to reconsider the poetry of William Butler Yeats. For how surely things fell apart, how surely the center did not hold.

His practice fell into a ruin. His colleagues made sympathetic allowances for him at first, but there are limits to these things. He made erroneous diagnoses, prescribed the wrong medicines not once or twice but as a matter of course.

Just as there is a deepening progression to misfortune, so too there is a point beyond which things can only get worse. They did. A middle-aged woman he was operating on died.

He had made an incision to remove a ruptured appendix and the incised flesh was clamped aside while he made ready to slice it out. It was not there. He stared in drunken disbelief. He began to search under things, organs, intestines, a rising tide of blood. The appendix was not there. It had gone into the abstract, atrophied, been removed twenty-five years before, he had sliced through the selfsame scar. He was rummaging through her abdominal cavity like an irritated man fumbling through a drawer for a clean pair of socks, finally bellowing and wringing his hands in bloody vexation while nurses began to cry out, another surgeon was brought on the run as a closer, and he was carried from the operating room.

Came then days of sitting in the armchair while he was besieged by contingency lawyers, action news teams, a long line of process servers. There was nothing he could do. It was out of his hands and into the hands of the people who are paid to do these things. He sat cradling the bottle of J&B with the marmalade cat snuggled against his portly midriff. He would study the window, where the light drained away in a process he no longer had an understanding of, and sip the scotch and every now and then stroke the cat's head gently. The cat purred against his breast as reassuringly as the hum of an air conditioner.

He left in the middle of the night. He began to load his possessions into the Lexus. At first he chose items with a great degree of consideration. The first thing he loaded was a set of custom-made monogrammed golf clubs. Then his stereo receiver, Denon AC3, $1,750. A copy of *This Side of Paradise* autographed by Fitzgerald that he had bought as an investment. By the time the Lexus was half full he was just grabbing things at random and stuffing them into the backseat, a half-eaten pizza, half a case of cat food, a single brocade house shoe.

He drove west past the hospital, the country club, the city-limit sign. He was thinking no thoughts at all, and all the destination he had was the amount of highway the headlights showed him.

In the slow rains of late fall the doctor's wife returned to the unfinished mansion. She used to sit in a camp chair on the ruined veranda and drink chilled martinis she poured from the pitcher she carried in a foam ice chest. Dark fell early these November days. Rain crows husbanding some far cornfield called through the smoky autumn air. The sound was fiercely evocative, reminding her of something but she could not have said what.

She went into the room where she had lost the child. The light was failing. The high corners of the room were in deepening shadow but she could see the nests of dirt daubers clustered on the rich flocked wallpaper, a spider swing from a chandelier on a strand of spun glass. Some animal's dried blackened stool curled like a slug against the baseboards. The silence in the room was enormous.

One day she arrived and was surprised to find the paperhanger there. He was sitting on a yellow four-wheeler drinking a bottle of beer. He made to go when he saw her but she waved him back. Stay and talk with me, she said.

The paperhanger was much changed. His pale locks had been shorn away in a makeshift haircut as if scissored in the dark or by a blind barber and his cheeks were covered with a soft curly beard.

You have grown a beard.

Yes.

You are strange with it.

The paperhanger sipped from his San Miguel. He smiled. I was strange without it, he said. He arose from the four-wheeler and came over and sat on the flagstone steps. He stared across the mutilated yard toward the treeline. The yard was like a funhouse maze seen from above, its twistings and turnings bereft of mystery.

You are working somewhere now?

No. I don't take so many jobs anymore. There's only me, and I don't need much. What has become of the doctor?

She shrugged. Many things have change, she said. He has gone. The banks have foreclose. What is that you ride?

An ATV. A four-wheeler.

It goes well in the woods?

It was made for that.

You could take me in the woods. How much would you charge me?

For what?

To go in the woods. You could drive me. I will pay you.

Why?

To search for my child's body.

I wouldn't charge anybody anything to search for a child's body, the paperhanger said. But she's not in these woods. Nothing could have stayed hidden, the way these woods were searched.

Sometimes I think she just kept walking. Perhaps just walking away from the men looking. Far into the woods.

Into the woods, the paperhanger thought. If she had just kept walking in a straight line with no time out for eating or sleeping, where would she be? Kentucky, Algiers, who knew.

I'll take you when the rains stop, he said. But we won't find a child.

The doctor's wife shook her head. It is a mystery, she said. She drank from her cocktail glass. Where could she have gone? How could she have gone?

There was a man named David Lang, the paperhanger said. Up in Gallatin, back in the late 1800s. He was crossing a barn lot in full view of his wife and two children and he just vanished. Went into thin air. There was a judge in a wagon turning into the yard and he saw it too. It was just like he took a step in this world and his foot came down in another one. He was never seen again.

She gave him a sad smile, bitter and one-cornered. You make fun with me.

No. It's true. I have it in a book. I'll show you.

I have a book with dragons, fairies. A book where Hobbits live in the middle earth. They are lies. I think most books are lies. Perhaps all books. I have prayed for a miracle but I am not worthy of one. I have prayed for her to come from the dead, then just to find her body. That would be a miracle to me. There are no miracles.

She rose unsteadily, swayed slightly, leaning to take up the cooler. The paperhanger watched her. I have to go now, she said. When the rains stop we will search.

Can you drive?

Of course I can drive. I have drive out here.

I mean are you capable of driving now. You seem a little drunk.

I drink to forget but it is not enough, she said. I can drive.

After a while he heard her leave in the Mercedes, the tires spinning in the gravel drive. He lit a cigarette. He sat smoking it, watching the rain string off the roof. He seemed to be waiting for something. Dusk was falling like a shroud, the world going dark and formless the way it had begun. He drank the last of the beer, sat holding the bottle, the foam bitter in the back of his mouth. A chill touched him. He felt something watching him. He turned.

From the corner of the ruined veranda a child was watching him. He stood up. He heard the beer bottle break on the flagstones. The child went sprinting past the hollyhocks toward the brush at the edge of the yard, a tiny sepia child with an intent sloe-eyed face, real as she had ever been, translucent as winter light through dirty glass.

The doctor's wife's hands were laced loosely about his waist as they came down through a thin stand of sassafras, edging over the ridge where the ghost of a road was, a road more sensed than seen that faced into a half acre of tilting stones and fading granite tablets. Other graves marked only by their declivities in the earth, folk so far beyond the pale even the legibility of their identities had been leached away by the weathers.

Leaves drifted, huge poplar leaves veined with amber so golden they might have been coin of the realm for a finer world than this one. He cut the ignition of the four-wheeler and got off. Past the lowering trees the sky was a blue of an improbable intensity, a fierce cobalt blue shot through with dense golden light.

She slid off the rear and steadied herself a moment with a hand on his arm. Where are we? she asked. Why are we here?

The paperhanger had disengaged his arm and was strolling among the gravestones reading such inscriptions as were legible, as if he might find forebear or antecedent in this moldering earth. The doctor's wife was retrieving her martinis from the luggage carrier of the ATV. She stood looking about uncertainly. A graven angel with broken wings crouched on a truncated marble column like a gargoyle. Its stone eyes regarded her with a blind benignity. Some of these graves have been rob, she said.

You can't rob the dead, he said. They have nothing left to steal.

It is a sacrilege, she said. It is forbidden to disturb the dead. You have done this.

The paperhanger took a cigarette pack from his pocket and felt it, but it was empty, and he balled it up and threw it away. The line between grave robbing and archaeology has always looked a little blurry to me, he said. I was studying their culture, trying to get a fix on what their lives were like.

She was watching him with a kind of benumbed horror. Standing hip-slung and lost like a parody of her former self. Strange and anomalous in her fashionable but mismatched clothing, as if she'd put on the first garment that fell to hand. Someday, he thought, she might rise and wander out into the daylit world wearing nothing at all, the way she had come into it. With her diamond watch and the cocktail glass she carried like a used-up talisman.

You have broken the law, she told him.

I got a government grant, the paperhanger said contemptuously.

Why are we here? We are supposed to be searching for my child.

If you're looking for a body the first place to look is the graveyard, he said. If you want a book don't you go to the library?

I am paying you, she said. You are in my employ. I do not want to be here. I want you to do as I say or carry me to my car if you will not.

Actually, the paperhanger said, I had a story to tell you. About my wife.

He paused, as if leaving a space for her comment, but when

she made none he went on. I had a wife. My childhood sweetheart. She became a nurse, went to work in one of these drug rehab places. After she was there awhile she got a faraway look in her eyes. Look at me without seeing me. She got in tight with her supervisor. They started having meetings to go to. Conferences. Sometimes just the two of them would confer, generally in a motel. The night I watched them walk into the Holiday Inn in Franklin I decided to kill her. No impetuous spur-of-the-moment thing. I thought it all out and it would be the perfect crime.

The doctor's wife didn't say anything. She just watched him.

A grave is the best place to dispose of a body, the paperhanger said. The grave is its normal destination anyway. I could dig up a grave and then just keep on digging. Save everything carefully. Put my body there and fill in part of the earth, and then restore everything the way it was. The coffin, if any of it was left. The bones and such. A good settling rain and the fall leaves and you're home free. Now that's eternity for you.

Did you kill someone, she breathed. Her voice was barely audible.

Did I or did I not, he said. You decide. You have the powers of a god. You can make me a murderer or just a heartbroke guy whose wife quit him. What do you think? Anyway, I don't have a wife. I expect she just walked off into the abstract like that Lang guy I told you about.

I want to go, she said. I want to go where my car is.

He was sitting on a gravestone watching her out of his pale eyes. He might not have heard.

I will walk.

Just whatever suits you, the paperhanger said. Abruptly, he was standing in front of her. She had not seen him arise from the headstone or stride across the graves, but like a jerky splice in a film he was before her, a hand cupping each of her breasts, staring down into her face.

Under the merciless weight of the sun her face was stunned and vacuous. He studied it intently, missing no detail. Fine wrinkles crept from the corners of her eyes and mouth like hairline cracks in porcelain. Grime was impacted in her pores, in the crepe flesh of her throat. How surely everything had fallen from her: beauty, wealth, social position, arrogance. Humanity itself, for by now she seemed scarcely human, beleaguered so by the fates that she suffered his hands on her breasts as just one more cross to bear, one more indignity to endure.

How far you've come, the paperhanger said in wonder. I believe you're about down to my level now, don't you?

It does not matter, the doctor's wife said. There is no longer one thing that matters.

Slowly and with enormous lassitude her body slumped toward him, and in his exultance it seemed not a motion in itself but simply the completion of one begun long ago with the fateful weight of a thigh, a motion that began in one world and completed itself in another one.

From what seemed a great distance he watched her fall toward him like an angel descending, wings spread, from an infinite height, striking the earth gently, tilting, then righting itself.

The weight of moonlight tracking across the paperhanger's face awoke him from where he took his rest. Filigrees of light through the gauzy curtains swept across him in stately silence like the translucent ghosts of insects. He stirred, lay still then for a moment getting his bearings, a fix on where he was.

He was in his bed, lying on his back. He could see a huge orange moon poised beyond the bedroom window, ink-sketch tree branches that raked its face like claws. He could see his feet book-ending the San Miguel bottle that his hands clasped erect on his abdomen, the amber bottle hard-edged and defined against the pale window, dark atavistic monolith reared against a harvest moon.

He could smell her. A musk compounded of stale sweat and alcohol, the rank smell of her sex. Dissolution, ruin, loss. He turned to study her where she lay asleep, her open mouth a dark cavity in her face. She was naked, legs outflung, pale breasts pooled like cooling wax. She stirred restively, groaned in her sleep. He could hear the rasp of her breathing. Her breath was fetid on his face, corrupt, a graveyard smell. He watched her in disgust, in a dull self-loathing.

He drank from the bottle, lowered it. Sometimes, he told her sleeping face, you do things you can't undo. You break things you just can't fix. Before you mean to, before you know you've done it. And you were right, there are things only a miracle can set to rights.

He sat clasping the bottle. He touched his miscut hair, the soft down of his beard. He had forgotten what he looked like, he hadn't seen his reflection in a mirror for so long. Unbidden, Zeineb's face swam into his memory. He remembered the look on the child's face when the doctor's wife had spun on her heel: spite had crossed it like a flicker of heat lightning. She stuck her tongue out at him. His hand snaked out like a serpent and closed on her throat and snapped her neck before he could call it back, sloe eyes wild and wide, pink tongue caught between tiny seed-pearl teeth like a bitten-off rosebud. Her hair swung sidewise, her head lolled onto his clasped hand. The tray of the toolbox was out before he knew it, he was stuffing her into the toolbox like a rag doll. So small, so small, hardly there at all.

He arose. Silhouetted naked against the moon-drenched window, he drained the bottle. He looked about for a place to set it, leaned and wedged it between the heavy flesh of her upper thighs. He stood in silence, watching her. He seemed philosophical, possessed of some hard-won wisdom. The paperhanger knew so well that while few are deserving of a miracle, fewer still can make one come to pass.

He went out of the room. Doors opened, doors closed. Footsteps softly climbing a staircase, descending. She dreamed on. When he came back into the room he was cradling a plastic-wrapped bundle stiffly in his arms. He placed it gently beside the drunk woman. He folded the plastic sheeting back like a caul.

What had been a child. What the graveyard earth had spared the freezer had preserved. Ice crystals snared in the hair like windy snowflakes whirled there, in the lashes. A doll from a madhouse assembly line.

He took her arm, laid it across the child. She pulled away from the cold. He firmly brought the arm back, arranging them like mannequins, madonna and child. He studied this tableau, then went out of his house for the last time. The door closed gently behind him on its keeper spring.

The paperhanger left in the Mercedes, heading west into the open country, tracking into wide-open territories he could infect like a malignant spore. Without knowing it, he followed the selfsame route the doctor had taken some eight months earlier, and in a world of infinite possibilities where all journeys share a common end, perhaps they are together, taking the evening air on a ruined veranda among the hollyhocks and oleanders, the doctor sipping his scotch and the paperhanger his San Miguel, gentlemen of leisure discussing the vagaries of life and pondering deep into the night not just the possibility but the inevitability of miracles.

Joy Beshears Hagy

Silver Man

He is silver before I ever get hold of him. Silver by his design. Metallic body paint in every nook and cranny. Robotic save the movements, which are round and smooth and bosom and hips. Aluminum bustier. Tin bootie shorts. Steel platforms. Disco-ball earrings swinging. Whistle ringing loud enough, siren singing. He looks and I wink, take him into the stall. He passes me a twenty spot. Open your mouth, I tell him, and his tongue unfurls like a red carpet. I grab him by the chin, raise the dropper, squirt a puddle in his mouth. They take him away in an ambulance, twirling, prancing in his shit-streaked underwear, sparkling.

Joy Beshears Hagy

Dinner Date

Ted Bundy arrives to pick me up before I can shave my legs, rings the doorbell with his left hand (his cast is on his right). I pop a pill before I answer. I open the door, red curls radiating and take his good hand, smiling pearly white fangs and thinking how I'm too hungry to wait for dinner. How nobody'd even miss him. How the crime rate would drop. How young ladies would be safer.

Greg Johnson

Crazy Ladies

Every Southern town had one, and ours was no exception. One year, my sister and I had an after-school routine that included watching the Mouseketeers on TV, holding court in the neighborhood treehouse we'd built, along with several other kids, in a vacant lot down the street, and finally, as dusk began and we knew our mother would soon be calling us to supper, visiting the big ramshackle house where the crazy lady lived. Often she'd be eating her own supper of tuna fish and bean salad, sitting silently across from her bachelor son, John Ray, who was about the same age as our parents. Becky would slither along through the hydrangea bushes, then scrunch down so I could stand on her shoulders and get my eyes and forehead—just barely—over the sill of the Longworths' dining-room window. After a few minutes I'd get down and serve as a footstool for Becky. More often than not we dissolved into a laughter so uncontrollable that we had to race back through the bushes, snapping branches as we went, and then dart around the corner of the house to avoid being caught by John Ray, who sometimes heard us and would jump up from the table, then come fuming out the back door. He never did catch us, and to my knowledge was never quick enough even to discover who we were. Naturally his mother didn't know, and didn't care. But there came a time—that summer afternoon, the year Becky was thirteen and I was eleven—when the crazy lady took her obscene revenge.

For me, that entire summer was puzzling. Our father, the town druggist, had begun keeping unusual hours. We could no longer count on his kindly, slump-shouldered presence at the supper table, and when he did join us there was a crackling energy in him, a playfulness toward Becky and me that he'd never shown when we were younger. And while our father, a balding and slightly overweight man in his forties, had taken on this sudden, nervous gaiety, our mother underwent an alarming change of her own. Her normally delicate features, framed by fine, wavy auburn hair, had paled to the point of haggardness. There was a new brusqueness in her manner—she scrubbed the house with a grim ferocity, she made loud clattering noises when she worked in the kitchen—and also a certain inattention toward her children, a tendency to focus elsewhere when she talked to us, or to fall into sudden reveries. This bothered me more than it did Becky, for it seemed that even she was changing. In the fall she'd be starting junior high, and she'd begun calling me "Little Brother" (with a slight wrinkling of her nose) and spending long hours alone in her bedroom. All through childhood we'd been inseparable, and Becky had always been called a tomboy by the neighborhood kids, even by our parents; but now she'd started curling her hair and painting her stubby nails, gingerly paging through movie magazines while they dried. What was wrong with everyone? I wanted to ask—but when you're eleven, of course, you can't translate your puzzlement into words. For a long while I stayed bewildered, feeling that the others had received a new set of instructions on how to live, but had forgotten to pass them along to me.

One humid afternoon in August, the telephone rang; from the living room, we could hear our mother snatch up the kitchen extension.

"What?" she said loudly, irritated. "Slow down, Mother, I can't make out—"

At that point she called to us to turn down the TV; from my place on the floor I reached quickly and switched the volume completely off, earning a little groan from Becky. She sat cross-legged on the couch with a towel wrapped tightly around her head, like a turban. We'd been watching *American Bandstand*.

"*You* turn it up," I said, with the same defiant smirk she'd begun using on me.

"Hush," Becky whispered, leaning forward. "I think something's wrong with Grandma."

We sat quietly, listening. Our mother's voice had become shrill, incredulous.

"Why did you let her in?" she cried. "You know she's not supposed to—"

A long silence. Whenever our mother was interrupted, Becky and I exchanged a puzzled look.

"Listen, just call John Ray down at the bank. The operator, Mother—she'll give you the number. Oh, I know you're nervous, but—Yes, you can if you try. Call John Ray, then go back in the living room and be nice to her. Give her something to eat. Or some coffee."

Silently, Becky mouthed the words to me: *the crazy lady.*

I nodded, straining to hear our mother's voice. She sounded weary.

"All right, I'll call Bert," she said, sighing. "We'll get there as soon as we can."

When she stopped talking, Becky and I raced into the kitchen.

"What is it, Mama?" Becky asked, excited. "Is it—"

"It's Mrs. Longworth," Mother said. Absent-mindedly, she fiddled with my shirt collar, then looked over at Becky. "She's gotten out of the house again, and somehow ended up in your grandmother's living room." Briefly, she laughed. She shook her head. "Anyway, I've got to call your father. We'll meet him over there."

But what had the crazy lady done? we asked. *Why was Grandma so frightened? Why were we all going over there?* Mother ignored our questions. Calmly she dialed the pharmacy, setting her jaw as though preparing to do something distasteful.

Within five minutes we were in the car, making the two-mile drive to Grandma Howell's. Dad was already there when we arrived, but he hadn't gone inside.

"Well, what's going on?" Mother asked him. She sounded angry, as if Dad were to blame for all this.

He looked sheepish, apprehensive. He always perspired heavily, and I noticed the film covering his balding forehead, the large damp circles at his armpits. He wore the pale blue, regulation shirt, with *Denson Pharmacy—Bert Denson, Mgr.* stitched above the pocket, but he'd removed his little black bow tie and opened his collar.

"I just got here," Dad said, helplessly. "I was waiting for you."

Mother made a little *tsk*ing noise, then turned in her precise, determined way and climbed the small grassy hill up to Grandma's porch. Dad followed, looking depressed, and Becky and I scampered alongside, performing our typical duet of questions. *Do you know what's wrong?* Becky asked him. *Why did you wait for us?* I asked. *Is Mother mad at you?* Becky asked. *Are you scared of the crazy lady?* I asked. *Scared to go inside?*

I asked this, of course, because *I* was scared.

Dad only had time to say, uneasily, that Grandma's St. Augustine was getting high again, and I'd have to mow it next Saturday. It was just his way of stalling; he'd begun evading a lot of our questions lately.

The front door was already open, and as we mounted the porch steps I could see Grandma Howell's dim outline from just inside the screen. Then the screen opened and I heard her say, vaguely, "Why, it's Kathy and Bert, and the kids . . ." From inside the room I heard a high, twittering sound, like the cries of a bird.

In the summertime Grandma Howell kept all the shades drawn in her living room; she had an attic fan, and the room was always wonderfully cool. It was furnished modestly, decorated with colorful doilies Grandma knitted for the backs of chairs and the sofa, and with dozens of little knickknacks—gifts from her grandchildren, mostly—set along the mantel of the small fireplace and cluttering the little, spindly-leg tables, and with several uninspired, studiously executed paintings (still lifes, mostly) done by my grandfather, who had died several years before I was born. A typical grandmother's house, I suppose, and through the years it had represented to us kids a sanctuary, a place of quiet wonder and privilege, where we were fed ginger cookies and Kool-Aid, and where Grandma regaled us with stories of her childhood down in Mobile, where her family had been among the most prominent citizens, or of her courtship by that rapscallion, Jacob Howell, who'd brought her northward (that is, to our town—which skirted the northern edge of Alabama) and kept her there. Grandma liked to roll her china-blue eyes, picturing herself as a victim of kidnapping or worse; through the years she refined and elaborated her act to rouse both herself and us to helpless laughter, ending the story by insisting tongue-in-cheek that she'd met, and adjusted to, a fate worse than death. (Grandfather Howell was a postal clerk, later the postmaster, and by all accounts a gentle, kind, rather whimsical figure in the town; it was always clear that Grandma had adored him.) Now, at sixty-one, she looked twenty years younger, the blue eyes still clear as dawn, her figure neat, trim, and erect, her only grandmotherly affectation being the silvery blue hair she wore in a tidy bun. On that day I decided she'd always seemed brave, too, even valorous in her quiet, bustling self-sufficiency, for that afternoon I saw in her eyes for the first time a look of unmitigated fear.

"Yes, come in, come in," she said, still in that vague, airy way, trying to pretend that our visit was a surprise. Then she turned back to the room's dim interior—her head moving stiffly, I thought, as if her neck ached—and said in a polite, tense, hostessy voice: "Why look, Mrs. Longworth, it's my daughter and her family. We were just talking about them."

Grandma Howell nodded, as though agreeing with herself, or encouraging Mrs. Longworth's agreement. The twittering birdlike sound came again.

By now we were all inside, standing awkwardly near the screen. Slowly, our eyes adjusted. On the opposite side of the room, and in the far corner of Grandma's dainty, pale-blue sofa, sat Mrs. Longworth: a tiny, white-haired woman in a pink dress, a brilliant green shawl, and soiled white sneakers, one of whose laces had come untied. The five of us stared, not feeling our rudeness, I suppose, because for the moment Mrs. Longworth seemed unaware of our presence. She kept brushing wispy strands of the bone-white hair from her forehead, though it immediately fell back again; and she would pat her knees briskly with open palms, as if coaxing some invisible child to her lap. It was the first time I had encountered the crazy lady up close, and my wide-eyed scrutiny confirmed certain rumors that had circulated in the town for years—that she wore boys' sneakers, for instance, along with white athletic socks; that her tongue often protruded from her mouth, like a communicant's (as it did now, quivering with a sort of nervous expectancy); and that, most distasteful of all, the woman was unbelievably dirty. Even across the dimmed room I detected a rank, animal odor, and there was a dark smear—it looked like grease—along one of her fragile cheekbones. The palms and even the backs of her hands were filthy, the tiny nails crusted with grime. Like me, the rest of my family had been stunned into silence at the very sight of her; it was only when her tongue popped back inside her mouth, and she cocked her head to begin that eerie, high-pitched trilling once again, that my mother jerked awake and abruptly stepped forward.

"Mrs. Longworth?" she said loudly, trying to compete with the woman's shrill birdsong. "We haven't met before, but I'm—"

She gave it up. Mrs. Longworth's head moved delicately as she trilled, cocking from side to side as if adjudging the intricate nuances of her melody—which was no melody at all, of course, but only a high, sweet, patternless frenzy of singing. (For it was clear that Mrs. Longworth thought she was singing; her face and eyes, which she still had not turned to us, had the vapid, self-satisfied look of the amateur performer.) She would stop when she was ready to stop. My mother stepped back, then drew Grandma closer. They began a whispered conference.

"How did she get in?" my mother said hoarsely. "Why did you—"

"It happened so fast," Grandma interrupted. Her face had puckered, in an uncharacteristic look of chagrin. "I was outside, watering the shrubs, and suddenly there she was, standing in the grass. Right away I knew who she was, but she looked so—so frail and helpless, just standing there. Then she asked for a glass of iced tea. She asked in a real sweet way, and it was so hot out, and she didn't *act* crazy. But once we got inside . . ."

Grandma's voice trailed away. I saw that her hands were shaking.

"You *know* what happened the last time she got loose," Mother said. She was almost hissing. “Wandered down to the courthouse and started screeching all kinds of things, crazy things, and then started taking off her clothes! In broad daylight! It took four men to restrain her before John Ray finally got there.”

Becky whispered, excitedly, “But doesn’t he keep her locked up? At school the girls all say—”

“Yes, yes,” Mother said impatiently, with a little shushing motion of her hand. “But she managed to get out, somehow. I’ve never understood why John Ray can’t hire someone to stay with her in the daytime, or else have her committed. My Lord,” she said, whirling back upon Grandma, “just imagine what could have happened. People like her can get violent, you know.”

“Ssh. Kathy, please,” Grandma said anxiously. She glanced back at the crazy lady, who had continued trilling to herself, though more softly now. “She isn’t like that, really. I don’t think she’d hurt anyone. In fact, if you’d heard what she told me—”

“Mother, the woman’s crazy!” my mother whispered, hard put to keep her voice down. “You can’t pay any attention to what she says.”

“What was it?” Becky asked, and though I was afraid to say anything, I seconded her question by vigorously nodding my head.

“Hush up,” Mother said, giving a light, warning slap to Becky’s shoulder blade, “or I’ll send you both outside.”

Now my father spoke up. “Listen, Kathy,” he said, “we ought to just call John Ray down at the bank. He’ll come get her, and that’ll be that.”

“I’ve a mind to call the police,” Mother said, and I looked at her curiously. She had sounded hurt.

“She hasn’t done anything,” Dad said gently. “And anyway, it’s none of our business.”

Grandma pressed her hands together, as if to stop their shaking. “Oh, if you’d heard what she told me, once I brought her inside. I gave her the iced tea, and a little saucer of butter cookies, and for a while she sat there on the sofa, with me right beside her, and she just talked in the sweetest way. Said she was just out for a walk this afternoon, but hadn’t realized how hot it was. She said the tea was delicious, and asked what kind I bought. Hers always turned cloudy, she said. And I'd started thinking to myself, This woman isn't crazy at all. She dresses peculiar, yes, and she should bathe more often, but people have just been spreading ugly gossip all these years, exaggerating everything. Anyway, I gave her more tea, and tried to be nice to her. She kept looking around the room, saying how pretty it was. She noticed Jacob's pictures, and couldn't believe he'd done such beautiful work. She asked if I still missed him, like she missed Mr. Longworth, and if I ever got lonesome, or frightened. . . . And it was then that she changed, so suddenly that I couldn't believe my ears. She started talking about John Ray, and saying the most horrible things, but all in that same sweet voice, as if she was just talking about the weather. Oh, Kathy, she said John Ray wanted—wanted to kill her, that he was going to take her into the attic and chop her into little pieces. She said he beats her, and sometimes won't let her eat for days on end, but by then she'd started using her husband's name—you know, mixing up the names. One minute she'd be saying Carl, the next she was back to John Ray. And pretty soon she was just spouting gibberish, and she'd started that crazy singing of hers. She said did I want to hear a song, and that's when I came to phone you. I didn't know what to do—I didn't—"

Tears had filled her eyes. Mother reached out, taking both her hands. "Never mind, you were just being kind to her," she said. "Bert's right, of course—we'll just call John Ray, and that'll be that."

Grandma couldn't speak, but her blue eyes had fixed on my mother's with a frightened, guilty look. It was then that Mrs. Longworth's eerie trilling stopped, and we heard, from the sofa: "Bert's right, of course, we'll just call John Ray. And that'll be that." The voice was sly, insinuating—it had the mocking, faintly malicious tone of a mynah bird.

I looked at Dad. His face had reddened, his mouth had fallen partway open.

"Would you like some more tea?" Grandma asked, in a sweet overdone voice. She inclined her head, graciously, though it was clear that she couldn't bring herself to take another step toward Mrs. Longworth. But the crazy lady didn't seem to mind. She cocked her head, and at the very moment I feared she would resume her weird singing, she said in a casual, matter-of-fact way, "No thanks, Paulina. I like the tea, but it isn't sweet enough." And she smiled, rather balefully; her teeth looked small and greenish.

Grandma began, "I could add more sugar—"

"Do you have Kool-Aid?" Mrs. Longworth asked. "That's my favorite drink, but my son won't let me have it."

"Yes, I think so," Grandma said, uncertainly. "I'll go and look."

"Red, please," Mrs. Longworth said. "Red's the best."

Grandma hurried back to the kitchen, leaving the rest of us to stare awkwardly at the old woman, while she looked frankly back at us. She had a childlike directness, but her eyes glittered, too, with the wry omniscience of the aged. Particularly when she looked down at Becky and me, her glance seemed full of mischief, as though she were exercising her right to a second childhood. And there was something in her glance that I could only feel as love, born of some intuitive sympathy. Young as I was, I remember sharing Grandma's thought: This woman isn't crazy at all.

For the moment, her attention had fixed on Becky. She held out a dirty, clawlike hand, as though to draw my sister closer by some invisible string.

"You're a pretty girl," she said, in the tone one uses for very young children. "Such pretty hair, and those cute freckles. . . . I used to have freckles, when I was young. *I* was a pretty girl."

She shook her head, as though hard put to say how pretty. "And I had nice dresses, cotton and gingham, all trimmed in lace. I'll bet you like pretty dresses. Your little nose is turned up, just like mine was."

Becky looked spellbound; her face had paled. "Thank you—thank you very much—" she stammered.

"Would you like to have some of the dresses I wore?" the old woman asked. "They're up in the attic, in a special trunk. We'll steal the key from John Ray. The dresses are safe, no bloodstains and none of them ripped. You could wear them to church, or when the young men come calling." She raised one finger of the still-outstretched hand. "But you'd have to bring them back. You couldn't steal them. We'll sneak them back late one night, when John Ray's asleep."

Becky tried to smile. I could see how scared she was, and I stood there hoping Mrs. Longworth wouldn't turn to me. Somehow I felt safer, being a boy.

"I—I don't know—It's real nice of you—" Becky couldn't put her words together.

"And you still have pretty clothes," my mother said suddenly, stepping forward. "That's a lovely shawl, Mrs. Longworth."

The crazy lady glanced down; she pulled the shawl tighter around her shoulders, as though she'd suddenly felt a chill.

"I had a cashmere shawl, pale gray," she said, "that my husband gave me. It was before John Ray was even born. Mr. Longworth went up to Memphis, and afterward he showered me with presents. An opal ring, too. And a set of hair combs. I was a pretty woman, you know. I still wear shawls, but it's not the same. This one's green."

She spoke in a circular, monotonous rhythm, as though reminiscing to herself; as though she'd spoken these words a thousand times. It was a kind of singsong. I thought again of her birdlike trilling.

"Well, it's very pretty," Mother said.

"It's *too* green," the crazy lady said, "but I think it hurts John Ray's eyes. He has weak eyes, you know. When he goes blind, I won't have to wear it."

Grandma came in from the kitchen, carrying a tray with six glasses and a large pitcher of Kool-Aid.

"It's raspberry, Mrs. Longworth," she said as she put the tray on the coffee table. Her hands still shook, and the glasses clattered together. "I hope you like it."

She poured a glass and held it out; Mrs. Longworth grasped it quickly, then took several long gulps. She closed her eyes in bliss. "Oooh!" she cried. "Isn't that good!"

Grandma maintained her brave smile. "Kathy, would you and Bert like—"

"No, Mother. We can't stay long, and Bert has a phone call to make. Don't you, Bert?"

"Yes—right," Dad said awkwardly.

"How about you kids?" Grandma said. She was trying gamely

to make all of this appear normal; then, perhaps, it would somehow *be* normal. That was always Grandma's way. But, much as I loved her, I was afraid to join in anything the crazy lady was doing. Like Becky, I stiffly shook my head.

Mrs. Longworth emptied her glass, then held it out to Grandma. "More, please," she said. While Grandma poured, she said (again in that matter-of-fact way): "You might not believe it, but I don't get good Kool-Aid like this. John Ray says it rots my teeth and my brain. I can drink water, or coffee without sugar." She made a face. "And if I don't drink it, John Ray gets mad. Now Carl, he never got mad. But my son is going to cut me with a long knife one of these days, and hide the pieces in the attic, all in separate trunks. When it starts to smell, he'll throw the trunks in the river."

She took the second glass of Kool-Aid that Grandma shakily handed her. Then she sighed, loudly, as if the details of her gruesome demise had become rather tiresome. "My son works in a bank," she said, "and his teeth are big and strong. So he can have sugar. If I try to sneak some, he pinches my arms, or hits me with a newspaper. That hurts, because he rolls it up first and makes me watch. The pinches hurt, too, but not always. He works in a bank, and so he knows all about locks and trunks and vaults. He has a map, so he can find the river when he needs it. I should be able to have red Kool-Aid, and to sing. I used to sing for Carl, and sometimes I sang to John Ray when he was a baby. Now, he's tired of taking care of me. He says, Don't I have a life to live? Don't I?" Again she spoke like a mynah bird, pitching her voice very low. "That's what he says, and that's why he wants to cut me into pieces, and why I have all these bruises on my arms. You want to see them? It's not fair, because my singing is pretty. Carl said I had a prettier voice than Jenny Lind, and he heard her in person when he was a boy. He's dead, though. You want to hear me sing?"

She stopped abruptly, her eyes widened. She waited.

"Would you like some more Kool-Aid?" Grandma asked, helplessly.

"Bert, you and Jamie go back into the kitchen. We'll wait out here with Mrs. Longworth." My mother gestured to her ear, as if holding a telephone.

Dad said, "Come on, sport," and I joined him gladly. I glimpsed Becky's look of envy and longing as we escaped into the dining room, and finally back into Grandma's tiny kitchen.

"What's wrong with her? Why does she say those things?" I asked breathlessly, while Dad fiddled with the slender phone directory. I tugged at his arm, like a much smaller child; my heart was racing. I wore only a T-shirt and short pants, and I remember shifting my weight back and forth, my bare feet unpleasantly chilled by the kitchen linoleum.

"Just simmer down, son," he said, tousling my hair in an absent-minded way. Frowning, he moved his eyes down a column of small print. "Ah, here it is. First National." He began to dial.

I didn't understand it, but I was on the verge of tears—angry tears. When Dad finished talking with John Ray, his eyes stopped to read the little chalkboard hanging by the phone. "I can't believe it," he said, shaking his head. "It's still there."

Grudgingly, I followed his gaze to the chalkboard, and for the hundredth time read its message, in that antique, elaborate hand: *Paulie, Don't forget Gouda cheese for dinner tonight. I'll be hungry at six o'clock sharp. (Ha ha) Jacob*. If Grandma was out when my grandfather came home for lunch, he would leave her a note on the chalkboard. But he hadn't lived to eat that Gouda cheese—he was stricken at four that afternoon, and died a short while later—and Grandma had insisted that his last message would never be erased. Mother disapproved, saying it was morbid, and more than once I'd seen Grandma's eyes fill with tears as they skimmed across the words yet another time. But she could be stubborn, and the message stayed.

"You'd know it was still there," I said, sniffling, "if you ever came with us to visit Grandma. But you're always gone."

The resentment in my voice surprised us both. My father's clear brown eyes flashed in an instant from anger, to guilt, to sorrow. He shook his head; the gesture had become familiar lately, almost a tic.

"Well, Jamie," he said slowly, licking his lips. "I guess it's time we had a little talk."

And for five or ten minutes he did talk, not quite looking at me, his voice filled with a melancholy dreaminess. He told me how complicated the grown-up world was, and how men and women sometimes hurt each other without wanting to; how they sometimes fell "out of love," without being able to control what was happening. He knew it must sound crazy, but he hoped that someday I would understand. Things were always changing, he said softly, and that was the hardest thing in the world for people to accept. Even my mother hadn't accepted it, not yet; but he hoped that she would, eventually. He hoped she wouldn't make it even harder for all of us.

The speech was commonplace enough, though startling to my young ears. As he spoke I kept thinking of Mrs. Longworth, and how she'd talked of her husband who had died, and how everything changed after that. I felt the cold, sickish beating of my heart inside my slender ribcage.

"But will Mother turn crazy, like Mrs. Longworth?" I asked, imagining myself, in a moment of terrified wonder, turning mean like John Ray. "Is it always the ladies who go crazy?"

Dad looked stymied; nor did I know myself what the question meant. I wouldn't even recall it until decades later, visiting my sister Becky in the hospital, where she was recuperating from a barbiturate overdose after the disappearance of her third husband. It would come back to me, in a boy's timid, faraway voice, like the echo of some terrible prophecy, a family curse. After a moment, though, my father reacted as though I'd said something amusing. Again, he tousled my hair; he smiled wearily.

"No, son," he said gently. "It's not always the ladies. You shouldn't let Mrs. Longworth get to you."

"But she said—"

"She's a crazy old lady, Jamie. She has nothing to do with us—don't pay any attention to what she says."

Hands stuffed in my pockets, one foot rubbing the toe of the other, I stood looking up at him. There were questions I wanted to ask, but I couldn't put them into words; and I somehow knew that he didn't have the answers.

"Now," Dad said, with a false heartiness, "why don't we—"

It was then that the kitchen door swung open, and there was my mother; she looked back and forth between Dad and me, as though she didn't recognize us.

"Honey? What is it?" Dad said, panicked.

"We—we couldn't stop her," Mother began, wildly. "She took off the shawl, then started unbuttoning her dress, that filthy dress—"

Dad crossed to her; he gripped her firmly by the upper arms.

"Calm down, Kathy. Now tell me what happened."

My mother was trembling. She said, haltingly, "Mrs. Longworth, she—she said she would show us, prove to us how cruel John Ray was. Before we could say anything, she started undressing. She undid the dress, then slipped it down to her waist. We—we just stared at her. We couldn't believe it. There were bruises, Bert, all over her arms and back. Big purplish bruises, and welts. . . . And she said, *John Ray did this*, in that little singing voice of hers—"

Dad had already released her arms. He went to the phone and dialed again. For a moment my mother's eyes locked onto mine. I'd never seen her lose her composure before, yet for some reason I was filled with a remarkable calm. From that moment forward, everything was changed between us.

"Oh God," she whispered, grief-stricken. "How I wish Becky hadn't seen."

Dad hung up the phone, then led us back into the living room; he kept one arm draped lightly around Mother's shoulder. John Ray had arrived, and sat on the sofa beside Mrs. Longworth. Her dress and shawl were in place, so it was hard for me to envision the scene my mother had described. Mrs. Longworth sat staring blankly forward, as if her mind had wandered to some distant place. John Ray held one of her hands, and sat talking amiably to Grandma. He was a big-chested man, almost entirely bald, and had teeth that were enormous, white, and perfectly straight. He smiled constantly. He was telling Grandma about all the times his mother had been "naughty," wandering into a department store, or a funeral parlor, or a private home. He hoped she hadn't been too much trouble. He hoped we understood that she meant no harm; that for years she hadn't had the slightest idea what she was doing or saying.

A small, terrible smile had frozen onto Grandma's face. She stood near the front door, her arm around Becky, who looked pale and dazed.

"She—she wasn't any trouble," my mother gasped.

"Oh no, none at all," said Grandma.

There were a few moments of silence, during which the five of us stared at the Longworths, John Ray giving back his imperturbable smile and Mrs. Longworth seeming lost in the corridors of her madness, her mouth slightly ajar, her hand resting limply inside her son's. I tried to picture John Ray beating her, or shouting his threats of a gruesome death. I decided it could not be true.

When the police arrived, neither John Ray nor his mother protested. The officer spoke to Mrs. Longworth by name, and returned a few pleasantries to the smiling John Ray. As he followed them out the door, the officer gave a knowing, barely perceptible look to my father, who nodded in acknowledgment, then turned his attention back to us.

"Well," he said, jovially, "why don't we all go out for an ice-cream sundae?"

Beyond that, I can't remember clearly. I don't believe that anyone, including myself, ever talked about the incident again; there was a tacit assumption between Becky and me that we would not resume our spying on the Longworths, but they continued to be tormented by other kids we knew. I remember feeling, for years afterward, that life had become disappointingly routine. Evidently the police hadn't charged John Ray: he was still working at First National by the time I left home for college. Nor had anything untoward happened to Mrs. Longworth: one night, about three years after wandering into our lives, she died peacefully in her sleep. It was whispered around town that John Ray was wild with grief.

By then, the tensions between my parents had all but vanished; my father's unexplained absences had stopped, my mother no longer seemed angry or depressed. Grandma stayed absorbed in her garden, her knitting, her memories. Becky had plunged headlong into her adolescent social career, and with great effort had obtained her obsessive goal: popularity. It seemed that I alone had changed. Violence had failed to erupt, and I became uneasy, tense, and vaguely suspicious. If I could have foreseen what would happen to my sister, I would not have been surprised. Like her, I left the South as soon as I was old enough, relocating to a big, overpopulated city where violence is commonplace. Although I often worry about Becky, and Mother, and even Grandma, I know there is no reason to feel guilty, just as there is no logic to the dream I've had, recurrently, for all these years: a dream in which I open a door to find the three of them perched on a sofa, cocking their heads from side to side, trilling their songs of madness and despair.

Jon Tribble

Cactus Vic and His Marvelous Magical Elephant

To take revenge on an enemy, buy him an elephant.
—Nepali adage

When Cactus Vic cruised up in his Wonder Bread truck,
it wasn't show business—not quite—but it was the closest thing to it
when I was six, seven, and eight. All the best birthday parties hired him
to arrive as we grew tired of pin-the-tail and kissing games,

the helium balloons no longer fascinating and floating away.
Wonder Bread furnished him with a merry-go-round for three,
sticky fruit pies and ding-dongs he pulled magically from behind our ears.
I doubt we'd have sat still without them. No rabbits or doves in his show,

instead he poured milk into rolled-up newspaper, waved yellowing white
handkerchiefs with a clown's flourish and grace, and he kept on reminding us
of "the importance of nutrition for a growing body" like a cafeteria worker
shilling Thursday's mystery meat. When I was eight, he'd already become

a depressing sideshow at parties you had to go to because your mother
was somebody's friend or she wanted into this club or that circle.
Wonder Bread retired him, took back the truck, merry-go-round,
and nutrition, and they almost got his name until he called a lawyer.

To make up for all he didn't have while he fought the bakery,
he started giving away plastic animals and miniature New Testaments.
As a gesture of goodwill to make the bad news go away, Wonder Bread
staged a retirement ceremony to award him a parting gift—a baby elephant,
Thaddeus. He emblazoned *Cactus Vic & His Marvelous Magical Elephant*

on the side of a horse trailer, and the first time he drove up to a birthday party
pulling it behind his new red van, he had our full attention.
It started out the same old stuff, though he seemed puzzled, out of sync,
kept repeating a tired needle through the balloon trick until it popped,

and he stared blankly at us, asked, "Why are we here?"
But then he opened the trailer, led Thaddeus out, and introduced us.
We circled the elephant, petting it shyly, tentative strokes barely making
contact with the strange skin, while Cactus Vic brought out cans of paint.

He pried the tops off, rolled back his sleeves and, with one hand dripping yellow
and the other trickling purple, invited us to join him. We rushed forward,
scooping and splattering handfuls of paint to slap and spread on the gray skin,
coating ourselves and Thaddeus until we were no longer children and elephant,

but orange and pink and green pygmies, rejoicing in screams and laughter
as we danced around our idol in living tribute like the Blue Men of Britain
celebrating fertility, like the Israelites in the Wilderness before the Golden Calf
while they were still unshackled from the tablets and the covenants to come.

Our tender hands caressed the hide, intertwined with other fingers
in our common supplication as the brush of trunk welcomed us closer,
steadied us together. When somebody's mother wandered out from iced tea
and highballs, Cactus Vic didn't work many more parties.

He faded into selling handpainted posters around town, and someone told me
he managed to get his son a job at Wonder Bread after the boy got back
from the Marines, though I heard it didn't work out. But more and more
I find myself wondering about Thaddeus. I hope he's somewhere better

than a zoo, uncaged, in a place he might find himself again in a circle
of worshipers caressing his heavy skin like Indian elephant handlers touch
their mounts to honor Ganesh, a god who reincarnated himself as an elephant,
willing to serve as a beast of burden and be praised for his quiet animal strength.

Jon Tribble

The Best Chicken in Arkansas

Before those words he started finished
I knew what wasn't coming from his lips

was this superior fowl of splendid plumage—
Rhode Island Red in my mind, but probably

dead white with a red comb if the feathered
semis streaming across the state are any real

indication of the king of the barnyard—
a bellows-keeled cock-of-the-walk scratching

across Grand Prairie coops where nitrate-
laced sluices shimmy past the slick pools

of nightsoil collecting the last trace of mountain
water the delta's cotton-poor fields need

to keep beans and rice from choking on
a stewardship of fertilizer and herbicide.

And I knew he wasn't smelling oil and rubber
burning on the ovals underneath the scream

of halogen peeling back the dark as muscle
in primer-coated, cut-angled metal shells

frees the beery crowds from the packed red
earth as demolition reverbs from the thrust

and grip of steel on steel, or the lonelier
knights careening down blank asphalt lanes

until the joust of nerves brakes and shames
back to life the sense all senselessness loathes.

And I knew those words weren't turning for
miniskirts flagging above dark legs in summer's

unforgiving age, merciless musk of locker talk's
bravado, the forty- and fifty-year-olds' bane

and brace for the turned head, long backward
glance those men who cross the line transform

into furtive Polaroids of the eighteen-year-old
girlfriend secreted upon them like a flask

to share sparingly, sin to confess only when
illusion shakes loose of mooring and drifts away.

And the adolescent taunt or curse was so far from
these words it was only a splinter of a memory

of a boy we would have named "Chicken Neck"
if he hadn't been "Weasel," his apocryphal

bathroom antics given wing on the jetstream
of teenage opinion, his strangled denials twisted

in whispervine which never cared he never
was invited anywhere by anyone before or after.

No, when those words defined themselves it was
salt and pepper, spices and juice, the crisp sizzle

seizing grease, flour, batter, and bird in a palm
of flavor's sharp rush of sustenance, so I listened

as he told me AQ Chicken was worth five hours
up the Pig Trail from Little Rock to Fayetteville,

if I was ever in Springdale we would share
the Sunday dinner served every day of the week.

Julianna Baggott

Birdfists

Today, at the neighborhood pool, there was a row of children and a row of mothers hovering behind them, rubbing lotion into their backs, dipping under straps, folding down ears. (I was one of the mothers in the row.) And then the children were fully polished, shined up, slick, and the mothers let go of them and they ran and jumped into the water.

And I eased myself into a deck chair and smiled and held my hand over my eyes like a visor. The chlorinated water beaded up on the children just so, and the lifeguards twirled whistles on white strings, clockwise and counter clockwise. One of the mothers named Pritzie, wearing a swimsuit with a gold buckle at the waist, sat down on one side of me and another mother named Marquette sat on the other. Marquette, blond and trim, was the one who'd set up the badminton net in the field on the other side of the tall chain-link fence. She leaned in close and said, "I have an emergency. I have to go home. Can you watch Missy?"

I said, "Well, sure. Is everything okay?"

She laughed a forced laugh. "I'm sure it will all be fine in the end, but, well..." She looked down at the striped towel in her lap that was wrapped around her hands. "This just started up," she said. "I'm not sure what it is." Marquette glanced around. A life guard was shaking the test tube to check the chlorine levels. Pritzie was yelling at her son for throwing Jujubes in the deep end. An old woman was climbing up the handicap stairs. Marquette lifted her hands out from under the towel.

At first I thought that her hands had tanned up, inexplicably, the rest of her being so pale. But then they rustled a bit, and the feathers on one hand stretched wide as if she were splaying her fingers—but she had no fingers—then these small wings crimped back up. I saw a beady eye on one hand and then on the other. The second one blinked.

She wasn't holding two birds. No, that's not what I'm saying. Her fists, I should clarify, her balled-up fists, were turning into birds. Common brown birds. Sparrows, maybe. I don't know much about birds. But they were beautiful this close up—soft-looking, delicate, like their bones would be as fine as twigs.

I looked at Marquette's face. She wasn't wearing any make-up. She never did, and this, I knew, was seen as impolite by some of the mothers at the pool, like Pritzie, for one, who always wore heavy coats fresh every day. I wear a bit, always, just a bit. And like the other mothers I hold my chin above the water and never wet my head. But I'd seen Marquette dive into the deep end. She would do laps. Now she looked worried, her blue eyes more vulnerable without the protection of mascara and eye shadow. "Are you going to the doctor?" I asked.

"I'm not sure what to do. Have you ever seen anything like it?" she asked.

"No," I said. "I've never even heard of anything like it." One of the birds opened a dark beak right where her thumb would have been. "Is it hungry?"

Marquette sighed and stared blankly across the pool. "Who can live in a place like this?" she asked. "Who can survive here?" She turned back to me. "Of course, they're both hungry. They're starving for something. Aren't we all starving for something?"

This kind of honesty scared the hell out of me. I thought of my husband, Tom, who was working in the automotive industry. I didn't know what he did, really. I just knew he'd turned doughy and tired. On the weekends, he stood in the shallow end, tossing the kids around, looking like he was wearing an inflatable ring around his waist, but it was merely a tube of fat. He was sad, I could tell. I was doughy and tired and sad, too, sometimes, like each time I cut crusts off of a sandwich, I felt like I was trying to cut off a part of myself—some excess, some wanting. But I didn't tell Marquette about the crusts though now I'm sure that I should have. It's not my fault that I kept that information to myself. I didn't know how to tell her, really. "You should go to the doctor," I said.

"I don't like doctors," Marquette said.

That's when Pritzie piped up. "My husband is a doctor," she said, without looking at us. She was wearing gold-trimmed sunglasses to match the buckle on her swimsuit.

"Sorry," Marquette said, covering up her balled-up bird-fists with the towel. "I thought he was a dentist."

"Dentists *are* doctors!" Pritzie said.

"I've heard Otum tell people he's a tooth farmer," I said, because I have. It's one of his favorite jokes.

"Well, he's being self-deprecating," Pritzie said, still refusing to glance in our direction. "I've told him a million times that people will think that he doesn't have enough pride in his occupation if he goes on saying that. And a lack of pride is a sign of weakness. People dislike weakness. Remember our dog Beeper? He had to have a leg removed because of cancer and then he started to get attacked by other dogs in the neighborhood. That's the way it is. We had to put him down."

I remembered Beeper for a moment, skirting the slats in their white fence, growling and snapping. I looked for my daughter in the pool, diving for pennies, coming up dolphin-slick. I saw Missy in line for the diving board. She was older than my girl, a little knock-kneed. I turned back to Marquette. "Well, you might should go to the doctor," I said quietly.

"Or the vet," Marquette said with a laugh then she whispered, "Maybe I should put the birds down, like Beeper. Put them out of their misery."

I wasn't sure how to respond. I thought her bird-fists were oddly beautiful—starving, yes, desperately starving, but beautiful. They terrified me, too—had the blinking eye been trying to send me a message? In any case, I didn't think the bird-fists were funny. "I'll look after Missy," I said. "She's never any trouble."

"Thanks," Marquette said. She rearranged the towel to hide her bird-fists and walked out of the pool area and across the field, past the badminton net—where no one ever played—to her house, just on the other side of the street.

The gunshot rang out during adult swim. I didn't hear it. Pritzie and a few other mothers had been standing in one corner with their hands on their hips. I usually joined them, but this time I was thinking about the birds. I'd decided that when I brought Missy home, I'd give Marquette an eye dropper so that she could feed the birds. I'd offer to look the birds up on the computer since she would surely have trouble typing anything. If it looked like she would need prolonged help, I decided I'd post a sign up sheet in the pool house where families could sign-up to bring meals.

I'd been in the water with a kickboard, scissoring across a lap lane. The ends of my hair had been brushing the water, and then I started thinking about Marquette, how she would spin around at the end of a lap, pushing off the sides of the pool, rocketing through the water. And, for no reason I can really explain, I abandoned the kickboard in the middle of a lap. I just put it on the side of the pool and dove down under the water—so low that my bathing suit skimmed the bottom of the floor. I was down there with only my blurry vision, without sound, and when I felt breathless, I pushed off of the bottom and propelled myself with my arms, as if my arms were wings. When I broke the surface, there was shouting.

The children were the first to the chain-link fence. They ran from the concession stand and clung to the fence, shouting at each other. The mothers heaved themselves to the pavement quickly, and shooed the children away from the fence. They gave them dollar bills and told them to buy more goodies. The lifeguards didn't do much at all. They were kids too, after all, teenagers who twirled whistles all summer.

"That was a gunshot," Pritzie said. "Didn't you hear it? It came from that direction." She pointed toward Marquette's house and then turned to me and flipped her sunglasses up on top of her head. "How did you get all wet?"

I didn't answer. I remembered Marquette telling me that maybe she should put the birds out of their misery, that we were all starving. I ran out of the pool area, across the field, past the badminton. I called to Pritzie over my shoulder to watch my daughter and Missy, too. I jogged across the street and reached the front door, breathless.

"Marquette?" I shouted. I wasn't sure what I would find. "Marquette? Where are you?"

And there she was on the sofa, slouched to one side. She was wearing the same clothes I'd seen her in that morning, her tennis shoes still neatly tied. The gun was on the floor. The floral cushions were blooming roses of blood. But the birds, the sparrows were flapping heroically, struggling to lift her limp arms above her head, as if she were still signaling for help.

When Tom came home, he'd already heard the news and told me as if breaking it to me—a suicide in the neighborhood.

I nodded. "That explains the sirens," I said. "There must have been a fleet of them." I didn't tell him that I'd been the one to find her, to call 911, to talk to the police in the yard while the pool mothers stood at the fence, their hands poised in the chain links like claws. I didn't tell him that Pritzie had watched our daughter for the afternoon, Missy, too. And that I'd taken a hot bath, sitting there until the water turned cold and I was shaking.

I knew that he'd find all of this out, probably that coming weekend at the pool in the shallow end. But I didn't care. I imagined him taking my hand at some point, saying, gently, "Why didn't you say something? Why didn't you tell me the whole story?" I would just shrug and tell him that I didn't know why. And, oh, how gently he'd treat me for a while after that. Is that what I wanted?

That night in bed, I knew the main reason why I didn't tell him. I knew that it was because of the sparrows—not that I was afraid he wouldn't believe me. No. But that I had some secret with Marquette. There was something I knew that no one else did. The sparrows, the starving sparrows. I wanted to hoard that. And I lay there in bed, wondering, for the longest time, what to do with my hands. Part of me wanted to lie there on my back like the living dead, hands crossed on my chest, inviting the birds into my fists, inviting the birds to rise.

But, in the end, I wasn't starving enough for this. Not enough. I thought of Tom in the pool, tossing my daughter out and reeling her back in, tossing and reeling, and I loved them. I rolled over and pinned my hands beneath my soft stomach, pinned them there and slept.

Joyce Carol Oates

The Bingo Master

Suddenly there appears Joe Pye the Bingo Master, dramatically late by some ten or fifteen minutes, and everyone in the bingo hall except Rose Mallow Odom calls out an ecstatic greeting or at least smiles broadly to show how welcome he is, how forgiven he is for being late—"Just look what he's wearing tonight!" the plump young mother seated across from Rose exclaims, her pretty face dimpling like a child's. *"Isn't* he something," the woman murmurs, catching Rose's reluctant eye.

Joe Pye the Bingo Master. Joe Pye the talk of Tophet—or *some parts* of Tophet—who bought the old Harlequin Amusements Arcade down on Purslane Street by the Gayfeather Hotel (which Rose had been thinking of as boarded up or even razed, but there it is, still in operation) and has made such a success with his bingo hall, even Rose's father's staid old friends at church or at the club are talking about him. The Tophet City Council had tried to shut Joe Pye down last spring, first because too many people crowded into the hall and there was a fire hazard, second because he hadn't paid some fine or other (or was it, Rose Mallow wondered maliciously, a bribe) to the Board of Health and Sanitation, whose inspector had professed to be "astonished and sickened" by the conditions of the rest rooms, and the quality of the foot-longs and cheese-and-sausage pizzas sold at the refreshment stand: and two or three of the churches, jealous of Joe Pye's profits, which might very well eat into *theirs* (for Thursday-evening bingo was a main source of revenue for certain Tophet churches, though not, thank God, Saint Matthias Episcopal Church, where the Odoms worshipped), were agitating that Joe Pye be forced to move outside the city limits, at least, just as those "adult" bookstores and X-rated film outfits had been forced to move. There had been editorials in the paper, and letters pro and con, and though Rose Mallow had only contempt for local politics and hardly knew most of what was going on in her own hometown—her mind, as her father and aunt said, being elsewhere—she had followed the "Joe Pye Controversy" with amusement. It had pleased her when the bingo hall was allowed to remain open, mainly because it upset people in her part of town, by the golf course and the park and along Van Dusen Boulevard; if anyone had suggested that she would be visiting the hall, and even sitting, as she is tonight, at one of the dismayingly long oilcloth-covered tables beneath these ugly bright lights, amid noisily cheerful people who all seem to know one another, and who are happily devouring "refreshments" though it is only seven-thirty and surely they've eaten their dinners beforehand, and *why* are they so goggle-eyed about idiotic Joe Pye! —Rose Mallow would have snorted with laughter, waving her hand in that gesture of dismissal her aunt said was "unbecoming."

Well, Rose Mallow Odom *is* at Joe Pye's Bingo Hall, in fact she has arrived early, and is staring, her arms folded beneath her breasts, at the fabled Bingo Master himself. Of course, there are other workers—attendants—high-school-aged girls with piles of bleached hair and pierced earrings and artfully made-up faces, and even one or two older women, dressed in bright-pink smocks with *Joe Pye* in a spidery green arabesque on their collars, and out front there is a courteous milk-chocolate-skinned young man in a three-piece suit whose function, Rose gathered, was simply to welcome the bingo players and maybe to keep out riffraff, white or black, since the hall *is* in a fairly disreputable part of town. But Joe Pye is the center of attention. Joe Pye is everything. His high rapid chummy chatter at the microphone is as silly, and halfway unintelligible, as any local disc jockey's frantic monologue, picked up by chance as Rose spins the dial looking for something to divert her; yet everyone listens eagerly, and begins giggling even before his jokes are entirely completed.

The Bingo Master is a very handsome man. Rose sees that at

once, and concedes the point: no matter that his goatee looks as if it were dyed with ink from the five-and-ten, and his stark-black eyebrows as well, and his skin, smooth as stone, somehow unreal as stone, is as darkly tanned as the skin of one of those men pictured on billboards, squinting into the sun with cigarettes smoking in their fingers; no matter that his lips are too rosy, the upper lip so deeply indented that it looks as if he is pouting, and his getup (what kinder expression?—the poor man is wearing a dazzling white turban, and a tunic threaded with silver and salmon pink, and wide-legged pajama-like trousers made of a material almost as clingy as silk, jet black) makes Rose want to roll her eyes heavenward and walk away. He *is* attractive. Even beautiful, if you are in the habit—Rose isn't—of calling men beautiful. His deep-set eyes shine with an enthusiasm that can't be feigned; or at any rate can't be entirely feigned. His outfit, absurd as it is, hangs well on him, emphasizing his well-proportioned shoulders and his lean waist and hips. His teeth, which he bares often, far too often, in smiles clearly meant to be dazzling, are perfectly white and straight and even: just as Rose Mallow's had been promised to be, though she knew, even as a child of twelve or so, that the ugly painful braces and the uglier "bite" that made her *gag* wouldn't leave her teeth any more attractive than they already were—which wasn't very attractive at all. Teeth impress her, inspire her to envy, make her resentful. And it's all the more exasperating that Joe Pye smiles so often, rubbing his hands zestfully and gazing out at his adoring giggling audience.

Naturally his voice is mellifluous and intimate, when it isn't busy being "enthusiastic," and Rose thinks that if he were speaking another language—if she didn't have to endure his claptrap about "lovely ladies" and "jackpot prizes" and "mystery cards" and "ten-games-for-the-price-of-seven" (under certain complicated conditions she couldn't follow)—she might find it very attractive indeed. Might find, if she tried, *him* attractive. But his drivel interferes with his seductive power, or powers, and Rose finds herself distracted, handing over money to one of the pink-smocked girls in exchange for a shockingly grimy bingo card, her face flushing with irritation. Of course the evening is an experiment, and not an entirely serious experiment: she has come downtown, by bus, unescorted, wearing stockings and fairly high heels, lipsticked, perfumed, less ostentatiously homely than usual, in order to lose, as the expression goes, her virginity. Or perhaps it would be more accurate, less narcissistic, to say that she has come downtown to acquire a lover? .. .

But no. Rose Mallow Odom doesn't want a lover. She doesn't want a man at all, not in any way, but she supposes one is necessary for the ritual she intends to complete.

"And now, ladies, ladies and gentlemen, if you're all ready, if you're all ready to begin." Joe Pye sings out, as a girl with carrot-colored frizzed hair and an enormous magenta smile turns the handle of the wire basket, in which white balls the size and apparent weight of Ping-Pong balls tumble merrily together, "I am ready to begin, and I wish you each and all the very, very best of luck from the bottom of my heart, and remember there's more than one winner each game, and dozens of winners each night, and in fact Joe Pye's iron-clad law is that *nobody's* going to go away empty-handed—Ah, now, let's see, now: the first number is—"

Despite herself Rose Mallow is crouched over the filthy cardboard square, a kernel of corn between her fingers, her lower lip caught in her teeth. *The first number is—*

It was on the eve of her thirty-ninth birthday, almost two months ago, that Rose Mallow Odom conceived of the notion of going out and "losing" her virginity.

Perhaps the notion wasn't her own, not entirely. It sprang into her head as she was writing one of her dashed-off swashbuckling letters (for which, she knew, her friends cherished *her—isn't Rose hilarious,* they liked to say, *isn't she brave),* this time to Georgene Wescott, who was back in New York City, her second divorce behind her, some sort of complicated, flattering, but not (Rose suspected) very high-paying job at Columbia just begun, and a new book, a collection of essays on contemporary women artists, just contracted for at a prestigious New York publishing house. *Dear Georgene,* Rose wrote, *Life in Tophet is droll as usual* *what with Papa's & Aunt Olivia's & my own criss-crossing trips to our high-priced $peciali$t pals at that awful clinic I told you about. & it seems there was a scandal of epic proportions at the Tophet Women's Club on acc't of the fact that some sister club which rents the building (I guess they're leftwingdogooder types, you & Ham & Carolyn wld belong if you were misfortunate enough to dwell hereabout) includes on its membership rolls some two or three or more Black Persons. Which, tho' it doesn't violate the letter of the Club's charter certainly violates its spirit. & then again,* Rose wrote, very late one night after her Aunt Olivia had retired, and even her father, famously insomniac like Rose herself, had gone to bed, *then again did I tell you about the NSWPP convention here ... at the Holiday Inn ... (which wasn't built yet I guess when you & Jack visited) ... by the interstate expressway? ... Anyway: (& I fear I did tell you, or was it Carolyn, or maybe both of you) the conference was all set, the rooms & banquet hall booked, & some enterprising muckraking young reporter at the Tophet* Globe-Times *(who has since gone "up north" to Norfolk, to a better-paying job) discovered that the NSWPP stood for National Socialist White People's Party which is (& I do not exaggerate, Georgene, tho' I can see you crinkling up your nose at another of Rose Mallow's silly flights of fancy, "Why doesn't she scramble all that into a story or a Symbolists poem as she once did, so she'd have something to show for her exile & her silence & cunning as well," I can hear you mumbling & you are 100% correct) none other than the (are you PREPARED???) American Nazi Party! Yes. Indeed. There is such a party & it overlaps Papa says sourly with the Klan & certain civic-minded organizations hereabouts, tho' he declined to be specific, possibly because his spinster daughter was looking too rapt & incredulous. Anyway, the Nazis were denied the use of the Tophet Holiday Inn & you'd have been impressed by the spirit of the newspaper editorials denouncing them roundly. (I hear tell—but maybe it is surreal rumor—that the Nazis not only wear their swastika armbands in secret but have tiny lapel pins on the insides of their lapels, swastikas natcherlly... .* And then she'd changed the subject, relaying news of friends, friends' husbands and wives, and former husbands and wives, and acquaintances' latest doings, scandalous and otherwise (for of the lively, gregarious, genius-ridden group that had assembled itself informally in Cambridge, Mass., almost twenty years ago, Rose Mallow Odom was the only really dedicated letter writer—the one who held everyone together through the mails—the one who would continue to write cheerful letter after letter even when she wasn't answered for a year or two), and as a perky little postscript she added that her thirty-ninth birthday was fast approaching and she meant to divest herself of her damned virginity as a kind of present to herself. *As my famous ironing-board figure is flatter than ever, & my breasts the size of Dixie cups after last spring's ritual flu & a rerun of that wretched bronchitis, it will be, as you can imagine, quite a challenge.*

Of course it was nothing more than a joke, one of Rose's whimsical self-mocking jokes, a postscript scribbled when her eyelids had begun to droop with fatigue. And yet... And yet when she actually wrote *I intend to divest myself of my damned virginity,* and sealed the letter, she saw that the project was inevitable. She would go through with it. She *would* go through with it, just as in the old days, years ago, when she was the most promising young writer in her circle, and grants and fellowships and prizes had tumbled into her lap, she had forced herself to complete innumerable projects simply because they were challenging, and would give her pain. (Though Rose was scornful of the Odoms' puritanical disdain of pleasure, on intellectual grounds, she nevertheless believed that painful experiences, and even pain itself, had a generally salubrious effect.)

And so she went out, the very next evening, a Thursday, telling her father and her aunt Olivia that she was going to the downtown library. When they asked in alarm, as she knew they would, why on earth she was going at such a time, Rose said with a schoolgirlish scowl that that was her business. But was the library even open at such a strange time, Aunt Olivia wanted to know. Open till nine on Thursdays, Rose said.

That first Thursday Rose had intended to go to a singles bar she had heard about, on the ground floor of a new high-rise office building; but at first she had difficulty finding the place, and circled about the enormous glass-and-concrete tower in her ill-fitting high heels, muttering to herself that no experience would be worth so much effort, even if it was a painful one. (She was of course a chaste young woman, whose general feeling about sex was not much different than it had been in elementary school, when the cruder, more reckless, more knowing children had had the power, by chanting certain words, to make poor Rose Mallow Odom press her hands over her ears.) Then she discovered the bar—discovered, rather, a long line of young people snaking up some dark concrete steps to the sidewalk, and along the sidewalk for hundreds of feet, evidently waiting to get into the Chanticleer. She was appalled not only by the crowd but by the exuberant youth of the crowd: no one older than twenty-five, no one dressed as she was. *(She* looked dressed for church, which she hated. But however else did people dress?) So she retreated, and went to the downtown library after all, where the librarians all knew her, and asked respectfully after her "work" (though she had made it clear years ago that she was no longer "working"—the demands her mother made upon her during the long years of her illness, and then Rose's father's precarious health, and of course her own history of respiratory illnesses and anemia and easily broken bones had made concentration impossible). Once she shook off the solicitous cackling old ladies she spent what remained of her evening quite profitably—she read *The Oresteia* in a translation new to her, and scribbled notes as she always did, excited by stray thoughts for articles or stories or poems, though in the end she always crumpled the notes up and threw them away. But the evening had not been an entire loss.

The second Thursday, she went to the Park Avenue Hotel, Tophet's only good hotel, fully intending to sit in the dim cocktail lounge until something happened—but she had no more than stepped into the lobby when Barbara Pursley called out to her; and she ended by going to dinner with Barbara and her husband, who were visiting Tophet for a few days, and Barbara's parents, whom she had always liked. Though she hadn't seen Barbara for fifteen years, and in truth hadn't thought of her once during those fifteen years (except to remember that a close friend of Barbara's had been the one, in sixth grade, to think up the cruel but probably fairly accurate nickname The Ostrich for Rose), she did have an enjoyable time. Anyone who had observed their table in the vaulted oak-paneled dining room of the Park Avenue, taking note in particular of the tall, lean, nervously eager woman who laughed frequently, showing her gums, and who seemed unable to keep her hand from patting at her hair (which was baby-fine, a pale brown, in no style at all but not unbecoming), and adjusting her collar or earrings, would have been quite astonished to learn that that woman (of indeterminate age: her "gentle" expressive chocolate-brown eyes might have belonged to a gawky girl of sixteen or to a woman in her fifties) had intended to spend the evening prowling about for a man.

And then the third Thursday (for the Thursdays had become, now, a ritual: her aunt protested only feebly, her father gave her a library book to return) she went to the movies, to the very theater where, at thirteen or fourteen, with her friend Janet Brome, she had met ... or almost met ... what were thought to be, then, "older boys" of seventeen or eighteen. (Big boys, farm boys, spending the day in Tophet, prowling about for girls. But even in the darkened Rialto neither Rose nor Janet resembled the kind of girls these boys sought.) And nothing at all happened. Nothing. Rose walked out of the theater when the film—a cloying self-conscious comedy about adultery in Manhattan—was only half over, and took a bus back home, in time to join her father and her aunt for ice cream and Peek Freans biscuits. "You look as if you're coming down with a cold," Rose's father said. "Your eyes are watery." Rose denied it; but came down with a cold the very next day.

She skipped a Thursday, but on the following week ventured out again, eyeing herself cynically and without a trace of affection in her bedroom mirror (which looked wispy and washed-out—but do mirrors actually age, Rose wondered), judging that, yes, she might be called pretty, with her big ostrich eyes and her ostrich height and gawky dignity, by a man who squinted in her direction in just the right degree of dimness. By now she knew the project was doomed but it gave her a kind of angry satisfaction to return to the Park Avenue Hotel, just, as she said in a more recent letter (this to the girl, the woman, with whom she had roomed as a graduate student at Radcliffe, then as virginal as Rose, and possibly even more intimidated by men than Rose—and now Pauline was divorced, with two children, living with an Irish poet in a tower north of Sligo, a tower not unlike Yeats's, with *his* several children) for the brute hell of it.

And the evening had been an initially promising one. Quite by accident Rose wandered into the Second Annual Conference of the Friends of Evolution, and sat at the rear of a crowded ballroom, to hear a paper read by a portly, distinguished gentleman with pince-nez and a red carnation in his buttonhole, and to join in the enthusiastic applause afterward. (The paper had been, Rose imperfectly gathered, about the need for extraterrestrial communication—or was such communication already a fact, and the FBI and "university professors" were united in suppressing it?) A second paper by a woman Rose's age who walked with a cane seemed to be arguing that Christ was in space—"out there in space"—as a close reading of the Book of Saint John the Divine would demonstrate. The applause was even more enthusiastic after this paper, though Rose contributed only politely, for she'd had, over the years, many thoughts about Jesus of Nazareth—and thoughts about those thoughts—and in the end, one fine day, she had taken herself in secret to a psychiatrist at the Mount Yarrow Hospital, confessing in tears, in shame, that she knew very well the whole thing—the *whole thing—was* nonsense, and insipid nonsense at that, but—still—she sometimes caught herself wistfully "believing"; and was she clinically insane? Some inflection in her voice, some droll upward motion of her eyes, must have alerted the man to the fact that Rose Mallow Odom was someone like himself—she'd gone to school in the North, hadn't she?—and so he brushed aside her worries, and told her that of course it was nonsense, but one felt a nagging family loyalty, yes one did quarrel with one's family, and say terrible things, but still the loyalty was there, he would give her a prescription for barbiturates if she was suffering from insomnia, and hadn't she better have a physical examination?—because she was looking (he meant to be kindly, he didn't know how he was breaking her heart) worn out. Rose did not tell him that she had just *had* her six months' checkup and that, for her, she was in excellent health: no chest problems, the anemia under control. By the end of the conversation the psychiatrist remembered who Rose was—"Why, you're famous around here, didn't you publish a novel that shocked everyone?"—and Rose had recovered her composure enough to say stiffly that no one was famous in this part of Alabama; and the original topic had been completely forgotten. And now Jesus of Nazareth was floating about in space ... or orbiting some moon ... or was He actually in a spacecraft (the term "spacecraft" was used frequently by the conferees), awaiting His first visitors from planet earth? Rose was befriended by a white-haired gentleman in his seventies who slid across two or three folding chairs to sit beside her, and there was even a somewhat younger man, in his fifties perhaps, with greasy quill-like hair and a mild stammer, whose badge proclaimed him as H. Speedwell of Sion, Florida, who offered to buy her a cup of coffee after the session was over. Rose felt a flicker of—of what?—amusement, interest, despair? She had to put her finger to her lips in a schoolmarmish gesture, since the elderly gentleman on her right and H. Speedwell on her left were both talking rather emphatically, as if trying to impress her, about *their* experiences sighting UFO's, and the third speaker was about to begin.

The topic was "The Next and Final Stage of Evolution," given by the Reverend Jake Gromwell of the New Holland Institute of Religious Studies in Stoneseed, Kentucky. Rose sat very straight, her hands folded on her lap, her knees primly together (for, it must have been by accident, Mr. Speedwell's right knee was pressing against her), and pretended to listen. Her mind was all a flurry, like a chicken coop invaded by a dog, and she couldn't even know what she felt until the fluttering thoughts settled down. Somehow she was in the Regency Ballroom of the Park Avenue Hotel on a Thursday evening in September, listening to a paper given by a porkish-looking man in a tight-fitting gray-and-red plaid suit with a bright-red tie. She had been noticing that many of the conferees were disabled—on canes, on crutches, even in wheelchairs (one of the wheelchairs, operated by a hawkfaced youngish man who might have been Rose's age but looked no more than twelve, was a wonderfully classy affair, with a panel of push-buttons that would evidently do nearly anything for him he wished; Rose had rented a wheelchair some years ago, for herself, when a pinched nerve in her back had crippled her, and *hers* had been a very ordinary model)—and most of them were elderly. There *were* men her own age but they were not promising. And Mr. Speedwell, who smelled of something blandly odd, like tapioca, was not promising. Rose sat for a few more minutes, conscious of being polite, being good, allowing herself to be lulled by the Reverend Gromwell's monotonous voice and by the ballroom's decorations (fluorescent-orange and green and violet snakes undulated in the carpet, voluptuous forty-foot velvet drapes stirred in the tepid air from invisible vents, there was even a garishly inappropriate but mesmerizing mirrored ceiling with "stardust" lighting which gave to the conferees a rakish, faintly lurid air despite their bald heads and trembling necks and crutches) before making her apologetic escape.

Now Rose Mallow Odom sits at one of the long tables in Joe Pye's Bingo Hall, her stomach somewhat uneasy after the TruOrange she has just drunk, a promising—a highly promising—card before her. She is wondering if the mounting excitement she feels is legitimate, or whether it has anything to do with the orange soda: or whether it's simple intelligent dread, for of course she doesn't want to win. She can't even imagine herself calling out *Bingo!* in a voice loud enough to be heard. It is after ten-thirty p.m. and there has been a number of winners and runners-up, many shrieking, ecstatic *Bingos* and some bellowing *Bingos* and one or two incredulous gasps, and really she should have gone home by now, Joe Pye is the only halfway attractive man in the place (there are no more than a dozen men there) and it isn't likely that Joe Pye in his dashing costume, with his glaring white turban held together by a gold pin, and his graceful shoulders, and his syrupy voice, would pay much attention to *her.* But inertia or curiosity has kept her here. What the hell, Rose thinks, pushing kernels of corn about on much-used squares of thick cardboard, becoming acquainted with fellow Tophetians, surely there are worse ways to spend Thursday night? ... She will dash off letters to Hamilton Frye and Carolyn Sears this weekend, though they owe her letters, describing in detail her newly made friends of the evening (the plump, perspiring, good-natured young woman seated across from her is named Lobelia, and it's ironic that Rose is doing so well this game, because just before it started Lobelia asked to exchange cards, on an impulse—"You give me mine and I'll give you yours, Rose!" she said, with charming inaccuracy and a big smile, and of course Rose had immediately obliged) and the depressingly bright-lit hall with its disproportionately large American flag up front by Joe Pye's platform, and all the odd, strange, sad, eager, *intent* players, some of them extremely old, their faces wizened, their hands palsied, a few crippled or undersized or in some dim incontestable way not altogether *right,* a number very young (in fact it is something of a scandal, the children up this late, playing bingo beside their mamas, frequently with two or three cards while their mamas greedily work at four cards, which is the limit), and the dreadful taped music that uncoils relentlessly behind Joe Pye's tireless voice, and of course Joe Pye the Bingo Master himself, who has such a warm, toothed smile for everyone in the hall, and who had—unless Rose, her weak eyes unfocused by the lighting, imagined it—actually directed a special smile and a wink in her direction earlier in the evening, apparently sighting her as a new customer. She will make one of her droll charming anecdotes out of the experience. She will be quite characteristically harsh on herself, and will speculate on the phenomenon of suspense, its psychological meaning (isn't there a sense in which all suspense, and not just bingo hall suspense, is asinine?), and life's losers who, even if they win, remain losers (for what possible difference could a home hair dryer, or $100 cash, or an outdoor barbecue grill, or an electric train complete with track, or a huge copy of the Bible, illustrated, bound in simulated white leather, make to any of these people?). She will record the groans of disappointment and dismay when someone screams *Bingo!* and the mutterings when the winner's numbers, read off by one of the bored-looking girl attendants, prove to be legitimate. The winners' frequent tears, the hearty handshaking and cheek-kissing Joe Pye indulges in, as if each winner were specially dear to him, an old friend hurrying forth to be greeted; and the bright-yellow mustard splashed on the foot-longs and their doughy buns; and the several infants whose diapers were changed on a bench unfortunately close by; and Lobelia's superstitious fingering of a tiny gold cross she wears on a chain around her neck; and the worn-out little girl sleeping on the floor, her head on a pink teddy bear someone in her family must have won hours ago; and "You won! Here. Hey! She won! Right here! This card, here! Here! Joe Pye, *right here!"*

The grandmotherly woman to Rose's left, with whom she'd exchanged a few pleasant words earlier in the evening (it turns out her name is Cornelia Teasel; she once cleaned house for the Odoms' neighbors the Filarees), is suddenly screaming, and has seized Rose's hand, in her excitement jarring all the kernels off the cards; but no matter, no matter, Rose *does* have a winning card, she has scored bingo, and there will be no avoiding it.

There are the usual groans, half-sobs, mutterings of angry disappointment, but the game comes to an end, and a gum-chewing girl with a brass helmet of hair reads off Rose's numbers to Joe Pye, who punctuates each number not only with a *Yes, right* but *Keep going, honey* and *You're getting there,* and a dazzling wide smile as if he'd never witnessed anything more wonderful in his life. A $100 winner! A first-time customer (unless his eyes deceive him) and a $100 winner!

Rose, her face burning and pulsing with embarrassment, must go to Joe Pye's raised platform to receive her check, and Joe Pye's heartiest warmest congratulations, and a noisy moist kiss that falls uncomfortably near her mouth (she must resist stepping violently back—the man is so physically vivid, so real, so *there). "Now* you're smiling, honey, aren't you?" he says happily. Up close he is just as handsome, but the whites of his eyes are perhaps too white. The gold pin in his turban is a crowing cock. His skin is very tanned, and the goatee even blacker than Rose had thought. "I been watching you all night, hon, and you'd be a whole lot prettier if you eased up and smiled more," Joe Pye murmurs in her ear. He smells sweetish, like candied fruit or wine.

Rose steps back, offended, but before she can escape Joe Pye reaches out for her hand again, her cold thin hand, which he rubs briskly between his own. "You are new here, aren't you? New tonight?" he asks.

"Yes," Rose says, so softly he has to stoop to hear.

"And are you a Tophet girl? Folks live in town?"

"Yes."

"But you never been to Joe Pye's Bingo Hall before tonight?"

"No."

"And here you're walking away a hundred-dollar cash winner! How does that make you feel?"

"Oh, just fine—"

"What?"

"Just fine—I never expected—"

"Are you a bingo player? I mean, y'know, at these churches in town, or anywheres else."

"No."

"Not a player? Just here for the fun of it? A $100 winner, your first night, ain't that excellent luck!—You know, hon, you *are* a real attractive gal, with the color all up in your face, I wonder if you'd like to hang around, oh say another half hour while I wind things up, there's a cozy bar right next door, I noted you are here tonight alone, eh?—might-be we could have a nightcap, just the two of us."

"Oh I don't think so, Mr. Pye—"

"Joe Pye! Joe Pye's the name," he says, grinning, leaning toward her, "and what might your name be? Something to do with a flower, isn't it?—some kind of a, a flower—"

Rose, very confused, wants only to escape. But he has her hand tightly in his own.

"Too shy to tell Joe Pye your name?" he says.

"It's—it's Olivia," Rose stammers.

"Oh. Olivia. Olivia, is it," Joe Pye says slowly, his smile

arrested. *"Olivia,* is it.... Well, sometimes I misread, you know; I get a wire crossed or something and I misread; I never claimed to be 100% accurate. Olivia, then. Okay, fine. Olivia. Why are you so skittish, Olivia? The microphone won't pick up a bit of what we say. Are you free for a nightcap around eleven? Yes? Just next door at the Gayfeather where I'm staying, the lounge is a cozy homey place, nice and private, the two of us, no strings attached or nothing..."

"My father is waiting up for me, and—"

"Come *on* now, Olivia, you're a Tophet gal, don't you want to make an out-of-towner feel welcome?"

"It's just that—"

"All right, then? Yes? It's a date? Soon as we close up shop here? Right next door at the Gayfeather?"

Rose stares at the man, at his bright glittering eyes and the glittering heraldic rooster in his turban, and hears herself murmur a weak assent; and only then does Joe Pye release her hand.

And so it has come about, improbably, ludicrously, that Rose Mallow Odom finds herself in the sepulchral Gayfeather Lounge as midnight nears, in the company of Joe Pye the Bingo Master (whose white turban is dazzling even here, in the drifting smoke and the lurid flickering colors from a television set perched high above the bar), and two or three other shadowy figures, derelict and subdued, solitary drinkers who clearly want nothing to do with one another. (One of them, a fairly well-dressed old gentleman with a swollen pug nose, reminds Rose obliquely of her father—except for the alcoholic's nose, of course.) She is sipping nervously at an "orange blossom"—a girlish sweet-acetous concoction she hasn't had since 1962, and has ordered tonight, or has had her escort order for her, only because she could think of nothing else. Joe Pye is telling Rose about his travels to distant lands—Venezuela, Ethiopia, Tibet, Iceland—and Rose makes an effort to appear to believe him, to appear to be naïve enough to believe him, for she has decided to go through with it, to take this outlandish fraud as her lover, for a single night only, or part of a night, however long the transaction will take. "Another drink?" Joe Pye murmurs, laying his hand on her unresisting wrist.

Above the bar the sharply tilted television set crackles with machine-gun fire, and indistinct silhouettes, probably human, race across bright sand, below a bright turquoise sky. Joe Pye, annoyed, turns and signals with a brisk counterclockwise motion of his fingers to the bartender, who lowers the sound almost immediately; the bartender's deference to Joe Pye impresses Rose. But then she is easily impressed. But then she is *not,* ordinarily, easily impressed. But the fizzing stinging orange drink has gone to her head.

"From going north and south on this globe, and east and west, traveling by freighter, by train, sometimes on foot, on foot through the mountains, spending a year here, six months there, two years somewhere else, I made my way finally back home, to the States, and wandered till things, you know, felt right: the way things sometimes feel right about a town or a landscape or another person, and you know it's your destiny," Joe Pye says softly. "If you know what I mean, Olivia."

With two dark fingers he strokes the back of her hand. She shivers, though the sensation is really ticklish.

"... destiny," Rose says. "Yes. I think I know."

She wants to ask Joe Pye if she won honestly; if, maybe, he hadn't thrown the game her way. Because he'd noticed her earlier. All evening. A stranger, a scowling disbelieving stranger, fixing him with her intelligent skeptical stare, the most conservatively and tastefully dressed player in the hall. But he doesn't seem eager to talk about his business, he wants instead to talk about his life as a "soldier of fortune"—whatever he means by that—and Rose wonders if such a question might be naïve, or insulting, for it would suggest that *he* was dishonest, that the bingo games were rigged. But then perhaps everyone knows they are rigged?—like the horse races?

She wants to ask but cannot. Joe Pye is sitting so close to her in the booth, his skin is so ruddy, his lips so dark, his teeth so white, his goatee Mephistophelian and his manner—now that he is "offstage," now that he can "be himself"—so ingratiatingly intimate that she feels disoriented. She is willing to see her position as comic, even as ludicrous (she, Rose Mallow Odom, disdainful of men and of physical things in general, is going to allow this charlatan to imagine that *he is* seducing *her—but* at the same time she is quite nervous, she isn't even very articulate); she must see it, and interpret it, as *something.* But Joe Pye keeps on talking. As if he were halfway enjoying himself. As if this were a normal conversation. Did she have any hobbies? Pets? Did she grow up in Tophet and go to school here? Were her parents living? What sort of business was her father in?—or was he a professional man? Had *she* traveled much? No? Was she ever married? Did she have a "career"? Had she ever been in love? Did she ever expect to be in love?

Rose blushes, hears herself giggle in embarrassment, her words trip over one another. Joe Pye is leaning close, tickling her forearm, a clown in black silk pajama bottoms and a turban, smelling of something overripe. His dark eyebrows are peaked, the whites of his eyes are luminous, his fleshy lips pout becomingly; he is irresistible. His nostrils even flare with the pretense of passion.... Rose begins to giggle and cannot stop.

"You are a highly attractive girl, especially when you let yourself go like right now," Joe Pye says softly. "You know—we could go up to my room where we'd be more private. Would you like that?"

"I am not," Rose says, drawing in a full, shaky breath, to clear her head, "I am not a *girl.* Hardly a girl at the age of thirty-nine."

"We could be more private in my room. No one would interrupt us."

"My father isn't well, he's waiting up for me," Rose says quickly.

"By now he's asleep, most likely!"

"Oh no, no—he suffers from insomnia, like me."

"Like you! Is that so? I suffer from insomnia too," Joe Pye says, squeezing her hand in excitement. "Ever since a bad experience I had in the desert ... in another part of the world.... But I'll tell you about that later, when we're closer acquainted. If we both have insomnia, Olivia, we should keep each other company. The nights in Tophet are so long."

"The nights *are* long," Rose says, blushing.

"But your mother, now; *she* isn't waiting up for you."

"Mother has been dead for years. I won't say what her sickness was but you can guess, it went on forever, and after she died I took all my things—I had this funny career going. I won't bore you with details—all my papers—stories and notes and such—and burnt them in the trash, and I've been at home every day and every night since, and I felt good when I burnt the things and good when I remember it, and—and I feel good right now," Rose says defiantly, finishing her drink. "So I know what I did was a sin."

"Do you believe in sin, a sophisticated girl like yourself?" Joe Pye says, smiling broadly.

The alcohol is a warm golden-glowing breath that fills her lungs and overflows and spreads to every part of her body, to the very tips of her toes, the tips of her ears. Yet her hand is fishlike: let Joe Pye fondle it as he will. So she is being seduced, and it is exactly as silly, as clumsy, as she had imagined it would be, as she imagined such things would be even as a young girl. So. As Descartes saw, I am I, up in my head, and my body is my body, extended in space, *out there,* it will be interesting to observe what happens, Rose thinks calmly. But she is not calm. She has begun to tremble. But she *must* be calm, it is all so absurd.

On their way up to Room 302 (the elevator is out of commission or perhaps there is no elevator, they must take the fire stairs, Rose is fetchingly dizzy and her escort must loop his arm around her) she tells Joe Pye that she didn't deserve to win at bingo and really should give the $100 back or perhaps to Lobelia (but she doesn't know Lobelia's last name!—what a pity) because it was really Lobelia's card that won, not hers. Joe Pye nods though he doesn't appear to understand. As he unlocks his door Rose begins an incoherent story, or is it a confession, about something she did when she was eleven years old and never told anyone about, and Joe Pye leads her into the room, and switches on the lights with a theatrical flourish, and even the television set, though the next moment he switches the set off. Rose is blinking at the complex undulating stripes in the carpet, which are very like snakes, and in a blurry voice she concludes her confession: "... she was so popular and so pretty and I hated her, I used to leave for school ahead of her and slow down so she'd catch up, and sometimes that worked, and sometimes it didn't, I just hated her, I bought a valentine, one of those joke valentines, it was about a foot high and glossy and showed some kind of an idiot on the cover, *Mother loved me,* it said, and when you opened it, *but she died,* so I sent it to Sandra, because her mother had died ... when we were in fifth grade ... and ... and."

Joe Pye unclips the golden cock, and undoes his turban, which is impressively long. Rose, her lips grinning, fumbles with the first button of her dress. It is a small button, cloth-covered, and resists her efforts to push it through the hole. But then she gets it through, and stands there panting.

She will think of it, *I must think of it,* as an impersonal event, bodily but not spiritual, *like a gynecological examination.* But then Rose hates those gynecological examinations. Hates and dreads them, and puts them off, canceling appointments at the last minute. *It will serve me right,* she often thinks, *if...* But her mother's cancer was elsewhere. Elsewhere in her body, and then everywhere. Perhaps there is no connection.

Joe Pye's skull is covered by mossy, obviously very thick, but close-clipped dark hair; he must have shaved his head a while back and now it is growing unevenly out. The ruddy tan ends at his hairline, where his skin is paste-white as Rose's. He smiles at Rose, fondly and inquisitively and with an abrupt unflinching gesture he rips off the goatee. Rose draws in her breath, shocked.

"But what are *you* doing, Olivia?" he asks.

The floor tilts suddenly so that there is the danger she will fall, stumble into his arms. She takes a step backward. Her weight forces the floor down, keeps it in place. Nervously, angrily, she tears at the prim little ugly buttons on her dress. "I—I'm—I'm hurrying the best I can," she mutters.

Joe Pye rubs at his chin, which is pinkened and somewhat raw-looking, and stares at Rose Mallow Odom. Even without his majestic turban and his goatee he is a striking picture of a man; he holds himself well, his shoulders somewhat raised. He stares at Rose as if he cannot believe what he is seeing.

"Olivia?" he says.

She yanks at the front of her dress and a button pops off, it is hilarious but there's no time to consider it, something is wrong, the dress won't come off, she sees that the belt is still tightly buckled and of course the dress won't come off, if only that idiot wouldn't stare at her, sobbing with frustration she pulls her straps off her skinny shoulders and bares her chest, her tiny breasts, Rose Mallow Odom, who had for years cowered in the girls' locker room at the public school, burning with shame, for the very thought of her body filled her with shame, and now she is contemptuously stripping before a stranger who gapes at her as if he has never seen anything like her before.

"But Olivia what are you *doing?* he says.

His question is both alarmed and formal. Rose wipes tears out of her eyes and looks at him, baffled.

"But Olivia people don't *do* like this, not this way, not so fast and angry," Joe Pye says. His eyebrows arch, his eyes narrow with disapproval; his stance radiates great dignity. "I think you must have misunderstood the nature of my proposal."

"What do you mean, people don't *do* ... What people..." Rose whimpers. She must blink rapidly to keep him in focus but the tears keep springing into her eyes and running down her cheeks, they will leave rivulets in her matte makeup which she lavishly if contemptuously applied many hours ago, something has gone wrong, something has gone terribly wrong, why is that idiot staring at her with such pity?

"Decent people," Joe Pye says slowly.

"But I-I—"

"Decent people," he says, his voice lowered, one corner of his mouth lifted in a tiny ironic dimple.

Rose has begun to shiver despite the golden-glowing burn in her throat. Her breasts are bluish-white, the pale-brown nipples have gone hard with fear. Fear and cold and clarity. She tries to shield herself from Joe Pye's glittering gaze with her arms, but she cannot: he sees everything. The floor is tilting again, with maddening slowness. She will topple forward if it doesn't stop. She will fall into his arms no matter how she resists, leaning her weight back on her shaky heels.

"But I thought—Don't you—Don't you want—?" she whispers.

Joe Pye draws himself up to his fullest height. He is really a giant of a man: the Bingo Master in his silver tunic and black wide-legged trousers, the rashlike shadow of the goatee framing his small angry smile, his eyes narrowed with disgust. Rose begins to cry as he shakes his head No. And again No. No.

She weeps, she pleads with him, she is stumbling dizzily forward. Something has gone wrong and she cannot comprehend it. In her head things ran their inevitable way, she had already chosen the cold clever words that would most winningly describe them, but Joe Pye knows nothing of her plans, knows nothing of her words, cares nothing for *her*.

"No!" he say sharply, striking out at her.

She must have fallen toward him, her knees must have buckled, for suddenly he has grasped her by her naked shoulders and, his face darkened with blood, he is shaking her violently. Her head whips back and forth. Against the bureau, against the wall, so sudden, so hard, the back of her head striking the wall, her teeth rattling, her eyes wide and blind in their sockets.

"No no no no *no."*

Suddenly she is on the floor, something has struck the right side of her mouth, she is staring up through layers of agitated air to a bullet-headed man with wet mad eyes whom she has never seen before. The naked lightbulb screwed into the ceiling socket, so far far away, burns with the power of a bright blank blinding sun behind his skull.

"But I—I thought—" she whispers.

"Prancing into Joe Pye's Bingo Hall and defiling it, prancing *up here* and defiling my room, what have you got to say for yourself, miss!" Joe Pye says, hauling her to her feet. He tugs her dress up and walks her roughly to the door, grasping her by the shoulders again and squeezing her hard, hard, without the slightest ounce of affection or courtesy, why he doesn't care for her at all!—and then she is out in the corridor, her patent-leather purse tossed after her, and the door to 302 is slammed shut.

It has all happened so quickly. Rose cannot comprehend; she stares at the door as if expecting it to be opened. But it remains closed. Far down the hall someone opens a door and pokes his head out and, seeing her in her disarray, quickly closes *that* door as well. So Rose is left completely alone.

She is too numb to feel much pain: only the pin-prickish sensation in her jaw, and the throbbing in her shoulders where Joe Pye's ghost-fingers still squeeze with such strength. Why, he didn't care for her at all... .

Weaving down the corridor like a drunken woman, one hand holding her ripped dress shut, one hand pressing the purse clumsily against her side. Weaving and staggering and muttering to herself like a drunken woman. She *is* a drunken woman. "What do you mean, people—What people—"

If only he had cradled her in his arms! If only he had loved her!

On the first landing of the fire stairs she grows very dizzy suddenly, and thinks it wisest to sit down. To sit down at once. Her head is drumming with a pulsebeat she can't control, she believes it is maybe the Bingo Master's pulsebeat, and his angry voice too scrambles about in her head, mixed up with her own thoughts. A puddle grows at the back of her mouth—she spits out blood, gagging—and discovers that one of her front teeth has come loose: one of her front teeth has come loose and the adjacent incisor also rocks back and forth in its socket.

"Oh Joe Pye," she whispers, "oh dear Christ what have you *done—"*

Weeping, sniffing, she fumbles with the fake-gold clasp of her purse and manages to get the purse open and paws inside, whimpering, to see if—but it's gone—she can't find it—ah; but there it *is:* there it is after all, folded small and somewhat crumpled (for she'd felt such embarrassment, she had stuck it quickly into her purse): the check for $100. A plain check that should have Joe Pye's large, bold, black signature on it, if only her eyes could focus long enough for her to see.

"Joe Pye, what people," she whimpers, blinking. "I never heard of—What people, where—?"

Kyle Minor

The Truth and All Its Ugly

1

The year my boy Danny turned six, my wife Penny and me took him down to Lexington and got him good and scanned because that's what everybody was doing back then, and, like they say, better safe than sorry.

He was a good boy and never got out of hand until he was seventeen years old and we got out of hand together. Around this same time Penny kept saying she was going to leave and stay with her sister in town. She said it enough that we stopped believing her, but the last time she said it, she did it. I remember the day and the hour. Friday, September 17, 2024. Quarter after five in the afternoon, because that's what time her grandmother's grandfather clock stopped when I kicked it over.

Danny heard all the yelling, and he came running downstairs and saw her standing there with her two suitcases and looked at me like I ought to do something. "Goddamn it, I'm not going to stop her," I said.

"It's your fault she's going," he said.

Penny hauled off and slapped his mouth. "I didn't raise you to talk to your father that way," she said, and at that moment I was of two minds, one of them swelled up with pride at the way she didn't let him mouth off to me.

It's the other one that won out. I reached back and gave her what she had coming for a long time now. I didn't knock her down, but I put one tooth through her lip, hit her just hard enough so she would come back to us when she was calmed down.

She didn't come back, though, and she didn't go stay with her sister, who claimed not even to know where she was. One week, two, then on a Saturday me and Danny had enough. We hauled Penny's mother's pink-painted upright piano out the front door and onto the porch and then we pushed it off and picked up our axes from by the wood pile and jumped down on it. "You got to be careful, Danny," I said. "There's a tension on those strings that'll cut you up bad you hit them wrong."

It was pure joy, watching him lift that axe and drive it into that piano. Up until then his head was always in books or that damn computer. Dead trees, I'd tell him, got not one thing on milkweed and sumac, horsemint and sweet William. But now I wasn't so sure, and now he'd caught on. "It's what you do with the dead trees," he said, like he was reading my mind.

I don't know what came over us after that, and it's not enough to blame it on our getting into the whiskey, which we did plenty. Penny had a old collection of Precious Moments figurines handed down from her own mama and grandmom. Children at a picnic, or playing the accordion to a bunch of birds, or hands folded in prayer, and nearly every little boy or girl wearing a bonnet. At first Danny said we ought to shoot at them—we had everything from assault rifles to a old Civil War service revolver that I'd be afraid to try firing—but then one Tuesday morning—by now it was November, and the old dog pens were near snowed under—he found some of the yellowjackets I had caught in glass Mason jars and forgot about. He found them dead in there and I saw him looking at them and he saw me watching but didn't say anything, just went upstairs and came down with my old orange tacklebox, which was where Penny kept her scrapbooking things.

"You gonna scrapbook those yellowjackets, buddy bear?" I said.

He said his plan was to shellac them. He couldn't near do it right, and I said, "Here, let me show you how," and showed him how to thin the shellac with turpentine and dab it on soft with the paintbrush bristles, which was something I knew from when things were better with Penny and I'd help her with her scrapbooks just so we could sit with our legs touching for a while.

He got good at it fast, and then we caught more yellowjackets and did what Danny had in mind all along, which was shellac them stiff, wings out like they were ready to fly, and set them on the Precious Moments figurines in a swarm.

After awhile that stopped being fun, and it kind of took the shock away when every Precious Moment in the house was swarmed like that, plus we were running out of yellowjackets. "We got to get more minimal," Danny said, and I could see what he meant. It's like when I served my country in the African wars. You get to see enough dead bodies and after awhile you get used to seeing them, and then you see another and it don't mean one thing to you. But you run into one little live black girl with a open chicken wire wound up and down her face and maybe three flies in her cut up eye, that gets to you.

So after that, we got strategic. We'd put three yellowjackets right by a brown marbly eye, eye to eye. Or one, stinger first.

Nobody but us had got to see what we had done to the Precious Moments until a few days later when Benny Gil, our postman, came by with the junk mail, and Danny saw him and invited him in for a glass of water, and he saw what it was we were doing with the wasps, and he said, "Son, that's sick," but he was smiling when he said it, and it was then I knew he was a person who could be trusted. Up until then, he'd always been asking about my methadone, which I got regular from the pharmacy at St. Claire's Hospital in town, on account of my back pain. He wanted to get some off me because he could trade it for other things he wanted.

This day I asked him, "Why is it nobody writes letters anymore?"

"It's a general lack of literacy," he said, and we started laughing because everybody knew that wasn't why.

"It's the government," Danny said, but he was just repeating what he always heard me say, and I wished he wouldn't get so serious in front of Benny Gil.

"They're spying," Benny Gil said, "listening in on us right now," but he wasn't serious.

"Best be careful," I said, because now was a time to keep it light. "Benny Gil here is on the government teat."

Benny Gil took a sip of his water and smiled some more. "That one," he said, "and maybe a couple two or three others."

Danny caught on. “It’s you we saw across the creek there, in the tall grass.”

“I been watching,” Benny Gil said. He leaned back in the wooden chair, put all his weight on the back two legs. I could see by the look on Danny’s face he was still thinking about how Penny would say not to lean back like that because it could put another divot in the wood floor, which was the kind of not important thing Penny was always worried about. There was a thousand or more divots in the wood floor, and by now another one just added a little extra character.

Benny Gil leaned forward again, put his elbows on his knees so his face was closer to mine. “I know where Penny can be found,” he said.

Danny’s ears perked up at that.

“She wants to be found,” I said, “and I don’t care to find her.”

“Irregardless,” Benny Gil said.

“Where is she?” Danny said, and I shot him a look.

“Maybe,” Benny Gil said, “me and your Dad ought to go out back and have a smoke.”

Danny watched us through the window, and I wonder what it is he was thinking and wonder to this day whether whatever it was he thought had anything to do with what he did later. Surely he saw something changing hands between me and Benny Gil, and he must have seen us shaking hands, too.

What he didn’t hear was Benny Gil saying, “God didn’t invent thirteen digit zip codes for nothing,” or me saying, “How many?” or him saying, “Sixteen,” or me talking him down to six. Six, I could spare, by careful rationing, and by grinding the white pills into white powder with my pocketknife, and snorting them instead of swallowing, which meant I could stretch out the supply until it was time for a new scrip.

Danny didn’t hear any of it, but maybe he knew something of it, because after Benny Gil left, he said, “You get to hurting again, I know somebody who can get you what you need.”

“Who?”

“Ben Holbrook,” he said.

“That’s the case,” I said, “I don’t want to hear of you talking to Ben Holbrook ever again.”

I meant it when I said it, but the problem was the methadone got better after I started grinding it up, and once I knew how much better it could get, I had a harder time rationing it, and ran out a week early.

Believe me when I say I know a thing or two about pain. I was wounded twice in Liberia, and got radiation poisoning from the Arabs in Yemen. Once in Minnesota I split a fourteen-point buck in half on a old fossil fuel motorcycle and broke nearly every bone in my body and knocked one eye crooked, and it stayed that way until I could afford to get it fixed. But, son, you don't know pain until you get what I got, which is a repetitive stress injury in my back from solar panel installations up there on roofs in the heat or the cold. So when the methadone ran out, I forgot about what I said before, and told Danny maybe if he knew somebody he ought to give him a call.

Ben Holbrook was a skinny son of a gun, no more than maybe eighteen years old, pimple-faced, head shaved bald so you could see its lumps. Money was not a problem for us. Benny Gil wasn't the only one on the government teat, he just had to work for his. Still, I didn't like the way this bald zitty kid came into our house thinking he was the only one who could set prices in America.

"Who do you think you are," I said, "Federal Reserve Chairman Dean Karlan?"

He was cool as a cucumber. "Supply and demand," he said, "is the law of the land in Kentucky, U.S.A."

Much as I didn't like it, I knew he was right, and I paid what he asked, which was considerable, and he handed over three brown-orange plastic bottles, which was supply enough for my demand and then some.

Soon as Ben Holbrook left, I went into the bathroom with my pocketknife and dropped two tablets on the sink counter and chopped them to powder and made a line. Then I put my nose low to the Formica and closed off my right nostril with a finger and snorted the line through my left.

I must have left the door open a crack, because I saw Danny there, just outside, watching. He knew it was a thing I was doing, but I don't think he ever saw me do it before.

I knew good and well that wasn't the type of thing I wanted him to see. Any other time I would have thrown a shoe at him if I caught him spying like that. But when you take your medicine through your nose, it hits your bloodstream fast and hard. That's why you take it that way. So my first thought was to throw a shoe, but before that first thought was even gone the juice hit my bloodstream, and there was my boy, his eyes looking at mine through the crack in the bathroom door, and if I ever loved him I loved him more in that now than in any ever, and right alongside that first thought was the second, which came out my mouth the same time it came into my head, even though I knew it was wrong as I thought it and said it. "Boy," I said. "Come on in here and try a line."

Some things you see like from outside yourself and from above, and that's how I see what happened next. Right there, below, there's big old me, and there's my boy Danny, and I'm coming around behind him, putting my arms around him like I did when I showed him how to line up a cue stick at Jack's Tavern or sink a putt at the Gooney Golf, and he's got the open pocketknife in his hand, and I've got his hand in my hand, pushing down on it, showing him how to crush without wasting anything, how to corral the powder, how a good line is made. That's me, leaning down, pantomiming to show him how. That's him, fast learner, nose to the counter, finger to nostril. There's the line, gone up like the rapture. Danny, standing up too fast because he don't know any better, and the trickle of blood down his lip and chin, and me, tilting his head back, cradling it in the crook of my arm, putting the old Boy Scout press on his nose with a wad of toilet paper, saying, "Hold still now, baby boy," and his eyes bright, and his cheeks flushed, and his voice like from a hundred miles away saying, "Lord, have mercy," then, "Weird," and us lying back, then, on the cold tile, his shoulder blades resting on my chest, both of us waiting for the hit to pass so we could take another.

The days and nights started going by fast after that, and sometimes there was no cause to tell one from the other. One morning or afternoon or midnight, for all I know, I went into my room and found Danny half-naked underneath the bed I shared for all those years with Penny, and when I asked him what he was doing under there, he said, "She's been after us all this time," and I said, "Who?" and he said, "Her," and hauled out a stash of scented candles his mother must have left under there, cinnamon and jasmine and persimmon-lemon.

At first I thought he was talking crazy, but then he pulled himself out from under the bed and walked real close and put the purple jasmine one under his eye and struck a blue tip match and lit the wick, and soon as it started to burn his eye went all bloodshot and swelled up. Even still, I wanted to take up her case.

"How was she to know?" I said, but he was looking at me hard. "Turn around," he said, "and look in that mirror." And sure enough, my eye was tearing up and swelling and all the blood vessels were turning red.

"Benny Gil," he said, "told you where she is."

"That's not strictly true," I said, except it was.

"The general area, then," he said.

"The general neck of the woods," I said.

He went into me and Penny's bathroom, then, and for some reason, even though we had being doing it together, I couldn't go in there just then and do it with him. I could hear him, though, and then I heard a few more sounds I knew but hadn't expected to hear, which were the sounds of him loading my old Browning 9mm, which I kept under the sink in case of emergencies. When I heard that, I got scared, because for a while now I had been feeling, like I said before, like things were getting out of hand, but now, him stepping out of the bathroom, hand around the grip of that nine, I had the kind of proof that makes it so you can't look the other way any more.

"Killing," I said, "isn't a kind of thing you can take back."

"I don't mean to kill her," he said. "I just mean to scare her a little."

That was more sensible talk than the talk I had been expecting from him, but still not altogether sensible. He was angry, I knew, after finding those candles, and I can't say I wasn't angry, either, but when you're young and full of piss and vinegar, caution is not a thing you take to naturally, and, besides, neither one of us was going through life in any kind of measured way at that particular point.

"I'm not saying she don't deserve a little scaring," I said. "When the time comes you'll see me front and center, taking the pleasure you and me both deserve after everything. But what I'm saying is that the time isn't come. Not yet."

"Look around," Danny said, and all around us was eighteen kinds of mess, some we'd made, and some that had just kind of grown while we weren't paying attention. "Sheila," he said, which was the name of a dog we'd had once who had abandoned her young before it was time, and all five of them had died, and who I had taken out back and shot because there wasn't one good thing about a dog who would go and do that.

"We're grown," I told him.

"Not me," he said.

There wasn't much I could say to that, because it was true, but I got him to hand over the Browning, and then he went upstairs and didn't come down for the rest of the night, and I figured he'd be down when he got hungry enough.

I went into the kitchen and made some pancakes and made some extra and wrapped them in foil and put them in the refrigerator so he could have them later. Then I put some butter and maple syrup over mine and ate them and drank some milk and fell asleep in front of a old Wesley Snipes movie and figured when I woke up I'd see if he didn't want to put on his boots and go out into the Daniel Boone National Forest and hike for a while and get cleared out the way the cold air will do you.

When I woke up, though, the car was gone, and the extension cord for the battery charger was running from the living room out the front door, and I followed it on out to the side of the house where we parked the car, which was sure enough gone, and with juice enough to go to Lexington and back probably. That's when panic kicked in, and I ran back into the house, toward me and Penny's bathroom, knowing the Browning was going to be gone, but hoping it wasn't, and when I got there and didn't find it where it should have been, I figured there wasn't any way I was going to see Penny alive again, but I was wrong.

2

It was Penny who found him. It took some time, but after awhile the authorities pieced together what had happened. Around six in the evening, they said, must have been the time I fell asleep. When the house got quiet enough, Danny went out to the shed and brought in the long extension cord and ran it to the car battery. While it was charging he loaded up three assault rifles, including the Kalashnikov 3000, the one made to look like a AK-47, but with the guts of a MicroKal, laser gun and flamethrower and all. He took the Browning, too, and my Bowie knife, and his old play camo war paint, and a cache of armor-piercing bullets, although he never did use any of it except the 9mm. Then he sat down and ate the pancakes I had made, and washed the plate and knife and fork he had used to eat them off, and left them out to air dry.

By the time he got to Benny Gil's house, he had worked himself up into something cold enough that Benny Gil didn't argue, didn't even need to be shown knife or gun to know it was in his best interest to give up Penny's location and get Danny on his way. I don't know what that means, exactly, except to say that Benny Gil is not a person I've ever known or heard of to be afraid of anyone or anything.

What Benny Gil told Danny was that Penny was staying with her sister's husband's nephew Kelly, a bookish boy we never knew well because he never came around to family things, probably because he, or more likely his mother, thought he was better than us, from what they call a more refined stock.

Kelly was, by then, well to do, UK law degree in hand, specialty in horse law. He even had a office at Keeneland and another at Churchill Downs, and if he thought as highly of himself as he seemed to every year on the television, sitting there next to some half-dead Derby owner who needed a oxygen tank just to breathe, sipping a mint julep, then I'm sure him and Penny made a fine pair.

There's no way to know it now, but my guess is that Danny, when he heard of it, came to the same idea I did when I first heard of it, which was something not right was happening between Penny and that boy, but I put it out of my head at the time because it was too horrible a thing to look at directly.

At any rate, what happened next is the part of the story that got out into the world. Danny drove east on Interstate 64, stopped at the Sonicburger in Mt. Sterling and ordered and ate a egg sandwich, then headed toward the big expensive stone houses by the airport, where Penny and Kelly was shacked up.

When he got there, he rang the doorbell three times—that's what Kelly's security company came up with later—and nobody was home, and I guess he didn't want to wait, and I guess he knew well enough what ended up being true, which was that there was something worse for a mother than to be killed by her son.

At the funeral, the preacher and everyone else said that wasn't the case, that Danny was sick in the head and that these things happen in the brain, something trips or snaps or misfires, and then somebody is doing something they wouldn't do if they were themself. But I think that's the kind of thing people say when what they want to do is make themselves feel better instead of look straight ahead at the truth and all its ugly. Because what I think and pretty near to know happened goes like this:

When he got there, he rang that doorbell three times, and nobody was home, and he got to thinking, and what he was thinking about was clear enough to him, and what he was thinking was that he had come all this way to hurt his mother, and his stomach was full from that egg sandwich, and that Browning 9mm was in his hand, and what if instead of killing her and just hurting her that one time, what if instead he did himself right there where she would have to come home and find him, and wouldn't that be something she would have to live with, and go on living and living and living? And wouldn't that be the way to hurt her again and again, the way she had hurt him and us by running off?

So that's what he did. He sat down in front of Kelly's front door, and put the muzzle to his right temple, and turned his head so his left temple was to the door, and when Penny came home that night, what she found was the worst thing you can ever find, and when I heard about it, I couldn't hate her the way I wanted to anymore.

At the funeral, they sat us both on the front row, but far apart from each other, with a bunch of her brothers and other male relatives between us so I would know clear as daylight that I was meant to stay away from her. But before the service got started, the preacher came over and asked if there were things each of us needed to say to the deceased, and we both said yes, but for me it wasn't because I had anything to say to Danny. He was dead and gone and wherever it is he ended up, and that was hard enough to bear without making a show of telling him something he wasn't ever going to hear. It was Penny I wanted to say some things to, and I thought maybe up there next to Danny she might in that moment have ears to hear them.

Her brothers didn't leave the room when the preacher asked, but they did go stand in the back and give what they must have thought was a respectful distance. Me and Penny went and knelt beside the casket, her near his head and me near the middle, maybe three feet separating us. She bowed her head to pray silently, and I did, too, although I didn't right then have any words to say, and then she said some things to Danny too personal for me to repeat, although I don't think it would be wrong to say that the things she said, if they were true, moved me in a way I didn't think I could be moved by her.

When she was done, she looked over at me. It seemed like she was able to keep from crying all that time until she looked into my eyes, and I was reminded that it was our looking into each other's eyes that was happening while we were about the business of getting him made in the first place, and maybe that's what she saw that finally broke her down when she looked over at me. Maybe that, and all the years we had together, the three of us, and how there wasn't anyone else in the world who knew what those years were, and how there wouldn't ever be anyone else again.

It was right then, though I didn't say anything at the time because it didn't seem like the right time, that I decided I couldn't live in a world where Penny would go on being as unhappy as she had been made to be.

First thing the next morning I went down to Lexington again and went to the place where we had taken Danny when he was six years old to get scanned. It was gone, boarded up, the part of town where it had been now all but forgotten by people in business to make money. The only place in the storefront where the lights were still on was the WIC food stamp place, and I went inside and was told where to go on the Loop, to a part of town I remembered as Lexington Green but which was now called Stonewall.

The business had changed its name too, was now called Livelong, and occupied a building the size of a city block. The woman at the front desk said my number was A83, gave me a smartpad to fill in and told me to take a seat.

By the time they called my name I had run my fingerprint and verified all my information and watched the screen that said the scan we had got was old technology, and while the guarantee we had bought was still good, the Danny we would get would eventually wear out, but would not age the way the ones they could make now could. We'd get him six years old, and six years old he would stay.

They made me meet with a kid in a suit and tie, and all he said was the same thing I had heard from the smartpad. He was looking at me funny, and I said, "All I want to get is the service I paid for eleven years ago, near to the day," and he lowered his head for just a moment, like he was ashamed, and then he said, "You're entitled to it, and we'll give it to you if you want, but what you need to know is sometimes what you want isn't the same as the thing we can give you."

Even though he was a kid, what he was saying was true, and I knew it then, and it made me want to pound the sense out of him, and even so I wanted what I wanted.

I walked out of that Stonewall storefront that afternoon holding the warm flesh hand of a thing that moved and talked and looked for the life of me just like Danny did at six years old, and it was nearly unbearable, at first, to touch him or hear him say, "Now we're going for ice cream, Daddy?" and to remember the bargain we had made with Danny the day we took him to get him scanned. *You be good through this,* we'd told him, *we'll take you to get whatever kind of ice cream you want.*

So I said, "Sure, buddy bear," and I took him to up the road to the Baskin Robbins, and he ordered what Danny always ordered, which was Rocky Road with green and only green M&M's sprinkled over top, and we got a high table for two, and I sat and watched him chew exactly the way he used to chew, and lick the spoon exactly the way he used to lick the spoon. He said, "Can we split a Coke, Dad?" and I said sure, and went up to the counter and ordered a large Coke, and when I forgot to get an extra straw, I regretted it the way I used to regret it, because he chewed the straw down to where you could hardly get any Coke out of it.

After that he wanted to go walk the old stone wall like we always did when we came to Lexington, so I took him down there and parked the car and got him out and hoisted him up on the wall, and held his hand to steady him as he walked on top of it, and he said, "Tell me about the slaves, Daddy," so I did what I used to do and told him about how all the black people in Kentucky used to belong to the white people, and how this very wall he was walking on had been made by their hands, one stone at a time, and the mortar mixed with probably some of their sweat and maybe some of their blood, too, still in it, and how even with all that Kentucky fought for the Union and could well have been the difference in that war. While I was saying it, I was remembering how I used to believe things like that, and the feelings that used to rise up in my chest when I said them, feelings of pride and certainty, and warm feelings toward my people I had come from. These were stories my own dad and granddad used to tell me and which I was now passing along to my own son, and this little Danny, walking along that wall, holding my hand, said the same thing the other little Danny had said in a moment a whole lot like this one but which couldn't have been, if you think about it, any more different if it was happening on the other side of the world. He said, "It wasn't right, was it, for people to keep other people to do their work for them? How did anybody ever think it was right?"

And I said the same thing I said then, which was, "People don't always do what's right, son, but you and me get the privilege of making our own choices, and we have to make good choices. That's what makes a person good, is the choices you make."

Right then is when we went off the script. Could be that something was wrong with his making, or could be that I wasn't leading him right, but right at that moment, he took a wrong step and fell. He didn't fall off the wall altogether, but he caught his shoe on a stone that was sticking up at a bad angle, and when he fell, he caught his arm on another stone, and it cut deep into his skin, and when he tried to stand up, he pulled away and didn't seem aware that his skin was caught on that rock. I guess they don't build those things in such a way that they feel pain the same way you and me do, because as he stood up, the skin of his arm began to pull away from what was underneath, which wasn't bone or sinew, but cold lightweight metal, what I now know they call the endoskeleton, and what began to drain from him warm wasn't his own blood, but somebody else's, and the reason it was in there wasn't to keep him alive, but just to keep his skin warm and pink, just to make him look and feel like someone alive.

"Danny," I said. He must have heard the alarm in my voice, and I could tell it scared him. He looked down and saw his metal arm, the skin hanging off it, and the blood pouring out in a way that wasn't natural, and then he gave me a look that sank my soul, and I realized what I should have realized before I signed what I signed, which was that I had got them to make a boy out of something that wasn't a boy. All that was in his head was all that was in Danny's head a long time ago, back when Danny was himself someone different than who he became later, and it wasn't his fault. He didn't know what he was, and the sight of it was more than he could handle.

His lip began, then, to tremble, in the way Danny's did when he needed comforting, and I lifted him down off that stone wall and took him in my arms and held him and comforted him, and then, in the car, I stretched the skin back to where it had been, and took Penny's old emergency button sewing kit out of the glove compartment and took needle and thread to it and got him to where none of the metal was showing. I didn't take him to Penny's like I had planned.

He was real quiet all the way home. He just stared straight ahead and didn't look at his arm and didn't look at me. Near

Winchester I asked him if he wanted to hear some music, and he said all right, but we couldn't find anything good on the radio. "How about the football game?" I said, and he said all right again, and we found the Tennessee Titans and the Dallas Cowboys, and I made a show of cheering for the Titans the way we always had, but when he said, "How come all their names are different?" I didn't have a good answer, and after that I asked if he wouldn't mind just a little quiet, and he said he wouldn't mind, and I leaned back his seat and said, "Why don't you just close your eyes and rest awhile? It's been a long day and I bet you're tired."

He did. He closed his eyes then, and after some time had passed and I thought he was asleep, I stroked his hair with my free hand and made some kind of mothering sounds.

It was dark when we got to the house. I parked the car by the bedroom window, then went around to his side and picked him up like I was going to carry him sleeping to bed. I held him there in the dark for a little while and thought about that, carrying him up to bed, laying him there, laying his head on the pillow, pulling the covers up around his shoulders, tucking him in. It would have been the easiest thing to do, and it was the thing I wanted to do, but then I got to thinking about Penny, and sooner or later, I knew, she would have to be brought in on this, and even though I thought I had done it for her, I could see now that I had really done it for me, like maybe if I showed up with this little Danny she would come back home and the three of us could have another go of it.

But already this little Danny was wearing out. I could feel it in his skin. He wasn't warm like he was when I had picked him up, I guess because the blood had run out of him on the stone wall. He was breathing, but he was cold, and a little too heavy compared to what I remembered. There wasn't any future for him, either. I got to thinking about how if I put him in school, everyone would get bigger than him fast, and it would get worse every year, the distance between who he was and who his friends were becoming.

He was stirring a little, so I put his head on my shoulder, the way I used to do, and patted his back until his breathing told me he was asleep again. Then I went around to the front of the house and reached up to the porch and took down my axe from the wood pile and went off into the woods, down the path I had mowed with my riding mower a few weeks back, and which was already starting to come up enough that I had to watch my step.

I kept walking, him on my shoulder, axe in my free hand, until I reached the clearing. Then, careful not to wake him, I unbuttoned my jacket and got it out from under him and took it off and laid it on the ground. Then I laid him down on it and made sure he was still sleeping. Then I lifted up the axe and aimed it for the joint where his head met his neck and brought it down. In the split second right before blade struck skin, I saw his eyes open, and they were wide, and what I saw in them was not fear but instead some kind of wonder, and then, fast as it had come, it was gone, and all I could tell myself, over and over, was *It's not Danny. It's not Danny.*

Cover Artist **Adela Leibowitz** was born in Hartford, CT, and now lives and works in New York, NY. In 2003, she had a solo show at the OK Harris Gallery in New York City; in 2004, her next solo was featured at Jack the Pelican Presents in Brooklyn, NY; 2006 at HPGRP Gallery in New York City; and 2007 at Gallery 10G in New York, in addition to a two-person show at Dabora Gallery in Brooklyn, NY. She has been in group shows at the Mobile Museum of Art in Mobile, AL, The Kashya Hildebrand Gallery in New York City, Jack the Pelican Presents Gallery in Brooklyn, NY and Julie Baker Fine Art in Nevada, CA, to name just a few. In addition, Ms. Leibowitz has been shown at Scope Art Fair; Kunst 05 Art Fair in Zurich, Switzerland; Art 212; Art Chicago; and the LA Art Show. Her work has been featured in *New American Painters, NY Arts Magazine*, and *Mastermind* magazine. She has been a previous recipient of the PS 122 space program and attended a residency at the Millay Colony. Adela will be featured in a forthcoming solo show at Jack the Pelican Presents Gallery in Brooklyn, NY.

"*Tulip* is riffing on themes of the female ability to attract strange phenomena. Specific animals, like the crow, can signify signs of the near end, or act as harbingers of doom. Dreams and nightmares are the sources for the background construction and color; the unreal is explored as potentially having more force and vitality than our current constructed realities. This painting was from 'The Cassandra Prophesies' series I exhibited in mid 2006, where each canvas explored a different aspect of dread and anxiety, as flailing octopus tentacles emerging from the black sea or deer trapped on an iceberg in the middle of nowhere were just a few of the sinister warning tales."

To see more of Adela's art, visit www.adelaleibowitz.com

Andrew Hudgins teaches at The Ohio State University. He's published five books of poetry and one book of literary criticism. His poems and essays have appeared in *Poetry, The American Scholar, The Hudson Review, The Washington Post, The New York Times,* and many other journals. (Photo Credit: Jo McCulty)

"'Mother' unites a couple of jobs that I had as a teenager and into my twenties and thirties, working as a gardener and yardboy for both people in the neighborhood and some who were wealthy. When I was the help, I knew I was the help, an understanding that both troubled me and didn't trouble me. But I noticed that my wealthy bosses were very often uneasy with the difference their wealth enforced. They were often embarrassed by, or overproud, of it. And there was occasionally a weird moment when they capitulated to the urge to impart wisdom to someone they imagined an avatar of their younger self."

Ann Pancake's collection of short stories, *Given Ground*, won the 2000 Bakeless award. Other prizes she has received include a Whiting Award, an NEA Grant, a Pushcart Prize, and creative writing fellowships from the states of Washington, West Virginia, and Pennsylvania. Her fiction and essays have appeared in journals and anthologies like *Glimmer Train*, *Virginia Quarterly Review*, *Shenandoah*, and *New Stories from the South*. She now teaches in the low-residency MFA program at Pacific Lutheran University. Her novel about mountaintop removal mining in southern West Virginia will be published by Shoemaker & Hoard in November 2007. (Photo Credit: Jim Moore)

"Parts of this story I scavenged from a failed novel, but the image around which everything finally coalesced came from a dream: me running up a snow-patchy hill to free a dog short-chained to a tree. I'll also say that almost every dog in 'Dog Song' is one I really knew."

Benjamin Percy is the author of two books of short stories, *The Language of Elk* (Carnegie Mellon University Press, 2006) and *Refresh, Refresh* (Graywolf, 2007). His fiction appears in *Esquire*, *The Paris Review*, *Glimmer Train*, *Chicago Tribune*, *Best American Short Stories*, and the *Pushcart Prize* anthology, among other publications. (Photo Credit: Daren Dummer)

"Like most of my stories, this one began with an image. When I was twelve, maybe thirteen, I was swimming in a lagoon. Nearby, a bunch of teenage girls were jumping off a cliff into the blue-green water. If I dipped my head below the surface, I discovered, I could watch as their bikinis tore away with the force of the fall. That enchanting image stuck with me over so many years: a young woman with her arms spread and her breasts bared, a column of bubbles surrounding her as if she made the water boil. From this seed grew a story of pained and isolated love. An editor once referred to my work as 'woodsy surrealism.' I suppose that's as good a label as any. I typically write about the West or the South, still-wild areas, where the vastness, the stillness, the ancientness of the mountains and deserts and forests and swamps call attention to human activity. These are mythic territories and I'm trying to write about them with a mythic voice."

Beth Ann Fennelly received a 2003 National Endowment for the Arts Award. She's written two books of poetry, *Open House,* which won The 2001 *Kenyon Review* Prize for a First Book and the GLCA New Writers Award, and *Tender Hooks* (W. W. Norton, 2004), as well as a book of essays, *Great With Child* (W. W. Norton, 2006). She has three times been included in *The Best American Poetry* series and is a Pushcart Prize winner. She is an Assistant Professor at the University of Mississippi and lives in Oxford, MS.

"When I wrote 'The River that Was My Father,' I was thinking about how we pretend the experience of time is both linear and logical, while it is actually neither. Take grieving, for example; it hasn't been my experience that grief gradually declines bit by bit until it's gone. I've found, instead, it's possible to go days, weeks, months without thinking of the departed—but suddenly one recalls him or her and all of the sadness and fury is right there, sometimes not one bit lessened. It's as if it has been there all along, running inside you like a river that you can dip into. A river that both terrifies and comforts.

"When I wrote 'Holding Pattern in the Ninth Month,' I was again thinking about the strangeness of measuring time—for example, how arbitrary it is that the baby's birth is considered its first day, as if nothing before that counts, but for the mother, who has been carrying the baby, feeling it move, speaking to it, and loving it, birth seems a false (although tidy) time to start keeping track."

Brad Vice was born and raised in Tuscaloosa, Alabama. His fiction has appeared in *The Georgia Review, The Southern Review, The Atlantic Monthly, Best New American Voices, New Stories from the South*, and many other journals and anthologies. In 2007 his short story collection *The Bear Bryant Funeral Train* will be printed by River City Publishing. He teaches creative writing for the University of West Bohemia's International Summer Language School in Pilsen, The Czech Republish. (Photo Credit: Maude Schuyler Clay)

"'The Bear Bryant Funeral Train' borrows conceptually from Guy Davenport's postmodern classic 'The Haile Selassie Funeral Train.' Like Davenport's story, 'The Bear Bryant Funeral Train' wears its postmodernism on its sleeve—yet my story still constitutes what I think of as regionalism, using Southern iconography to replace the icons of high modernism present in Davenport. Charles Reagan Wilson's essay 'The Death of Bear Bryant: Myth and Ritual in the Modern South' provides much of the iconography used to decorate my 'The Bear Bryant Funeral Train.' Wilson's essay also provides a certain epic regional sensibility that I hope carries over to my story, and indeed my entire book. It was my purpose to replace Haile Selassie, the Ethiopian demagogue and messianic figure of the Rastafarian religion, with the messiah of my hometown—the god of the gridiron—Bear Bryant. The story 'The Bear Bryant Funeral Train' is not only a story about Southern iconography, it is an ars poetica of sorts, a Rosetta stone placed at the end of the text that calls into question the coherence, reliability, and dangers of all stories. It points out the fictive nature of all the narratives that have preceded it, both in my book and throughout the evolution of literature and history. The last line of 'The Bear Bryant Funeral Train' is 'Back and to the left.' Many readers will hear an echo of Oliver Stone's conspiracy thriller film *JFK*.

"It is yet another appropriated line.

"It also might be read as a set of directions."

Chris Offutt grew up in Haldeman, Kentucky, a former mining community of 200 in the Appalachian Mountains. He attended grade school, high school, and college there—all within a ten mile radius of his home. He is the author of two books of stories, *Kentucky Straight* and *Out of the Woods*; two memoirs, *The Same River Twice* and *No Heroes*; and one novel, *The Good Brother*. Two books are forthcoming: *Luck*, a collection of stories, and *Hit Monkey*, a novel. He's written screenplays, a pilot for HBO, and comic books for DC and Dark Horse. He's also written three jokes.

His work is widely translated and has received many honors, including a Lannan award, a Guggenheim fellowship, and a literature award from The American Academy of Arts and Letters for "prose that takes risks." His short fiction appears in many anthologies including three editions of *New Stories of the South* and *The Best of the South, Second Decade*.

He lives with his family, and writes in half of what would normally be the front room of his house. He has a dog. He loves people but prefers to be alone. He has never held a full-time job. He has a level 70 Paladin. He collects taxidermy and rocks with holes in them. (Photo Credit: Sandy Dyas)

"This is chapter two of a novel called *Hit Monkey*. I began writing it after learning that in 2003, the Federal Bureau of Investigation made its top national priority the investigation of animal rights activists. I believe we live in a far more surreal era than Rene Magritte could have imagined. For example, the mullet is making a comeback as a hairstyle."

Daniel Woodrell was born in the Missouri Ozarks and lives there again. He graduated from the University of Kansas and has a graduate degree from Iowa. He has published eight novels. (Photo Credit: Bruce Carr)

"A buddy had his dog shot out in Booger County by a fella who deserved shooting himself."

Dean Paschal is originally from Albany, Georgia, but has lived in New Orleans for the past twenty years. His academic background is in electronic engineering, zoology and medicine. He has worked as an ER physician for most of his time in New Orleans. "Like all such physicians, I have benefited enormously from the recent television shows describing the sorts of things that we do. Years ago, when I would tell people I was an ER physician, absolutely no one knew what that was.

"For many, if not most of my stories, I have no idea where I am going when I begin to write. That was not the case with 'Sautéing the Platygast.' I knew exactly where I was headed when I wrote the first sentence. Specifically, I knew that the story would be built around a skeleton—or more precisely within an exoskeleton—of highly stylized language: the language of science, the language of a cookbook, and the King James version of religious/biblical language. The biblical language only shows up in the final paragraphs, since I didn't want to reveal my overall trajectory too soon. Religious symbols and allusions are used throughout the story, however, so that the final linguistic shifting of gears makes a sort of subliminal sense. The story is, of course, a fantasy, with an otherworldly feel to it. But what would probably most intrigue a zoologist/ paleontologist reading it, is how few facts are actually made up. There is a lot of real science in 'Platygast,' and it is an unending series of inside jokes. If these animals actually existed, this would be the correct way to describe them—and the guesses and observations made about their physiology would be the correct ones.

"I know a lay reader will miss fully a third of what is going on in the story. But I am also aware that he/ she will not be much troubled by that fact. The same thing happens to most of us when we read nautical stories, where we quickly lose track of the various masts and spars, and the location of the skysails and topgallants. In truth, we may have forgotten what a belaying pin is but, by God, we want it in there if it's an old-fashioned story about the sea. I was using the same sort of reasoning when I did not tone down the technical details of my narrative. Only my scientific readers will actually know what a diplocaulus is and why they look pious. It is enough for my other readers to feel they can trust me on that observation, and they can."

George Singleton has published over 100 stories in magazines such at *The Atlantic Monthly, Harper's, Playboy, Book, Zoetrope, Glimmer Train, Georgia Review, Shenandoah, Southern Review*, and *North American Review*. His stories have been anthologized in seven editions of *New Stories from the South*, plus *Writers Harvest 2, A Dixie Christmas, They Write Among Us, 20 Over 40*, and *Behind the Short Story: from First to Final Draft*. Singleton's the author of four collections of shorts stories*: These People Are Us* (2001), *The Half-Mammals of Dixie* (2002), *Why Dogs Chase Cars* (2004), and *Drowning in Gruel* (2006). His novel, *Novel*, was published in 2005. A new novel, *Work Shirts for Madmen*, will be published by Harcourt in the fall of 2007. Singleton lives in Dacusville, South Carolina, and teaches at the South Carolina Governor's School for the Arts and Humanities. (Photo Credit: Glenda Guion)

"I was in the middle of a bunch of connected stories concerning Stet Looper and his awkward travails in regards to completing a low residency master's degree in southern culture studies, so I drove around aimlessly. I happened across a place between Pumpkintown and Marietta, South Carolina—the next towns over—called Laurel and Hardy Lakes: All Day Fishing $5. How had I never seen this sign before, or taken the road back there? I ended up driving along the Saluda River, through what appeared to be a summer resort circa 1940. The road then followed a ridge, and I passed—not that I'm an expert on such things—a number of vintage house trailers that could only be used, I thought, for meth labs. There were No Trespassing signs, and rebel flags, and so on. I kept driving. The road finally dead-ended into what looked like a thick forest hit by a tornado, the trees clipped twenty feet up. I thought of fat lighter. On the drive back down, a man stood in the road, waiting for me. He asked what I was looking for. I kind of turned into Ned Beatty from *Deliverance* and hollered out, 'I don't mean no harm.' His eyes were absolutely shot. He wore a stars and bars t-shirt. I drove on home, and started writing."

Greg Johnson is the author of twelve books of fiction, non-fiction, and poetry. His most recent book is *Women I've Known: New and Selected Stories* (Ontario Review Press). He teaches in the graduate writing program at Kennesaw State University and lives in Atlanta. (Photo Credit: Mimi Fittapaldi)

"'Crazy Ladies' is partly autobiographical but mostly fiction. The autobiographical part is that when I was about ten, a 'crazy lady' did wander into my grandmother's house, and we were summoned to help my grandmother; eventually the police were called, etc. The family situation, however, is entirely invented in order to highlight the theme of 'craziness' and isolation in the small-town South. The final passage necessarily shades into the surreal, as the narrator imagines a less than happy fate for the female members of his family."

Jacinda Townsend, the 2003-04 Carol Houck Smith fiction fellow at the Wisconsin Institute of Creative Writing and a 2002 Hurston Wright Award finalist, has published fiction in numerous literary magazines, such as *Carve Zine*, *Obsidian II*, *Passages North*, and *Xavier Review*, and in anthologies such as *Telling Stories: Fiction by Kentucky Feminists*. A former Fulbright fellow to Cote d'Ivoire and graduate of both Harvard University and the Iowa Writers' Workshop, she teaches at Southern Illinois University. (Photo Credit: Phil Bankester)

"In 2001, I went to Africa and took up residence in a 200-year-old residence on the beach. Every evening, I bolted my antechamber, turned down my lights, dropped my mosquito net, and tried in vain to sleep despite the ghosts that fermented my imagination. I lived there for almost a year but never quite got used to sleeping there, and never quite got over the feeling, when the sun rose, that I was a hero for having survived. 'Night' is my attempt to capture this feeling."

Jon Tribble was born in Little Rock, Arkansas. He grew up in Aldersgate Camp just outside of Little Rock (at that time), a church camp devoted to medical and social services programming. He currently lives in Carbondale, Illinois, with his wife, Allison Joseph, and teaches literature and writing at Southern Illinois University Carbondale. He is the Managing Editor of the literary journal *Crab Orchard Review* and is the Series Editor of the Crab Orchard Series in Poetry from SIU Press. (Photo Credit: Allison Joseph)

"'Cactus Vic and His Marvelous Magical Elephant' and 'The Best Chicken in Arkansas' both draw upon the mythic elements often present in my memories of childhood and adolescence in the South. The strange stories and turns of phrase in conversation always seemed ready to find older roots of worship, pain, blood, loss, and wonder. Though the New South may be increasingly losing touch with these things as the "Anywhere America" of corporate chains and McMansions take away so much of the region's uniqueness, there still are vestiges of the good and bad character of the South in its backroads and people, its dinner tables and taverns."

Joy Beshears Hagy lives on High Rock Lake in Lexington, NC, with her husband, two dogs and a cat. Hagy holds a BA from Salem College, where she is the director of the Writing Center, and an MFA in Creative Writing from Queens University of Charlotte. Her poetry has appeared in or is forthcoming from various journals and anthologies including *Main Street Rag*, *Southern Gothic Online*, *R-KV-R-Y Quarterly*, *In the Yard: A Poetry Anthology*, *Mountain Time* and *Caesura*. Her poem, "Rapture" was chosen by Kathryn Stripling Byer as Honorable Mention in the 2006 NC State Poetry Contest.

"Believe it or not, the 'Silver Man' character really exists, though clearly in an alternate universe: the rave scene of the early 90s. Anyone who has attended a rave has seen the variety of costumes, but this guy glowed—literally. This poem is my attempt to share Silver Man—in all his glory—with you.

"My entire life I have been attracted to the bizarre and grotesque. My childhood reading included topics such as Big Foot, aliens, spontaneous human combustion and true crime novels about people, such as serial killer Ted Bundy, who lured many of his victims away by wearing a fake cast and asking for help lifting something into his car. 'Dinner Date' is the first in a series of poems about serial killers. In it I imagine turning the tables on Ted."

Joyce Carol Oates is a recipient of the National Book Award and the PEN/Malamud Award for Excellence in Short Fiction. Author of the national bestsellers *We Were the Mulvaneys, Blonde*—which was nominated for the National Book Award—and *The Falls*, which won the 2005 Prix Femina, Oates is the Roger S. Berlind Distinguished Professor of the Humanities at Princeton University. She has published a number of story collections featuring surreal/Gothic work, namely *Night-Side, Haunted: Tales of the Grotesque, The Collector of Hearts*, and *The Female of the Species*. Having lived in upstate New York—in the "Snow Belt"—for the first two decades of her life, she is well acquainted with surreal America. (Photo Credit: Raymond Smith)

"The Bingo Master," according to Oates, is "a surreal excursion into an alternative universe in which a youngish woman not unlike Flannery O'Connor has an experience appropriate to O'Connor's curious blend of naivete and schoolgirl sadism."

Julianna Baggott is the author of four novels, including *The Madam* and *Which Brings Me to You* (co-written with Steve Almond) and three books of poems, most recently *Lizzie Borden in Love* and *Compulsions of Silk Worms and Bees*. She writes novels for younger readers under the pen name N.E. Bode, namely *The Anybodies* trilogy. She teaches at Florida State University's Creative Writing Program. (Photo Credit: David G.W. Scott)

"In July of 2004, I found the dead body of my dear friend who had shot herself in the jaw. We lived across the street from the community pool and, that summer, had played daily badminton matches. She had two daughters, two step-children. She was one of the funniest, and her intelligence was vast. I've tried to get at this deep loss through poems and essays, but the straightforward attempts have always failed me. For some reason, this more surreal approach has been the truest—in a strange way that I can't quite explain. I'm sure I'm not finished dealing with this death. I may never."

Kathy Conner was born in Birmingham, AL but grew up in Jackson, MS where she has spent most of her life. She earned a Masters in Creative Writing at the University of Southern Mississippi and currently lives in Tallahassee, FL where she is working on a PhD at Florida State University. Her short stories are forthcoming in *The Chattahoochee Review*. (Photo Credit: Thomas Cooper)

"In 2004, a friend gave me a coffee table book which consists of photos from the Mütter Museum, a medical museum in Philadelphia. Many of the photos are of mutations—fetal skeletons with club feet and two-headed babies. My friends would flip through it, cringe, set it aside. Depressing, they said. And it is. But I was fascinated. It was all so odd, so grotesque. My favorite: a full page photo of a wax model—an old woman with a large horn growing out of her forehead. The caption next to the photo claims the model represents 'Madame Dimanche, or Widow Sunday, who lived in Paris around the beginning of the nineteenth century. The horn on her forehead attained a length of 9.8 inches. . .' Widow Sunday was real. But other than what the book tells me, I know virtually nothing about her. I also know virtually nothing about living with a deformity. But I wanted to write about it; I wanted to write about her especially, the Widow Sunday. I knew I couldn't pretend to understand, so I put it off. Finally, in the fall of 2005, I took the risk and 'The Widow Sunday' turned out to be the most difficult story I have ever written. I couldn't give it up; I had to get it right. Finally, I realized something: the story was not so much about the Widow Sunday as it was about Milla, a woman obsessed with the deformities she herself does not possess. It took drastic revision, four complete drafts and several months, but at last I understand: the story is not about living with a deformity; it's about coping without one."

Katie Estill received her BA from Kenyon College and her MFA from the Iowa Writer's Workshop. She lived in Greece for five years, the setting of her first novel, and currently resides in the Ozarks with her husband, Daniel Woodrell. Her second novel, *Dahlia's Gone* (St. Martin's Press), was published January 2007. (Photo Credit: Edward Biamonte)

"My husband and I live in an old house that is rumored to have been part of the Underground Railway and was built over a large cave in our hillside. We've been told that once the cave could be reached from the basement, but that entrance, as well as the one in the yard, has been closed. We may open the cave again and allow it to breathe."

Kyle Minor's most recent work appears in *The Gettysburg Review*, *The Mid American Review*, and the Random House anthology *Twentysomething Essays by Twentysomething Writers*.

"I wrote the first draft of this story on my father-in-law's mountain in Rowan County, Kentucky. That draft was a sweetly thing about love and robots, but by this draft, number eleven, it had grown dark as the emotional material that originally informed its making. This story is for my old teacher Lee Abbott, who gave me permission to not let my world grow too small, and whose stories make me want to make mine better."

(Photo Credit: Jay Fram)

Laura Benedict is the author of the novel, *Isabella Moon*. Her short fiction has appeared in *Ellery Queen Mystery Magazine* and several anthologies. A second novel is forthcoming from Ballantine in 2008. For the past decade, she's worked as a freelance book reviewer for *The Grand Rapids Press* in Michigan and other newspapers. She lives in Southern Illinois with her husband, Pinckney Benedict.

"Angela Carter's story collection, *The Bloody Chamber*, is one of my favorite books. In it, she re-imagines folk tales and fairy tales and exposes them for what they are: thinly veiled monster stories that reveal and celebrate our deepest desires and darkest fears. I love a good monster story. 'Witches, All' is my homage to the late Ms. Carter. As to the story's plot, I've always had a sort of grudging admiration for the bold women who present themselves at dressing room doors, ready for what ever lies behind them."

Lee K. Abbott is the author of seven collections of short stories, most recently *All Things, All at Once: New & Selected Stories* (Norton, 2006). He's been published nearly everywhere: *Harpers*, *Atlantic*, *The Georgia Review*, *The Kenyon Review*, *The Southern Review* among them. His work has been reprinted semi-regularly in *Best American Short Stories* and *The Prize Stories: the O'Henry Awards*, as well as the *Pushcart Prize* volumes. He teaches in the MFA Program at the Ohio State University in Columbus. (Photo Credit: Emma Dodge Hanson)

"'The Era of Great Numbers' is one of what I call my 'trash compactor' stories: stuff—lines, characters, situations, images, exchanges of dialogue—that wouldn't fit in anything else and be quite the test of the imagination that the future is or demands. I also enjoyed the chance to pursue illogic and the irrational in a landscape that will be ours if we don't, as my dad put it, straighten up and fly right. I like the surd made ab-, not to mention the opportunity to have folks declaim. I love a mad orator, especially one who finds significance in the slight and the nearly ephemeral. I am a fan, finally, of the deadpan, the understatement. And, yes, football must be among the most surreal sports we have."

Pinckney Benedict grew up on his family's farm in Greenbrier County, WV. He has published two collections of short fiction and a novel. His stories have appeared in, among other magazines and anthologies, *Esquire*, *Zoetrope All*-Story, the *O. Henry Awards*, *New Stories from the South*, *Ontario Review*, the *Pushcart Prize*, and *The Oxford Book of American Short Stories*. He is the recipient of, among other prizes, a Literature Fellowship from the National Endowment for the Arts, a Literary Fellowship from the West Virginia Commission on the Arts, a Michener Fellowship from the Writers' Workshop at the University of Iowa, the *Chicago Tribune's* Nelson Algren Award, and Britain's Steinbeck Award. He is a professor in the English Department at Southern Illinois University in Carbondale, Illinois.

"Pig Helmet is based on a buddy of mine who's a sheriff's deputy, a surreal mix of the entirely pragmatic (even hard-hearted) and the mystical. The Wall of Life is based on an act that appeared during an evangelical rock concert my daughter not long ago attended. The act resembled a spiffed-up version of the Wall of Death I frequented as a kid at the state fair. I wanted to write about them both, so why not put the two together, I thought."

Robert Olen Butler has published ten novels and four volumes of short fiction, one of which, *A Good Scent from a Strange Mountain*, won the 1993 Pulitzer Prize for Fiction. His most recent collection is *Severance*, from Chronicle Books, which contains 62 short short stories in the voices of newly severed heads. Butler has also published a volume of his lectures on the creative process, *From Where You Dream*, edited with an introduction by Janet Burroway. Among his numerous other awards are a Guggenheim Fellowship in fiction, the Richard and Hinda Rosenthal Foundation Award from the American Academy of Arts and Letters, and two National Magazine Awards in Fiction. His stories have appeared widely in such publications as *The New Yorker*, *Esquire*, *Harper's*, *The Atlantic Monthly*, *Zoetrope*, and *The Paris Review* and have been chosen for inclusion in four annual editions of *The Best American Short Stories*, eight annual editions of *New Stories from the South*, and numerous college literature textbooks. He teaches creative writing at Florida State University in Tallahassee, Florida. (Photo Credit: Elizabeth Dewberry)

"As with all the stories in my collection *Tabloid Dreams*, 'Help Me Find My Spaceman Lover' was inspired by the lower rack of the supermarket tabloids. I long thought that those papers were getting the headlines right but the stories all wrong, and so I chose to set the record straight. Not incidentally, Edna and Desi stuck with me and insisted on their fuller story being told—which I did in my novel *Mr. Spaceman.*"

Rodney Jones is the author of nine books of poetry, including *Transparent Gestures,* winner of the National Book Critics Circle Award, and *Elegy for the Southern Drawl,* a finalist for the Pulitzer Prize. His most recent book, *Salvation Blues: 100 Poems, 1985-2005,* was selected for the 2007 Kingsley Tufts Poetry Award.

"'Willows' came from two journal entries that I made at separate times in the early nineties: one about three thirteen-year-old girls, who are middle-aged women now; the other about willows. Both related recurring memories that somehow grew together to form one image. The subject of 'The Swan' is my long-enduring and uncomfortable relation with surrealism, which I distrust and adore."

Ron Rash is the author of three novels, three volumes of poetry and three story collections. His latest story collection, *Chemistry and Other Stories*, was published by Picador in 2007. In 2005 he received the James Still Award from the Fellowship of Southern Writers. He teaches at Western Carolina University. (Photo Credit: Mark Haskett)

"In the Southern Appalachian mountains, the owl has traditionally been viewed as a harbinger of death, and this belief was one I heard growing up in Western North Carolina. One day near Halloween, I decided to write a story about a man who lives in a secular culture where much of what he has been taught to believe is not just rejected but ridiculed. How would such a man react if the old beliefs suddenly impinged on the secular world he now inhabited? How much would have to be at stake before he would actually act upon those beliefs? Those were the questions I mulled as I began 'The Corpse Bird.' My favorite ghost story is Joyce's 'The Dead,' and that story was also on my mind as I wrote this one."

Susan Woodring is a graduate of the Master in Fine Arts program at Queens University in Charlotte. Her fiction has appeared in a number of journals, including *Isotope: A Journal of Literary Nature and Science Writing, Passages North, turnrow,* and *Ballyhoo Stories*. Her first novel, *The Traveling Disease,* was published by Main Street Rag Press. Susan currently lives in Drexel, North Carolina, with her husband and her children. (Photo Credit: Danny Woodring)

"I've been trying to put a traveling salesman in a story for the last couple of years. I don't have a good reason for my obsession with this particular profession except that I felt a traveling salesman could be an agent of change in another character's life, or in the life of an entire community. Discovering that the salesman of my dreams was an alien from a distant planet made a huge difference—it allowed me to keep the aspects of the slick salesman I had envisioned, but it allowed me to bring the character into the light of the bizarre, which really opened the story for me. The other important piece came when I was talking to a friend about how, though I certainly enjoy my children, I felt they really should come with on/off switches so I could turn them off when the phone rang or when I was just too tired to deal with them. She said, oh you should write about that, and I started to imagine what might be the downsides of such an invention, and how ultimately, that sort of convenience might go disastrously wrong."

Tom Franklin, from Dickinson, Alabama, has published a collection, *Poachers*, and two novels, *Hell at the Breech* and *Smonk*, all from William Morrow. His short fiction and essays have appeared in *The Oxford American*, *The Southern Review, New Stories from the South* and *Best American Mystery Stories of the Century*. Winner of a 2001 Guggenheim Fellowship, Franklin is a writer-in-residence at Ole Miss and lives in Oxford with his wife, poet Beth Ann Fennelly, and their two children. (Photo Credit: Maude Schuyler Clay)

"Smonk isn't human. Without giving away secrets ('Smonk' is an excerpt from a novel of the same name), I can't say more than that, except to say that E. O. Smonk isn't a werewolf, vampire, homunculus, warlock, demon, alien, the missing link, bigfoot or any other normal 'monster.' But he isn't human, either. He seemed to fit a landscape that came together from a number of influences, Cormac McCarthy's amoral *Blood Meridian*, Charles Portis' hilarious and profound *True Grit*, David Milch's stunning *Deadwood* and Barry Hannah's anti-western *Never Die*."

William Gay is the author of the novels, *The Long Home* and *Provinces of Night*, as well as a collection of stories, *I Hate To See That Evening Sun Go Down*. His novel, *Twilight*, was published in the winter of 2006. He lives in rural Tennessee where he is completing a novel. (Photo Credit: Chris John)

"The plotline and the last paragraph came to me one day while I was at work. I was painting a house, and contributing factors were an officious homeowner and a plumber's large wooden toolbox. I wrote the story that night, seeing it as a sort of Gothic fairytale. The origins of the paperhanger himself remain a mystery to me, and, to paraphrase Cash Bundren, it is perhaps better so."

Printed in the United States
91408LV00005B/28-60/A